Y0-AGK-679

Grosset's **UNIVERSAL** *Library*

CHRIST STOPPED AT EBOLI by Carlo Levi (UL-1)

THE DANCE OF LIFE by Havelock Ellis (UL-2)

THE GOOD SOCIETY by Walter Lippmann (UL-3)

THE LATE GEORGE APLEY by John P. Marquand (UL-4)

MAN AND HIS GODS by Homer Smith (UL-5)

THE MEASURE OF MAN by Joseph Wood Krutch (UL-6)

MELBOURNE by Lord David Cecil (UL-7)

OSCAR WILDE by Hesketh Pearson (UL-8)

THE PURITAN OLIGARCHY by Thomas Wertenbaker (UL-9)

QUACKERY IN THE PUBLIC SCHOOLS by Albert Lynd (UL-10)

REVEILLE IN WASHINGTON by Margaret Leech (UL-11)

THE WEB AND THE ROCK by Thomas Wolfe (UL-12)

THE IDES OF MARCH by Thornton Wilder (UL-13)

NOBLE ESSENCES by Sir Osbert Sitwell (UL-14)

WHY WAS LINCOLN MURDERED? by Otto Eisenschiml (UL-15)

YOU CAN'T GO HOME AGAIN by Thomas Wolfe (UL-16)

THE SHOCK OF RECOGNITION (*Vol. I—The 19th Century*),
edited by Edmund Wilson (UL-17)

THE SHOCK OF RECOGNITION (*Vol. II—The 20th Century*),
edited by Edmund Wilson (UL-18)

SIR OSBERT SITWELL

Noble Essences

A BOOK OF CHARACTERS

Grosset's UNIVERSAL *Library*

GROSSET & DUNLAP · NEW YORK

ATLANTIC—LITTLE, BROWN BOOKS
ARE PUBLISHED BY
LITTLE, BROWN AND COMPANY
IN ASSOCIATION WITH
THE ATLANTIC MONTHLY PRESS

PRINTED IN THE UNITED STATES OF AMERICA

I dedicate this book
to those friends of mine
who figure in its pages.

Contents

I	Portfolio	3
II	Sir Edmund Gosse	40
III	Ronald Firbank	77
IV	Wilfred Owen	101
V	Gabriele D'Annunzio	125
VI	Ada Leverson	143
VII	Walter Richard Sickert	182
VIII	W. H. Davies	230
IX	Violet Gordon Woodhouse	272
X	Rex Whistler	293
XI	Arnold Bennett	317
XII	Colophon	335
	Appendix A: From *Things that Have Interested Me*, by Arnold Bennett	341
	Appendix B: "The Poet and the Mirror," by Sacheverell Sitwell	343
	Acknowledgments	345
	Index	347

NOBLE ESSENCES

CHAPTER I

Portfolio

ROBUST old country neighbor, one of the last of the squires, was heard during a severe thunderstorm thus to address his faithful and aging servant: "Alec, you damn fool, don't stand about there, doing nothing! Climb up the lightning conductor, can't you, and see if it's working!" The man who climbs such an instrument naturally leads a more exciting life than does he who watches the hurricane and writes about it: in short, as I have argued before, a writer's life is duller than that of a man of action. Yet would I rather read an account of the storm by one who had watched it than by one who climbed the lightning conductor; and further, I would rather read a book which concerned Leonardo, let us say, and Baudelaire or a lesser artist, than the most circumstantial and detailed volume devoted to the Battle of Waterloo, or a prize fight. . . . The chapters, then, that follow deal with character and atmosphere more than with action, and though during the course of my autobiography I have more than once stated the main themes of the whole work, yet it is better, perhaps, to recapitulate here, in general, as well as to state plainly and in particular, my conception of this final and very different volume. My aim throughout the thousand or so preceding pages has been to portray the age in which history came to life again, the stirrings and then the great storms that followed the historic halcyon epoch (for the Victorian Age into which I was born constituted what is termed by farmers in Derbyshire a "weather breeder": the false calm — but none the less calm and sweet for that — of a golden day in winter). I have tried to stabilize for the audience of the future, as much as of today, the very scents and feeling and quiddity of the time. This I endeavored to accomplish by providing an account of my own experiences, by building up a portrait of myself, and by adumbrating through these the outlines and characteristics of the epoch. But now, in the ensuing chapters, in order to provide the reader with a further mirror of that age, in which he can check and tally what has gone before, I retrace my steps and try, obversely, to delineate the era and myself through the portraits of others, portraits of people of exceptional talent, wit or genius.

It has long been my conviction that only by the magic of art, or of individuality, can men save themselves. Evil and ugliness are the same thing (as we recognize by such phrases as "It was an ugly thing to do"), and dullness is the mother of both. It is not the material conditions of the time so much that darken the hues of the future, but man's self-satisfaction in the midst of the cataclysms he provokes by his aimless monkey-cleverness, his inability to foresee the effects of the tricks he plays, his refusal to trust his eyes, to rely on his senses, or to allow what he sees or feels to loosen the bonds that confine his spirit. Thus only the artist, who is compelled by his nature and profession to a very opposite attitude, is free to cast out fear from his being. Every artist is his own Marco Polo, lost to terror in the discovery of new wonders in nature or man. And one of the strange sights observed by this prototype I may mention here, for it carries its own lesson. Reaching the side, if I recall it rightly, of a great mountain range, somewhere forgotten in antiquity and the mammoth spaces of Asia, he saw, stretched beneath him to the east, under the counterfeit gold of the sun, an enormous plain, filled with ants, very active and manifestly engaged in some particular occupation. He asked one of his attendants, a native of the region, what work they might be employed on, and the man replied that they were digging for gold. . . . Similarly, today, a traveler arriving from the west would see, looking eastwards, a vast territory engulfing about a fifth of the world, in which millions of ants are burrowing or scratching the ground, or just running busily to and fro — though gold is dug no more, but minerals more dingy and useful, that give off fumes or energy and enable yet more ants to work yet more ant-hours, until the final ant-hour comes for them to die, and be incinerated into oblivion. No more is man to labor for a vision — even if it be only the base vision of great personal wealth — but instead, merely for the day's food: for the new barbarism decrees an equal share of misery, ugliness, hebetude, shame, and ultimately of nihility, for each and all.

To the ant, the individual is the enemy. But it is precisely in individuality that Western Europe has excelled. Not for us of the Occident the schools of poets and painters, almost indistinguishable one from another in style, and continuing for millenniums: our works of art are sharply differentiated and defined. In our countries — the imaginative greatness of which was built, as was that of Greece, from happy and illustrious combinations of sea with land — even this age, which threatens to end so catastrophically, has been endowed with genius in abundance, though Everyman, now so opprobriously termed Little or Common Man, has failed to respect it or to pay attention. Yet, even apart from its productions, the spectacle of genius or of exceptional talent or personality, of lives spent happily or unhappily in the service of an ideal, and of the application of the rare, yet essential, *common sense* of art towards life may possess its own practical, no less than moral or semihistorical, value.

To indicate, in its ordinary yet highest range of poetry, the sort of common sense I strive to indicate, let us consider an anecdote; what might be termed — except that it is true — the Fable of Arthur Waley and the Frog. We must picture that remarkable poet and scholar sitting, very alert under an aloof and impassive manner, at a semiscientific, semipsychic meeting organized by the late Dr. Harry Price — another friend of his; for Arthur Waley has perhaps the greatest range of friendship of any person I know, extending from dons and savants to spiritualists and members of Parliament, from his own kind, poets, painters, musicians, to those who practice their obsolete Eskimo tricks in winter on the topmost slopes of mountains. The hall was crowded with an enthusiastic audience. While everywhere Science was engaged in such feats of imaginative charity as cutting off a dog's head, and keeping that part of it alive in a saucer for weeks or even months, the brain still functioning, Superstition, her illegitimate sister, was, to the contrary, here occupied in the more harmless task of trying to make a frog go to sleep or fall into a trance. Up on the platform, a celebrated expert in hypnotism and paranormal manifestations faced a frog, clammily palpitating, which had been carried hither on a tray by an attendant, and then set on a table. The Professor first made a few perfunctory passes over the creature with his hands, in order to lull it, and then continued his work with an air of more busy concentration. The frog perhaps felt dizzy, and closed his eyes. In any case, he appeared soon to become too frightened to stir. The Professor then quickly popped over his motionless victim a tightly fitting bell-glass, and continued to wave his hands soothingly above it. After a time, all movement ceased within the cover, and the learned hypnotist stopped his antics and announced:

"You will observe, ladies and gentlemen, that the frog has now ceased to breathe."

Everyone seemed immensely impressed by this evidence of the Professor's psychic powers — everyone, that is, except Arthur Waley, who, without anger, but with decision, spoke up, or snapped out rapidly the words:

"Naturally, it can't breathe, poor little beast, when it's

under a glass case! You couldn't, could you? If you'd give it some air, it would soon be able to breathe all right!"

This clinical view, so typical of the speaker and of an artist, upset the audience. The initial uneasy silence was later broken by a good deal of hissing directed at the interloper. The Professor, though at first he had seemed rather stunned, soon roused himself and, in his turn, glared down at his challenger. He thus regarded him for several seconds. Then, perhaps at a loss what to reply, he made a slip. In order to show how foolish and unwarrantable the interruption had been, he unwisely lifted the cover. The frog, who could first be seen to breathe deeply, thereupon took a flying leap into the audience, and landed in the lap of an elaborately dressed lady in the second row. The meeting thereupon ended in uproar and confusion.

Artists in general, then, though they may not be noted for common sense in all its varieties, often possess this most rare form of it; and we shall meet with it again, I hope, in the course of these pages, in which I have tried to demonstrate by those persons to whom I call attention the variety and range of English Genius. Indeed I have essayed to make this book, to which I have given as subtitle the label *A Book of Characters,* into a gallery devoted to a few people of the period in which I was born and have lived. It is a volume which, in consequence, has required a very different technical approach by the author, though the standards remain the same. In the full-length portraits, which begin with the next chapter, I have tried to collect all the details *I* have noticed, and many that I have been able to gather, and weld them into a solid likeness of the person I knew: of the person *I* knew, not so much an objective likeness as the one I saw; but I have recorded, so far as is possible, without fear or favor. I have tried to perpetuate, in especial, the memory of those belonging to categories unlikely to recur in other centuries: Gosse, the archetype of Victorian Professor, roguish, sprightly, but with a deadly spring; Ada Leverson, experienced and witty; Sickert, possessed of his very individual and epochal collection of talents. With certain exceptions, the originals belong to a generation previous to my own, since it is easier to watch those older than oneself with the proper studious, uninterrupted and fastidious attention; whereas those younger than oneself remain children, and artists of one's own age, if they share the same aims, often distract one with their ideas, or, if they follow other paths, betray one into showing prejudice. Nevertheless, there are in this book those who died young, and those who lived to a considerable age. Indeed, only a single denominator do they share: each is, in his own manner and degree, an artist. In every respect but this, they differ. Some, like Gosse, are erudite and pernickety, like Firbank, fantastic as a drawing by Callot, or like Ada Leverson, of wit, originality and warmth of feeling. There is Sickert, a great man in the grand manner, but spiced with its own mockery; Wilfred Owen, a poet rationed by fate to three or four months only in which, his temperament and various talents having been fused into genius by emotion, to write at his highest power, but during that brief period, nevertheless, destined to compose poems that qualify him for immortality; W. H. Davies, a natural character, who never lost through sophistication the capacities he brought into the world; and Arnold Bennett, a child turned businessman.

The people whom these portraits represent must, it should be remembered, be judged by the tenets of their own time, and not by those of a world governed by the various terrors that control men's minds today, whether Atom Bomb, or Starvation, or Mass Dullness. While the reader looks at this book, his mind should dwell in another age. The large portraits, again, might be regarded as the chief works hanging in a gallery, but, before entering it, one will first turn over some sketches that have been collected in a portfolio in an antechamber. In these, I have aimed — and how difficult a task it has been! — to recapture the most volatile of essences, the very spirit of a moment that makes it live and sparkle, or some mental or physical characteristic, or some trait of out-look — as is illustrated, for example, in the foregoing anecdote of Arthur Waley; to record these incidents, in themselves so evanescent, which yet impregnate the mind, so that when idly the memory turns to them they invariably and at once distill again their aroma. I have engaged myself to make fast these ephemera, impressions of a particular time or a particular person, who happened typically in that instant to display himself or to be displayed. A few of those who might have posed separately for a large portrait in these pages — I would give as an instance William Walton — have made their appearance already, having been integrated into the main body of the autobiography: but in this preliminary chapter I add further final touches to some, allow them to be gazed at from a new direction; especially is this done to illustrate some aspect hitherto, in the author's opinion, in-sufficiently stressed. Thus, to take Lytton Strachey, who bowed to us in *Laughter in the Next Room*, it is true that his books, in which learning and natural and cultivated talent were so manifest, turned a new light on to the preceding epoch; but also — and this would not be obvious to those who had not known him personally — in an age when people tended to look the same, his emergence into any scene, whether street or drawing room, lifted it to a new plane, investing it with a kind of caricatural Victorian interest. I do not think I have so far emphasized enough this difference that his physical presence created: the lanky, bearded figure, with his high, incisive gift of few words; for in company he spoke little and to the point — though sometimes to a point that only he saw. Before going on to catch a further glimpse of him, we might recall what he said to a clever, charming, rather noisy young man who had once been taken to stay with him. I do not know whether the visit could be considered a success, but when the guest next saw his former host, a whole lustrum had passed.

"Mr. Strachey, do you realize it's five years since we met?" the young man asked. He received the reply: "Rather a nice interval, don't you think?"

Usually, however, he was kind, and somewhat silent. I have seen him sit with a kind of eager silentness and sense of waiting in several countries, for our paths were apt to cross. I have watched him, as I have described, sitting by my bed in Queen Alexandra's Military Hospital at Millbank; I have taken the opportunity to observe him in Florence, or having luncheon with us at Montegufoni, or in Paris, where he unexpectedly materialized, in the genial company of Cyril Connolly, one Whitsun, at Foyot's, where I was staying. It was a quiet, ceremonious call, and I recollect that he refused all refreshment (Cyril Connolly, I am sure, adopted a more yea-saying attitude) and remained without speaking but plainly appreciative. But, to show him as he looked in his life, and as he is most certainly to be seen, too, in the portrait of him by Henry Lamb — for many years exhibited in the Tate Gallery — I choose this time to make him pose for an instant, by no means easy to set down, against a Spanish background.

* * *

In April 1919 my brother and I had gone to Spain, as a symbol to ourselves of our newly won independence, since we had just left the Army — I, after seven years of it. We had chosen Spain of all other countries, because we had never hitherto visited it, and because, throughout the First World War, it had seemed an unattainable island of peace, and, as always, to be compact of idiosyncrasy and austere beauty — as well as of a kind of masculine and aristocratic common sense, because, so long as it is not a matter of religion, the Spaniard is always willing to mind his own business. . . .

Even the journey over the frontier, from Hendaye to Irun, was exciting, unlike any other: the great mountains, the towering clouds overshadowing them, and suddenly releasing bursts of dramatic sunlight, the women, who could be seen carrying pitchers to the wells, the men, with enormous straw hats as big as wheels, the hog skins filled with wine, the sub-Alpine dwarfs — all possessed the indefinable tang of an ancient and historic country that was new to us. Nor, above all, will the memory of our arrival at Irun itself ever leave me. During four years of war we had forgotten how to be tourists, and as one result had omitted to have our baggage examined at Hendaye, on the French side of the frontier. In consequence it had remained there. But at Irun, a Basque, whom naturally we had never seen before, sized up the situation and took entire charge of us. In type he belonged to the music-hall-stage peasantry, with thick eyebrows, a snub nose and a structure of chin and forehead that made him resemble a drawing of the earliest man, reconstituted from bits of a lately discovered skull by an ill-equipped draughtsman of one of those illustrated weekly journals devoted in equal parts to disasters, science and sport. He was wearing a beret, a plaid shawl, a velvet coat and corduroy trousers, and carried a vast green umbrella. He talked no language, I think, but Basque, but could make himself understood without any such aids. No trouble was too much for him. Within a few minutes of assuming responsibility for us, he had arranged for me to travel back across the frontier in a dilapidated free-hand version of a hansom cab, had contracted for the fare and then further contrived for me to halve it by organizing matters so that I was able to share the vehicle with a priest, also involved in some kind of difficulty with his luggage (though he had with him, and hugged it, a large black canvas trunk). The cabman was given instructions how to find our bags. In the interval our new friend looked after my brother, bought our tickets, met me on my safe return, and was obviously delighted that my brother's anxiety could now be relieved. In fact that man constituted himself a kind of super-courier, such as could only be provided by guardian angels, and for all this kindness, all this peasant cleverness and good will he had lavished on us, he would accept no reward. He refused absolutely all offers of money, though he stayed with us and saw us off. As we could not speak to him, we could not even adequately thank him. . . . But in discussing this prehistoric and enchanting survival, I wander far from the portrait I intend to paint. Unfortunately, I was about to say, after the long ordeal by boredom and null agony that the war had constituted, the very abruptness and delightful violence of the change affected my nervous system, and I fell ill in Madrid, whither we had gone first.

This prevented us from continuing our journey to Seville, where we had intended to pass Easter. It was too far away: and so we decided to visit Toledo instead, because, on the map, the journey looked short and easy. But that ancient city, though situated only some seventy miles from Madrid, proved to be a spiritual terminus, especially difficult either to reach or to leave. The truth is that, thirty years ago, all Iberian towns were divided from each other by stretches of time so immense as to dwarf any mere measurement in miles. Toledo, for example, was in its essence, no less than in superficial characteristics, as far removed from the metropolis as the most obscure town in Andalusia. The capital, albeit more individual than Paris or Berlin — though the light and air there were different from those of any other place, and although goats on their way to be milked still marched in small herds through the outer streets lined with shacks made of petrol tins — yet, with its display of wide boulevards and green parks, and of palaces, remained securely tied to the burgess civilization of the epoch. Toledo, on the other hand, with its even more vivid alternations of blazing sun and mountain-cold winds, with its lion-colored bridges, its synagogues and mosques, now converted into churches (but some of them still painted a blinding African white), with its severe and architectonic landscape, the contours of which seem to exercise an influence on the shapes and shadows of the men and animals who stand in it or move through it, pulling their lines out, distorting them, so that still, over every hill and valley, every building and human being, broods the mysterious and pervasive spirit of El Greco — Toledo, I felt, might well have been a city in a different planet. No less singular and memorable were the sounds of its cobbled streets, the behavior of its inhabitants, the taste, even, of its food. The people of Toledo must, I suppose, have been inbred for centuries. At the gates, and in the *calles*, were whole companies of the infirm and cretinous, crawling along on boards, hopping, twitching. On the great terrace laid across the ramparts above the Tagus, every evening a dwarf would race at full speed, singing with an unexpected fullness and strength of lung, and parting the sauntering sunset crowds with the stiff, hurtling stride of his short legs and top-heavy body. In spite of physical abnormality, his was a jolly and high-spirited performance; but none of the dignified men — the women were indoors — in their cloaks would deign to notice him or register any change in the expression of their faces. To foreigners, however — and my brother and I seemed, so soon after the war, to be the only strangers there — they did not extend the same charity. . . . Holy Week, with its bursts of hot sunshine exploding on bare hills streaked rarely with the most shrill young green, and with its air of somber holiday, proved a particularly typical and, indeed, sensational festival. Many services were held in the Cathedral and churches, and on the early afternoon of Saturday took place the traditional procession of gigantic grotesques, representing for the most part personages in the Christian story of whom the populace particularly disapprove, Pontius Pilate or Iscariot. One of these carved and painted effigies, however, crystallized an historical rather than religious passion and prejudice: the resentment felt by the proud Castilians who were his contemporaries at the behavior of King Henry VIII to Catherine of Aragon. Named Anna Boliña, the ridiculous image borne high by four men in hoods portrayed, though I think few in the crowd now identified her, the Protestant Usurper, Anne Boleyn.

The narrow streets leading up to the Plaza from the Cathedral were lined with two threads of people, who on this occasion alone allowed themselves to grow excited. Between them, like a slow-moving stream, passed the procession. Then, after it had gone, in one of those moments of anticlimax, of burst bubble, common to all great annual civic events the world over, the threads coalesced into a disappointed but still hurrying and jostling throng. In one of the confined streets my brother and I stood and waited, to watch the effigies carried by. Our height afforded us our usual advantage in crowds, but more than ordinarily to be noted in this city of the anomalous and stunted. At first our eyes had been occupied entirely with the procession, and it was not until half of it had passed us that I beheld opposite, across the narrow stream, a figure more striking than any that had so far been exhibited for us, but this time totally unexpected and, in addition, alive, able to move, to turn and look: the lean, elongated form of Lytton Strachey, hieratic, a pagod as plainly belonging as did the effigies to a creation of its own. Well muffled, as usual, against the wind, and accompanied by his faithful friend and companion Carrington — she was always known as Carrington, *tout court* — who, with fair hair and plump, pale face, added a more practical, but still indubitably English-esthetic, note to the scene, he was regarding the various giants and giantesses with a mute and somewhat phlegmatic air of appreciation. He did not see us, and this was another opportunity I enjoyed of examining Lytton carefully, at my leisure, and unobserved by him in return. For several minutes I thus studied him, because, even

then, I intended or hoped, one day to write a description of
him.

His head was crowned with a wide-brimmed brown hat.
He had by nature a narrow, long-shaped face, and his narrow, rather long beard, which extended it in similar fashion
and showed itself to be chestnut-colored in the sun, exaggerated this characteristic. Though, unlike André Gide,
whom I had met on a few occasions recently, he did not wear
a cloak (Gide's cloak, animated by his bustling French walk,
had to my eyes then almost become the outward symbol of
his genius, albeit, even with these aids, the rational Protestant
cut of his features suggests a great French lawyer or doctor
rather than a great French writer), Lytton's long brown tweed
coat seemed no less typical of a literary man, and since he
held his arms in an inert way, the effect was, notwithstanding,
of a cloak. Humor and wit were very strongly marked in the
quizzical expression of his face, and also, I think, a kind of
genuine diffidence as well as a certain despair and, always, a
new surprise at man's follies. . . . While I stared at him,
noting various physical traits, I reached several conclusions
about his appearance. Though of a type so rare, and therefore
unnational, as well as deliberately un-English in style, he yet
could have belonged to no other country, and was as pre-
eminently Anglo-Saxon in result as was his companion. His
long nose, the color of his face and beard, his rather arched
angular eyebrows, and his brown eyes, the sense of a cultured,
scholarly man that permeated his entire outward aspect, all
these characteristics and qualities were, though highly individual, essentially English. It is important to look the part
one plays, and he gave consummately the impression of a man of
letters perhaps rather of one in the immediate past than in the
present; a Victorian figure of eminence, possibly. Yet, examining him carefully, it became clear too that he would have
been at ease in the England of an earlier age, when his beard
might have been tinted a carnation hue. It was an Elizabethan

as well as a Victorian head that peered from aloft over the darker, more obviously excited people. . . . Again, I noticed that, while no crowd is more full of individuality than a Spanish, nevertheless, as he stood there, thinly towering, impressive undoubtedly, but with an undeniable element of the grotesque both in his physique and in his presentation of himself, it was at him one looked, and not at anybody else; while, on the other hand, the citizens of Toledo, whose courtesy, famous as it was, never proved strong enough to prevent them from mocking at foreigners, accepted and seemed in no manner inquisitive about this strange individual, to them particularly new in type. Certainly his personal quality triumphed. . . . Suddenly, he saw us, and a look of friendly and amused recognition came into his eyes. But unfortunately that was just the moment when the two lines of spectators broke behind the procession, and whirled and eddied into a single crowd. We remained for several minutes, trying to reach each other, two isolated groups of English, until finally we were swept along in opposite directions and were lost. Nor were we subsequently able to find out where our friends were staying, and this was disconcerting since Lytton had, as I have mentioned, been so kind in coming to visit me when I had been in hospital, only two months before. . . . We did not see him again until we returned to England, and perhaps in consequence that glimpse of him has retained for me a clarity of outline that is unusual, especially in a country where there were so many new impressions, all strongly defined, to supersede and erase it.

*   *   *

If the foregoing was a stubborn moment, not easy to set out, the next transcends it in this same respect, though full, too, of an *ambience* that is unforgettable. It arose out of a Saturday to Monday visit I paid to Frank Schuster at Bath, for I had known that among my fellow guests were to be my

friends Madame Vandervelde and Reginald Farrer. And I welcome my task, difficult as it is, because it affords me the opportunity of writing at greater length about one who, though
his name rather fitfully occurred in *The Scarlet Tree*, has been
somewhat slighted, considering both the originality of his mind
and the usefulness — how he would have deplored that this
last should be said of him! — of his life: since he was an author
of talent, both as novelist and as a writer of books of travel
and of gardening, and a great plant collector, so remarkably
successful especially in his discovery of rock plants in China,
Tibet, Burma and elsewhere, that he is, indeed, sure of immortality in the world of flowers.

Reginald Farrer, then, was my second cousin, his mother
and my father being first cousins. He was born in 1880, and
was thus twelve years older than I. Perhaps because of this
separation in age, we had seldom met, except for a few casual
minutes at the house of some relative, until the latter years of
the First World War, which brought him back to England
from one of his expeditions to the East in search of new dis-
coveries for the garden. At the time of which I speak, he was
working in the Foreign Office, and I was stationed in London.
During this period we often saw each other, and soon became
friends; a result no doubt helped by the fact that my sister
knew him well, and liked him. She used to stay with his father
and mother in Yorkshire, and had grown greatly to appreciate
his wit and unusual talents. But, to go back, if it had so happened that I had seen but little of him until now, I had, it is
true, heard of him throughout my life, in the earlier stages with
a certain warmth, with commendation, if with an air of "boys
will be boys" (for he had published a novel at an early age,
and my grandmother Sitwell did not *approve* of fiction,
though an author of any kind was for her invested with a
certain romantic aura) — in the later with a notable lack of
enthusiasm, for which had been substituted a cold and almost
apprehensive curiosity. While I was still a small boy, my

grandmother had quoted his sayings to show that he was clever; she applauded his interest in flowers — a taste which, in lesser degree, she shared — and from time to time had made it evident that she entertained hopes of "dear Bessie's elder boy" embarking upon a career of Low Church devotion. To that the novel had put a stop. Still, even if he showed a worldly side, he had grown more expert in gardening, and perhaps he would alter. (The Lord had His own methods of getting to work, and under her breath she sang a favorite hymn: "God moves in a mysterious way.") In any case, no background could have offered her more hope of a chance of his conversion to a militant if unmuscular Christianity; for his mother shared the same fervent disposition as herself, and Reginald had been brought up in an austere if opulent world, where you could have possessions so long as you did not enjoy them, and where each Sunday dragged after it a weary, weekly train of charitable village functions, jumble sale or jamboree, and the more purely domestic orgies of missionary meeting and simple family prayer. . . . Yes, there had been hope of the dear boy developing along sound orthodox lines, and the report had percolated, who knows from what source, that he was beginning to turn his attention more seriously to religious matters. . . . It can be imagined, therefore, with what a wealth of sad religious resignation and with what a subdued polar shivering of disapproval the news was received, when I was still at school, that Reginald was indeed at last taking religion seriously, but had as his creed adopted Buddhism! Henceforth the consternation which reigned made every rumor become fact when repeated, and still more did the air of frigid grief which hung over Gosden, and especially over the Indian Room, where my grandmother reclined on her sofa with a Samoyed dog on guard each side of it; still more, I say, did it become augmented, so as almost to grow palpable, when a relative came to break the news — false, as it turned out later — that Reginald had returned to England as a

Buddhist missionary. The impression thus created was never quite dispelled. When he arrived to stay, his mere presence in the house struck a chill to the bones of the faithful (and, indeed, I suspect that was why we met so seldom; I must have been sent away during his visits, lest he should attempt to capture my soul). An indignant shudder passed through every gathering of relatives for prayer when, with an accompanying tremble in their voices, they besought the Lord that the heathen might be permitted to see the true light. The only member of the family to be pleased, as might have been expected, was my father, who had suffered similar exhortations to faith as a young man. He never attended family prayers, but he had received the news with a chuckle, and always thereafter paid special attention to Reginald when he met him, and took trouble in the young man's absence to praise to his other cousins his books and various activities.

The new convert was the son of J. A. Farrer, who owned the estate of Ingleborough, situated near Clapham in Yorkshire, and celebrated for its mountains and caverns and lakes and streams. Mrs. Farrer had been a strikingly handsome woman, the background was wealthy and cultivated, and her husband was the author of a number of immemorable books, and had several times been a Liberal Member of Parliament. In his circumstances, therefore, Reginald was fortunate. When he grew up, he was able to go where he wished, to finance his own expeditions, and to make his garden at Ingleborough famous. On the other hand, he had from infancy suffered a drawback so grave that it might have deprived him, had he possessed less courage, character and persistence, of all ambition as of all achievement: he was born with a cleft palate — the result, it was held, of his mother being frightened before his birth by seeing unexpectedly a chimney sweep. Already as a small child Reginald had undergone several most painful operations to remedy his defect, but without success. In addition, his stature was stunted, and his health was delicate, and the first impression his presence created was one of discomfort. Over these severe personal disadvantages he singularly triumphed. A certain hardiness which he developed as he grew older overcame his delicacy, so that he could travel and reside for months in the most out-of-the-way parts, beyond the reach of doctors; his vitality was immense, and the activity of his mind remarkable. Yet it will be recognized, as we examine his aims, that his natural disabilities were precisely those most calculated to defeat them. In spite of his protestations to the contrary in letters and books, in spite of his frequent statements that mountains and solitude were the only things he craved, and though, too, it is obvious that this side to his character also existed, nevertheless he was sociable by disposition, and I believe he designed particularly to shine in the world of talk and manners. With this purpose in view, he had been obliged to become highly stylized, almost affected, in his manner of conversation, since it would have been of no use for him to pretend to be ordinary. His wit, therefore, while it was spontaneous in essence, was artificial in mode; and he had rendered himself in addition an accomplished and agreeable talker, so that dullness was ever banished by his presence.

Now, in the spring of 1918, with which I deal, he was middle-aged, and though his voice, when he spoke, was at first as startling as the discordant cry of jay or woodpecker, so alert and vivacious a mind did he possess, and with so exact and often ludicrous an expression was he able to formulate his thoughts, that, after a single meeting with him, his vocal and bodily anomalies were completely overlooked. Nor, indeed, was his appearance now altogether unprepossessing, though it remained still grotesque. His complexion, formerly sallow, had assumed a more florid tinge, and he had grown rather fat, which caused him a little to resemble the Chinese God of Good Fellowship, or a Western Silenus painted by a Chinese artist. From his birth, he had carried a slightly Mongol look, which in turn had been emphasized — though in this instance

[20]

not acquired, as is often the case — by long periods spent in China. (After my own visit there, subsequent to his death, I began to wonder, too, whether one reason why he so greatly loved the Orient might not have been that in China he did not look so exceptional, while, in addition, the tones of his voice were less noticeable when Mandarin Chinese was being spoken round him.) His hair was black, and grew rather low on the forehead, his dark eyes were, in hackneyed phrase, speaking eyes, beyond any I have seen. They shone with that particular and urgent light that is only to be noticed in the eyes of the deaf or of those who encounter some physical difficulty in utterance. Yet this in his case was unaccountable, for he possessed no hesitation in his speech, which, at its worst, sounded like one of those early gramophones fitted with a tin trumpet. His manner was bland, but, albeit possessed of the capacity to be extremely considerate, he was impish by nature, and so, since he had also the power of identifying, with an intimidating speed and certainty, hypocrisy and pretentiousness, there were, even at his most clement, occasional sly digs and prods for all in his conversation. He was vain, it must be admitted, in several directions, and liked to air the contents of a well-stored and observant mind. Just as, in his novels, he had developed a complex, sub-Meredithian style, so he had cultivated an intensely personal method of talk, in which he made evident his liking for effects, for epigrams and fireworks.

At Bath, on the day of which I write, all the qualities of his I have mentioned were in evidence, and at their best. It was a day of early spring, full of an illusive enchantment such as in England occurs when, once in a while, May seems to come two months too soon and to bring with it the suggestion that it will stay, and that all the rest of the year will be of a similar beauty and gaiety. So strongly armed in its own atmosphere was that Sunday morning, calling one out of doors into the glittering opalescent crescents and terraces, where the young opening leaves were beginning already to deck the tall eighteenth-century trees with their green calligraphy, that, leaving the house quickly — for Madame Vandervelde, Reginald and I found our own company congenial — we wandered, aimless with the pleasure of the air, until we discovered ourselves to be in the country, and eventually reached an inn. Entering, and discovering that it had a garden facing the sun, we proudly asserted our status as bona fide travelers, and there drank glasses of a peach brandy, fragrant and delectable, and basked no less in its warmth than in that of the pale yellow sunshine. In my mind's eye, I can still picture Madame Vandervelde and myself sitting there, while our fantastic companion strutted up and down on the green lawn, talking, telling us of many things, homely or exotic, for the conversation ranged from his parents to the uplands of China and Tibet. To his mother and father he always referred as "the Watsons," for he maintained that, in the fashion of Sherlock Holmes's celebrated, if stolid, friend, they followed on events, making their own deductions, and arrived on the scene in the end, late, from the wrong direction, and amazed at every new development, but still safe and still sure of the essential rightness of their methods. He talked of them now, and of various other relations we had in common, of whose ways we had both made a study. In describing his various travels, he told us, I remember, of an interview he had been granted some years before by a Living Buddha. This Incarnation resided in the interior of Ceylon, and Reginald had gone to see him there, taking with him an interpreter, through whom — for he had been informed he might disturb the Holy Man to that extent — to put a few questions. On the way they had been alarmed by rumors of a man-eating tiger in the jungle which they had been obliged to traverse, so Reginald, directly he entered, demanded to be told what he ought to do if, in the course of his return journey, he encountered the ferocious beast. For a long while the Living Buddha pondered, and then he spoke. The interpreter thus conveyed his message:

"His Holiness is of the opinion that if, after every other method of persuasion has been exhausted, and every exhortation has failed, the tiger still continues to threaten you, then you are at liberty to enter into argument with him."

When the matter had been thus disposed of, Reginald had left the Living Buddha's presence, and had been fortunate enough to return home in safety.

Similarly, much of what he said that morning was tinged by the experience he had gained during long sojourns in the East. He had already discovered — and this was a year before his last journey — an amazing number of new plants, including the famous gentian named after him. And he brought to bear on every flower, and on even the most ordinary pleasures of everyday life, what I can now see, after my visit to China, to be a Chinese gift of appreciation. It was precisely this quality which made his company often so delightful, and imparted so much atmosphere to the hour or so that I describe. The unfolding of each leaf, the falling of the light, attained an importance unusual in the West in the scheme of a day, and the easy and convivial party spirit of the Chinese prospered in the sparkling air round us. As the morning wore on — and fortunately, though enjoyable, it tarried and lingered as is rarely the way — and as the peach brandy in the bottle diminished, and because Madame Vandervelde was wearing a leopard-skin coat, we decided to stage an impromptu *Bacchanale*. We twined for our heads, I remember, garlands of ivy, as a plain British substitute for the authentic vine, while, too, Reginald borrowed from me the enormous Brigade of Guards gray greatcoat I was wearing. I still recall with pleasure the sight of him thus garbed and wreathed, prancing about, the full skirts of my magnificent coat trailing behind him on the grass, so that he looked as if he were a child dressed up in the clothes of his parents. More than ever he resembled an Oriental version of Silenus.

His writings to a large extent make permanent the qualities

of his personality. The manner of his books no doubt possesses its faults; it lacks the repose, for example, to be found in the novels of Jane Austen, for whom he cherished so great a veneration. It may be thought, in addition, to have started the rhapsodical hyperboles of the modern flower worshiper. Nevertheless, a most genuine love of beauty permeates his books; they are stamped with his unusual individuality, and in all of them is to be found a powerful surge of original humor and of wit. He was a prolific author, and of his various novels and other works,[1] in some ways the most interesting and representative is *The Rainbow Bridge*, published posthumously. For, only two years after the glimpse we have caught of him, he died in Burma, it was said of diphtheria, though since no doctor could reach him, and he was unattended save by his native servants, this is not certain.

The letter which follows was written during his last months, and I append it here because it reveals a little of what both he and I had suffered in the war years, though at the time we had apparently differed in our opinions, or at least in our expression of them.

C/o T. Cook   Nyitadi, Via Kongha, Via Fort Herz
Phayre Street   Via Myitkyina
Rangoon   Upper Burma

My Dear Osbert,

How do you do, all the long while — although you never answered my valedictory note? The other day, or rather, now, quite a long time since, I came across a photograph of you in the paper, looking more than ever like an elder brother of Princess Charlotte of Wales. But this did not so much inspire my craving for a chat with you, as pour fuel on its fire: chats with you are

[1] The following list of Reginald Farrer's books is not by any means exhaustive: *The House of Shadows*, 1906; *The Sundered Streams*, 1907; *My Rock Garden*, 1907; *The Ways of Rebellion*, 1908; *In Old Ceylon*, 1908; *The Dowager of Jerusalem*, 1908, *Alpine and Bog Plants*, 1908; *The Anne-Queen's Chronicle*, 1909; *A Yorkshire Garden*, 1909; *On the Eaves of the World*, 1917; *The Rainbow Bridge*, 1921.

things I've very rarely had and always so much wanted that I grudge the way we always met only in crowds or in circumstances false and non-conductive. You might indeed, have sent me *Argonaut and Juggernaut* [2] (what a dreadful jingle that will be in the mouths of the vulgar). You mistake, if you think I am not interested and sympathetic; remember in how unrepresentative an atmosphere we found each other. Where usually we met, nobody ever really reads anything, you know: the atmosphere, for all its pretentiousness is as obstinately ἀπειρόκαλος [3] as a coalheaver's. Even the most esthetic is not of any excessive enthusiasm towards other people's efforts as creating beauty. For I do hope you are still and primarily concentrating on this: under the stress of war there was a danger you might incline too excessively to contempt and hate. Indignation may make verse, as Juvenal claims: it certainly don't make poetry. There is nothing in the whole world worth while except the creation of beauty, in some form or other: scorn and rage are mere distractions of the devil. I speak feelingly, for though unfashionably aged by now, I have hated, and do still hate a number of things, with an intensity I believe you have never surpassed, except in so far as youth's fire surpasses in evidentness the settled glow of the forties. I hate lies and humbug, journalism, Christianity, domesticity, dulness and European civilisation in general, with a fury that, if I let it, makes me feel quite ill. But what is the use of fighting and raving? The only thing to do for a wise man, is to sit under the wall while the dust storm of mortal folly drives by. My refuge is to come away up here, among "the stars and the great silences," where never a murmur of that noxious nonsense can come to my ears and, for a healing season or two, I can forget all about it, and escape unto myself. It is all so tiring in its hopelessness: nothing but a new Attila, followed by a new Buddha, will do any good. You have the advantage, or disadvantage, of years. I too fought in my time and way, though then, in the particular circles which you and I adorn, it was as *mal-vu* to be young as it is nowadays to be anything else. But nothing's any good. I now ask only for peace, and a chance to go on trying to make something beautiful for myself in this desert

[2] The author's first book, a volume of poems.
[3] Ignorant of the beautiful, without taste, or vulgar.

of falseness and hideousness. And it tires me and saddens me, in a
way, to see the same generous furies that I used to have, still at
work in the new young; and the endless circle going on just the
same. You, too, will arrive at my contemptuous and remote resignation: but nothing can ever make good the loss of our twentieth
years, with their divine and noble folly.

You will be surprised at this outburst of peevishness against the
claptrap and slumgullion of the world, when you remember how
loyally I clung by just that very slumgullion during the war. But
this was not done blindly, but of choice, knowing the claptrap and
falsehood for what they were, but finding them the only possible
drugs for a delirious disease. You cannot go on doing beastly
things without buoying yourself up on beastly thoughts, wicked
madnesses to match the madness by which you are driven. War is
a wholly beastly irremediable evil, let it be as defensive, as chiv-
alrous, as all-the-rest-of-the-rot ever preached by the wildest war
profiteer: at its very best, it is a doing of unimaginable harm in
the theory that a possible good may result. It is fatal, then, in the
course of such a crime, to look to right or left, to ponder reason,
mercy and justice: the only thing is to make oneself deliberately
drunk with the DAILY MAIL, so as to be able to live through the
dreadful drunkenness of everyone else. If one stops to think of
the utter sham one knows the whole thing to be, everything collapses, and one can't go on: it's like Peter on the Sea. No, one
must [clamp] shutters to all thought, admit only the maddening
and deafening clamour of the time. At least, if the thing is to be
carried through. It is one of the world's pet pretences that you
can gather grapes of thorns and figs of thistles: even as our dear
families believe that you can make a thing so by calling it so.
You can no more have an amicable lawsuit or a clean-hearted war
than you can have a white black or a dry wet. Evil is always evil
and can only breed true: the bye-products are no more relevant
than the anemones that might spring up round the thistle. Therefore, if one's got to be ugly, let us deliberately and frankly be it.
I don't want to use the Military Representative's argument — but
while you're at lethal grips with a tramp — no, let's say, merely,
without invidiousness, an enemy — it is no use thinking of anything but how to kick him in the guts or gouge out his eyes.

These are the beautiful fruits that enmity inevitably breeds, be it in a cause no matter how apparently, or pretendedly, or really noble. Once you begin thinking instead about the adversary's domestic virtues, or other desirable qualities, you slacken, and either he kicks you in the guts, or else the enmity collapses and comes to an end. And how dreadful that would be! To keep stark in hate you have to go on making yourself drunk with it, the state being, fortunately, abnormal. Let no-one say I didn't do *my* best. But *how* greatly I loathed myself, and life, and everything all the time: It was like going straight forward, desperately, along a tight-rope, over Hell. No wonder if one's nerves were strained to snapping point.

These are extremely belated meditations with which to assail you from afar. But, out of the fantasmagoric nightmare of hysteria, you do emerge to me as a possibly real person. Our circumstances and relationship have given us two minds not wholly unlike, and developing on lines as similar as the difference of incidents and generations have allowed. So, now, in the solacing calm of solitude, I feel a certain freedom to sit down and prattle. Neither of us, praise be, is to be judged and valued, I think, by our distraught selves of 1917–18. Also, of course, this unfathomable remoteness gives me a yet more naked boldness in unveiling the nudities of what I really think. Far and far beyond posts and railways, far beyond Ultima Thule, right away over on the far side of the uttermost edge of nowhere, I sit in a little bamboo shanty, open at every pore to all the winds that blow, surrounded, far overhead, by inky black peaks like flames in a tempest, frozen suddenly. No letters, no papers, no news, nothing to remind me of the mad world I hate, nothing but the enormous embalming peace of the Alp, where little thoughts and selves have no more place — as indeed, the wise and holy of history have always found and proclaimed. It is extraordinarily, incomparably, delicious and restorative, amid loneliness and the gigantic company of mountains and their silences and great haunting presences. So that I'm now happy as the days are long, working hard among the plants, and camping on high passes, full of snow and midges, incidentally with two immortal works on hand, to vary my employments — of which at least one, I am convinced, will defy all rivalry from

our cousins in the way of unpleasantness. Yet though I so ex-
cruciatingly detest European civilisation, I love the component
molecules, and am very often at home with you all in spirit. In
absence, indeed, people are extremely present: one can play with
them untrammelled and make them what one likes them, after the
image of one's own heart's desire that they should be.

I ought to be down out of this at the year's end: then for
Peking: and then home. — R. F.

*   *   *

As well as talents of this, and no mean, order, I have been
privileged to catch sight of genius, and in some rare instances
to contemplate it at my leisure. The next character I present
was, even at first sight, impressive. My brother has written of
him elsewhere [4] with such understanding that I am obliged
to paraphrase what he has written, but I could not omit so
remarkable a friend from the pages of my autobiography.

Bernard van Dieren, to whom I thus refer, bore the stamp
of his altogether exceptional nature in his appearance. My
brother and I had first met him in the house of Mr. and Mrs.
Jacob Epstein, just opposite the grounds of the Foundling
Hospital, in 1913. The composer had written to the eminent
sculptor about the exhibition of his work then to be seen in
the Twenty-One Gallery in the Adelphi, and shortly after this
the two men had become acquainted. Now van Dieren and
his wife were on a very cordial footing with the Epsteins, and
were often to be seen with them in Guildford Street. And a
year or two later, van Dieren served as the model for Epstein's
celebrated "Christ." It would have been impossible, I think,
for anyone of intelligence to see van Dieren or hear him talk,
and not to wish to know him better: and we were fortunate in
that, after our first meeting, a friendship soon sprang up
between the composer and ourselves, and for several years we
saw a great deal of him. Ten years later, he honored us with
the dedication of his setting of Heine's *Der Asra*.

[4] In *The Hunters and the Hunted*.

By birth, van Dieren came of a noble Dutch family, though French blood too flowed in his veins, for he was the great-great-grandson of Madame de Lamotte de Valois, the adventuress implicated in the notorious scandal of the alleged purchase by Queen Marie Antoinette of the famous Diamond Necklace. Through this ancestress van Dieren descended illegitimately from Henri II. But as a young man — he was thirty-three years of age when we first saw him — it was of the Bonapartes, rather than of the House of Valois, that he put one in mind, since he bore a certain resemblance, in the cut and tint of his face (he suffered from a painful and recurrent malady which accounted for this rather floury or ivory pallor), to the young Napoleon, though he was slighter in build and a little taller. His manners were fine, and the touch of charlatanism which the short brown velvet smock he habitually wore suggested to English eyes in no way impaired his look of high breeding. Even if he had not adopted this garment, his appearance — more Latin than Dutch, though he was not very dark — would still have been vivid and interesting enough to be unlike that of anyone else: but with it he exhibited, as my brother has remarked, some likeness to a youthful alchemist or necromancer of medieval times. Albeit in his make-up there were elements of the dramatic, the obscure, almost of the unbelievable, these in no fashion predominated. It is to the clear working of his intellect, and to the level but luminous reaches of his conversation, that one looks back. His vocabulary in English was rich and varied, he spoke it with no accent, but rather slowly and with a Dutch intonation. He laughed seldom, but when he smiled his expression was particularly charming, and his eyes, which were apt to be serious, and penetrating in their gaze, altered in the most striking manner.

In his art, no slightest trace of charlatanism or ostentation was to be found, and to it he devoted his life, and what little health he had, with a singular integrity and selflessness. It was a far from sensuous music, of bone and spirit, and of the highest contrapuntal virtue and complication. He pursued his own path, made no effort to compromise, and remained aloof, undeterred by lack of popular appreciation and understanding: though it is true that he was supported by the affection, faith and esteem of a band of true musicians and fervent admirers, and that he was most fortunate in having for his wife Frida Kindler, the pianist. She is the sister of the late Hans Kindler, the celebrated Dutch cellist and conductor, and her great intelligence and devotion must have been able to ease for her husband those moments of loneliness and frustration which doubtless came to him, as they come — and with less reason — to most artists. . . . Concerning his music, my testimony must be that of one technically unequipped to pronounce. I can only say that it was easy to appreciate the often exquisite beauty of his songs, and that in his other compositions I seemed to catch sight, at a great distance from me, of beauties the existence of which I had not hitherto divined. I wish I could live long enough to hear the verdict of posterity: but it will not be delivered yet awhile. Finally, I may add on this subject that it seems to me impossible that a man of such plainly exceptional gifts, and one who gave himself so seriously to his task, should have failed to transfer to his creations something of his own genius, or something conveyed through it from beyond.

Everything about van Dieren was rare, fine, unusual. With his weak health he combined unusual muscular strength, no doubt inherited from his mother, who, when he was the victim of one of the crises of his illness, would, though she was an old lady of over seventy or more, carry him up and down stairs. His memory was of such a quality that once in my brother's presence he was able to recite by heart the whole of an article he had been reading in the newspaper, while his friends had been talking and he, seemingly, had been listening to their conversation. His hands, with their particularly well-shaped nails, were individual, long and most sensitive: and it was difficult, looking at them, to realize that he was an expert carpenter in practice: though to the contrary one was in no way surprised by the beauty of his handwriting or the exquisite precision of his elaborate scores. Nor did it require any effort to believe that he made his own marble end papers, or himself repaired the many volumes in his library — remarkable in both quality and quantity for one of his means — or that he engaged, generally, in the most difficult technical feats of bookbinding. Indeed, looking back, I seem always to recall him in his brown velvet smock, and with his flopping, black bow tie, sitting surrounded by the gleaming array of his bookshelves, with their calf-bound volumes in prime condition, and their lettering a-glitter with gold.

As fitting colophon to this account of him, I here repeat from my brother's *The Hunters and the Hunted* the story of an incident which occurred towards the end of van Dieren's life. The periodic agonies he suffered grew no less as the years went by, and it may be mentioned that towards the crisis of his illness his temperature is said to have been known to register as much as 112 degrees Fahrenheit. The scene I go on to describe was pitched in the null, noncommittal surroundings of a rehearsal room at the B.B.C. The composer had come hither to hear his own music. With all the appearance of being too ill to stir, he was lying on a sofa, while the orchestra went through a piece of his. Suddenly, at a passage of extreme difficulty, van Dieren called to the conductor to stop, asked the first violin for his instrument, took it, and demonstrated how the music ought to be played. The rehearsal then continued, and when, a moment later, the conductor looked round to ask a question of the composer, he saw him lying back exhausted on the sofa, with steam rising from his head.

This was the last time that he was present in the flesh to hear a performance of his own music. . . . But it may not have constituted his final appearance on such an occasion; for a singular story is current in musical circles. Some years ago, but also a year or two after van Dieren's death — which occurred in April 1936 — a concert was given at the Mercury Theatre, Notting Hill Gate, and the program included his Third Quartet. In the audience were two old ladies, who, though they were friends, happened to be sitting in different quarters of the theater. Neither of them was musical, and they were only present because a younger friend of theirs, a well-known woman musician, was to take part in an item later in the evening. After van Dieren's quartet had been played, one of the old ladies went up to her younger friend and remarked casually:

"I thought a quartet always meant that four people played."

On being asked to explain, she said she had seen five men on the platform — and one was a very remarkable-looking man, pale, with a face that somehow recalled the young Napoleon. He was wearing a brown velvet smock, she noticed, and he had seemed to take all the applause at the end, and had come forward and bowed. . . . During the conversation, the other old lady had joined them, and now she also testified to having seen the same figure.

Thus we take leave of a strange, delightful, supremely endowed individual, possessing many high faculties in the most eminent degree — including the gift of becoming a legend in his own lifetime, and a presence after it. And, indeed, his appearance after his death is hardly less surprising than the occasion I have just described at the end of his life. Everything about his personality was unusual, fabulous almost, and would incline even the most skeptical to be credulous in this one instance.

In a letter accompanying the copy of *Der Asra* he sent to Sacheverell, Bernard van Dieren wrote:

It has taken ten years before my slight tribute to you and your brother has, within the narrow limits of my very modest fame, become a relatively public one. But since it has, I should be unhappy to think that you were ignorant of the almost pathetic fact. Were it only because it may remind you of much affectionate appreciation that remained steadily alive through these intervening years. My inscription is as sincerely conceived as it would have been today, and as much — if not more — an act of deep regard for your talents, now, as it was then.

The warmth and charm of the reference may make the reader wonder about my brother, and what he was like at this time to which van Dieren refers. . . . Sacheverell, then an officer in the Grenadier Guards, was nineteen years of age, and it would be difficult, I think, to say which was the more striking personality, the composer or the young poet. Six feet three inches in height, he had a somewhat fair tawny skin, a regular profile, and his hair waved at the temples, so that his appearance united something of the Norman or Gothic saint, Saint Sebastian perhaps, with something, too, of the young Bacchus. Yet he could have been mistaken for no one but an Englishman and — though at present in the guise of an English officer — if aiming at a more strict classification, an English poet. There was an untidy grace about him, and a faunal *faroucheness* which constrained him to silence in the company of those he did not know well, and made some think, groundlessly, that it was founded on arrogance. His mind was as alive and as brilliantly colored as a tropical bird. His craving to learn was almost as strong as his passion for beauty, and his head was full of abstruse matters and of lore concerning the arts. The enthusiastic generosity and affectionate recklessness of his disposition were most unusual. His temper, though it flashed easily and fiercely, was forgiving, but often, if angered, he would refuse to eat. (In later years, I recall his remarking to me, "I *never* lose my temper unless someone does something to annoy me.") In pursuit of his intellectual or esthetic interests, to see a building or a picture, he would be capable of indefatigable effort, but, when young, he would not raise a finger to do something that did not appeal to him. He possessed all the energy and strength and all the indolence of his giant's frame, but *mental* laziness, or even repose, was an impossibility to him. The next year — 1918 — was to be published his first book,[5] containing poems of an original and astonishing loveliness.

THE MOON

The white nightingale is hidden in the branches
And heavy leafage of the clouds.
She pours down her song —
Cascades threaded like pearls,
And the winds, her many-noted flutes,
Flood forth their harmony. —
But the Earth turns away
Swinging in its air and water-rocked cradle.

The ardent nature and extraordinary capacities of the two beings who were nearest to me, my brother and sister, provided me with matter for continual observation in my own home. And at this point I offer, as equipoise to the foregoing account of Sacheverell as a young man, and to end the introductory chapter to this book with a fanfare, an incident of Edith's early youth. Rescued from the already nigh obliterated records of childhood, yet it certainly belongs to these pages. It occurred a few months after I was born and was, therefore, not a personal recollection: but it formed an episode too perfect, too complete, to be included in the chapters devoted to prenatal or infantine character-planting in the first volume of this autobiography, or to be incorporated in the general fabric of the remainder. Although I may not count it among my own reminiscences, nevertheless, it almost ranks as such, so well can I recall the few people who figure on this particular stage, so clearly can I summon up the scene itself, and so frequently did I hear the occasion alluded to in after years with the particular tones of regret, shame and condem-

[5] *The People's Palace* (Blackwell, Oxford, 1918).

nation reserved for it. The childish lack of modesty, the childish directness and certainty it exemplified, at the time made a wound, and subsequently left a scar, on the family consciousness. In her circle, it was generally held that my mother had on this occasion exhibited a commendable restraint. . . . After it had taken place, there had been an instant's pause, and then she had said to our nurse:

"Davis! You had better take Miss Edith out for a walk!" And thereupon the child had been led out into the great spaces of the sunlight. . . . But though I often heard the matter discussed in low voices, it was never, I believe, spoken of outside the walls of our home until now: when I produce it here because it may furnish a clue — and self-confessed — to my sister's subsequent achievement.

Though when I first remember her, a few years later, my sister was recognizable as the youthful version of what she still is, the same carriage, long limbs, and Byzantine or Sienese profile, yet some two or three years earlier, at the moment in which I am trying to paint her, she was only just emerging from babyhood, and possessed an almost unidentifiably different appearance, as different as a young eagle, soft and downy, is from its grown-up self. Then she was a sturdy, indeed — let us be frank — a fat child of four, dressed in dark green serge and wearing buttoned boots and gaiters. Her lank golden hair curled at the end and framed a full-moon face: only the deep-set, hooded, tragic eyes of the poet she was to become peered out from this mask of childhood, telling us of her own future and of the world's. The eyes seemed to contemplate with a full consciousness, and dwell upon with a brooding compassion, the forces at work to shatter the gay and glittering surfaces round us and to dispose of those who walked or sauntered across them, while the green glance of those gray-blue eyes was, in addition, directed within, directed towards the infinities of the human soul, as well as towards the exterior aspects.

[35   ]

The room in which the action takes place was the rather large drawing room on the first floor of our Scarborough house, decorated in elegant mandarin taste, with Chippendale chairs and flimsy Chippendale tables and looking glasses, a piece of Flemish tapestry, and in the corners of the room misty sea-green vases, made of Venetian glass and tall as a man. These were shaped like an enormous trumpet, standing upright on its mouthpiece, but the outer rim was frilled and indented so as the better to hold the blossoms and branches. On the table, too, were placed smaller bowls and vases of flowers. Below the windows — wide open, for it was a warm afternoon in the middle of May — showed a flat floor of green tree-tops, as though cut specially for the summer winds to race along, and beyond this, a vast expanse of light blue sea, merging into the light blue sky that covers us, covers all. Here, today, was to be detected no trace of the possibility of the winter's rage, when, so loud is the roaring tumult and turmoil of the waves, so persistent the never-ending pounding of their great rams against the base of the cliff, that even in the center of the town, and enclosed by the walls of a room, it is difficult to hear a human voice. Here, today, came no echo, either, of the scarecrow's cry, "*Rags and Bones! Rags and Bones!*" borne on the gale's edge, under the creaking chimney pots in a crepuscular dawn. On such a long, lacquered, aromatic afternoon as this, there was to be perceived as yet no hint of the windy, desolate spaces of the future:

> . . . where Man's threatening shadow
> Red-edged by the sun like Cain, has a changing shape,
> Elegant like the Skeleton, crouched like the Tiger,
> With the age-old wisdom and aptness of the Ape.

The only sound to reach this room today was a cheerful and inane music: somewhere, far away in the town, a barrel organ was rattling out *Ta-ra-ra-boom-de-ay!* and, under this lively din, and louder in the interval between it and the next item in the mechanical repertory, there was tapped out the good-natured but formal repartee of croquet ball and mallet.

Within this room, my mother was sitting in the light sunshine and shadow, while beyond her a figure — Rita, a friend of ours who had come to stay — was outlined in the center window against the splintered glory of the sun: she was dressed in pale, luminous colors, and though she was not beautiful as was my mother, her waist was renowned for its slenderness, and, as she stood there, she seemed to possess an ineffable modishness, in line the elegance of a Minoan priestess-acrobat, in color the gay dappling and speckling of a painting by Seurat. My mother was wearing clothes of a more sporting cut, for she always, if possible, marred in the daytime the warm perfection of her Italian looks with this hard, inappropriate yet characteristic style. In opposition to it, however, she carried, just above the waist, a large bunch of tuberoses, edged with sweet geranium leaves. My father, who was in the background, was lifting up the smaller vases, to see if too much water had been poured into them, and whether it was running down the sides to leave on the polished surfaces of the tables an ashy or mildewed ring of lighter color. The simple work necessary for the detection of this possible misdemeanor by gardener or housemaid, the raising up on an even keel, so that more water should not upset, he accomplished with a somewhat furtive air, for he knew that, if she noticed it, it would irritate my mother ("Fussing again, George!"); but he could not refrain from so favorite an occupation. For the rest, he did not seem to pay much attention to what was in progress in the room — where, indeed, it was unusual for him to be present at this hour — or to what was being said.

My mother rang the bell, and when the footman answered it, told him to "send for Davis and Miss Edith." Not that she wanted herself to see the child, who at times roused in her a kind of fear so that she almost hated her, for the little creature possessed a striking personal dignity. She used words, on occasion, of which at her age — four — she could hardly comprehend the meaning, and in general she seemed disagreeably unlike the children of friends and relations. Her way of seeing things was surprising, unsuitable and, as my father thought, tended to destroy the charm that, for parents, should invest childhood with a sticky but romantic gloss. Her truthfulness, in particular, was objectionably truthful, while in addition she showed a love of music that seemed to him so excessive as almost to be dangerous. . . . But Rita, who had not long arrived, had always evinced a fondness for the strange child, whom she had not yet seen on this visit. She had asked for her to be brought in, and so my father and mother had been obliged to pretend to want to see her also.

After a moment or two, the door had opened, and Davis in her black bonnet, and gray alpaca coat and wide skirt, ushered the little girl in, and stood apart, a kindly, impassive figure, her head held a little on one side, as was her wont, with her eyes full of the devotion she felt for her small charge, and, in addition, of a chronic and almost constitutional bewilderment. The child advanced — I nearly wrote, swept — into the room and seemed to fill it with her personality, so that it vanquished even the strong individual atmosphere created by my mother and father.

"Well, little E.," the guest inquired, "do you remember me?"

For a full minute the child regarded her attentively, with large, melancholy eyes, considering the matter, and then spoke firmly the uncompromising monosyllable:

"No!"

My mother laughed uneasily: my father put down a vase so quickly that he nearly himself spilled the water, and observed, with his own species of tact, "The memory of children is often deficient in tenacity: Herbert Spencer, whom I was reading the other day, has made some interesting deductions

[38]

in the matter. . . . Perhaps you'd like to look at the book, Rita?"

The others did not pay much attention to what he was saying. The child held the limelight; though she had made a bad beginning. Worse was to come.

Rita shifted the conversational ground so as to hide her smiling dismay. She spoke again, inclining kindly, as much as her figure would allow, towards the little girl who stood there with singular isolation.

"And what are you going to be when you grow up?"

This time the reply came without any pause for reflection, straight, clear, final:

"A Genius!"

With this summoning up of a moment from the past, we have finished looking at the preliminary sketches in the portfolio. The doors of the picture gallery are thrown open, we leave the antechamber and enter. It is hung with eleven portraits, and the guide, as he comes to each one in turn, calls out the name. In some cases the identity attached to it may not at once be plain to all, but the first will be familiar to many, and some there will be, no doubt, who will experience at the sound of it the identical thrill of pleasure and tremor of apprehension that used to make themselves felt when in his lifetime the same person was announced in a drawing room.

CHAPTER II

Sir Edmund Gosse

SIR EDMUND GOSSE! Though, in a sense, till you examined him, Sir Edmund Gosse was ordinary to look at, his entry would never have passed unnoticed. His presence made itself felt. Thus, though it is easy for the young critics of the present day to mock at him, they would not have found it so easy were he alive; *he* would have seen to that. The last survivor of an age that has passed, he constituted the lingering, final spark of the Pre-Raphaelite comet which had flashed through the darkness of the Victorian small hours, and it is for this reason that I set myself to the task of trying to present a momentary glimpse of his personality. Of his literary remains I shall here say little, except that all who have read *Father and Son* must by now be convinced that it is a truly remarkable work, and that it soars on a sudden flight of wings high above the level that he generally achieved. It was a book ahead of the time, to the same degree that its author was sometimes behind it. (Shaw, indeed, proclaimed that it entitled its writer to burial in the Abbey.[1]) But his poetry is of a kind that does not

[1] In a letter to Dr. Philip Gosse, Sir Edmund's only son, dated 18th January 1929, a few months after Gosse's death, Shaw tells him that when he last saw Sir Edmund, at Thomas Hardy's funeral, he had said to him of *Father and Son*, "It is one of the immortal pages of English literature," to which Gosse had replied, "Oh, my dear Shaw, you are the *only* one who ever encourages me." Shaw ends his letter, "In my opinion he, too, should have been buried in the Abbey; for the little room that is left there should not be reserved for Best Sellers whose work has been fully recognised and rewarded during their lifetime, but allotted for preference to those workers who have loved literature for its own sake and done the things for it that only scholars appreciate, leaving big-drum celebrity for people like myself,

appeal to me, and I detest conventional literary criticism. Nevertheless, for it has been so much disparaged, I must briefly enter various pleas on his behalf in this respect.

Gosse's understanding of dead authors was perhaps more sure than his comprehension of living; when, for example, he wrote of the minor Elizabethan dramatists, he was impeccable in feeling, if not always, it appears, in fact. His knowledge, along its own lines, was wide and deep. Above all, his opinions were prejudiced — as I like an author's to be. His writings upon modern authors were biased and fiery, in both denunciation and praise, but he never endeavored to play for Safety First by balancing both in the same composition. Myself, I divide critics into two flocks, *hedgers* and *ditchers*. One living critic, for example, a discriminating faint-heart with a gift for phrase, I have watched for a long time past at work as a *hedger*, noticing how, when a work of a controversial order emerges, or, better still, a man of genius dies, D. H. Lawrence or Joyce, he will devote articles to this particular book or to the whole body of the dead man's writings for two weeks running; in the first he will praise, in the second condemn, thereby securing in the same lobby the votes of *ayes* and *noes*. He is a man, in fact, after Humpty Dumpty's own heart and pattern, a coalition, and both sides are required to buttress the walls upon which he sits with the incomparable skill born of a full generation of uneasy equipoise. . . . But Gosse was a *ditcher*, a bold and combatant ditcher.

It is true that it often took him many months, even years, to choose his ditch, but, once he had selected it, he threw himself into it with fury, and, if attacked, would carry out a series of brilliant sorties and counterattacks. Never would he abandon his position. The fact of his punctilio, and love of ceremonious manners, and of his humor, blinded many to his

---

for whom literature is only a means of self-expression." (*The Life and Letters of Sir Edmund Gosse*, by The Hon. Evan Charteris, K.C. London, William Heinemann, Ltd., 1931.)

very combative nature. This always to me appeared to be an essential part of him, and I see Shaw alludes to it in the same letter to which I have referred in the previous footnote. In fact, though Gosse was, and liked to be, a man of the world, and enjoyed the pleasure of prestige and the various dignities that came his way, at any time he was ready, as it were, to throw down his gloves and top hat, tear off his frock coat, and rush to take a hand in the battle. If it was not raging fiercely enough for his liking, he could be depended upon to quicken it into fury.

I first met Mr. Edmund Gosse, as he then was, in 1916, at a luncheon party given in his honor and that of his wife, at the Royal Automobile Club, by Robert Ross. It would have been impossible to meet him under more agreeable circumstances: for the particular deference Ross paid him, the subtle flattery of his address, made the eminent Victorian expand and glow, and rise to more than his own stature: he was rather small and neatly built. In spite of his somewhat ordinary appearance, he manifested, when you came to examine him, a certain panache all the more effective because it was not too obtrusive. Above the puritan foundations, solid and belonging to the mid-Victorian epoch, which were at once evident, and in addition to his obvious integrity or rectitude,[2] could be detected also an air of gaiety and dash, most attractive, and seldom to be met with in one of his age, for he was nearing seventy. He was fine in profile, in the texture of his fair skin, of his gray hair that had been yellow, and of his slightly drooping *chinoiserie* mustache; *refined* in the proper sense of the word. Indeed his name itself, *Gosse*, if you came to think of it, suggested something of him, something of his sprightly, elusive *gossamer* quality, something also of *un Gosse*. But this mild and frail exterior offered as well certain indications of strength, albeit

[2] This was so plain a feature of his character as to make the suggestion that he was in any degree whatsoever cognizant of Thomas Wise's forgeries ludicrous in the extreme to all those who knew Gosse.

of the coiled-spring, rather than of the dumbbell, variety. Moreover, he could make it menacing, for it disguised a true fighting spirit, a nature perhaps a little feline, but most certainly daring and even aggressive — and it must not be forgotten that tigers and leopards and lions all belong to the cat tribe. In Gosse's anger — and, when displeased, he liked, I think, the world to know it — you could watch the cat pounce, the tiger spring, the lion both play and roar. He gave no quarter and implored none. He brooked no rivals. . . . Yet all this that I have described as panache was, notwithstanding, ever subtly tinctured with the atmosphere of an English Sunday.

Even more important than this fine but pernickety distinction, however, was the impalpable aura of power that emanated from him. Young writers were not introduced to him, they were brought up to be *presented*, and beforehand they would feel nervous — if they did not, he could be trusted to see that they felt nervous afterwards. The distinction, then, was innate; the aura owed its glow to several component causes. There was his friendship with the Pre-Raphaelites, and with other great and interesting men, there was his introduction of Ibsen to the English-speaking world, there was his eminence as a critic, and there was, finally, his learning. In the past his accuracy had often been impugned, his authority challenged, but these times were long over. So, too, that happy, never-to-be-forgotten afternoon, when, still smarting from the murderous attack made upon him in the *Quarterly* a day or two earlier by Churton Collins — one whom he had considered his friend — he had arrived, in fulfilment of a promise made long before, to stay at Aldworth with Lord Tennyson. Tennyson was forty years older, and in the full blaze of his great fame, and involuntarily Gosse trembled before the ordeal. It was teatime when he had arrived, and he found the poet at the head of a long table crowded with guests, and at the other end a place empty. He said. "How do you do?" and sat down. The poet surveyed him, and then called down the table between the ranks of attentive ears:

"Gosse, shall I tell you what *I* think of Churton Collins?"

Gosse could not refuse the challenge, and had apprehensively assented, whereupon he heard the great man roll at him the following alliterative and assuaging sentence: "He is a louse upon the locks of literature." [3]

But now Churton Collins or "Shirt and Collars," as Gosse always called him if he had to refer to him, was dead — he had been found drowned, and it was widely believed that he had committed suicide, though the verdict recorded was one of accidental death; Tennyson, too, was dead, and as a consequence, in one way and another, his own aura had grown brighter. Attacks on his learning had ceased, and his successors knew little of how intensely he had suffered. His stature, as it were, had increased of itself, year by year, until now he was a prince of professors. The lights that had, in their lifetime, dimmed the luster of his smaller flame had gone out, and his, as a result, seemed brighter. Honors had poured in upon him and continued to do so; C.B. and knighthood, honorary degrees from St. Andrews and Cambridge, Strasbourg and Gothenburg and the Sorbonne, the orders of St. Olaf in Norway, the Polar Star in Sweden, and of the Danish Dannebrog; honors awarded to his own merits, as much as by proxy to the dead, poets and painters of originality, whose gifts he had been one of the few to appreciate in their own time, but who had themselves received little from their country or from its rulers except abuse and mockery. But though Gosse loved the world and loved honors, he still rated above all the arts

[3] Dr. Philip Gosse has pointed out to me that Tennyson's celebrated phrase derives from Smollett. In *Humphry Clinker* (letter from Matthew Bramble to Dr. Lewis, dated *June 8*) occurs the following passage: ". . . he damns all the other writers of the age with the utmost insolence and rancour. One is a blunderbuss as being a native of Ireland; another a half-starved louse of literature, from the banks of the Tweed; a third an ass, because he enjoys a pension from Government. . . ."

and literature. Now like a king he could surround himself with favorites, his chosen heirs, men and women of promise. At a good word from him — and at this time, from him alone — the sales of a young author's books, even of a poet's, mounted higher, while the insolence he would naturally otherwise have had to encounter would diminish or altogether disappear.

The younger poets in whose work he took an interest were well exemplified in a reading, organized on behalf of some charity by the late Robert Ross and Madame Vandervelde, in the autumn of 1917. It was held at the house of Lady Colefax in South Kensington — Onslow Square, if I am not mistaken. Gosse was in the chair, and the poets who were invited to read their own poetry were, so far as I can remember, Robert Graves, the late Robert Nichols, Siegfried Sassoon, Irene Rutherford McLeod, Sherard Vines, T. S. Eliot, Aldous Huxley, Edith Sitwell, Sacheverell Sitwell and myself. Sassoon failed to materialize; but the others were there. It was on this occasion that I first realized how nervous Gosse was, for, though an excellent chairman, he would glance with plain exasperation if anything went wrong and, as I have related in *Laughter in the Next Room*, he took such umbrage at Eliot — who had been delayed at his bank — arriving a few minutes late on the platform, that I doubt he ever forgave him. Fortunately he was easily distracted temporarily. He loved all little ceremonies and gracious formalities, and so was for the moment easily mollified when Robert Nichols, as planned, stepped forward and proceeded to recite a poem of Gosse's — I forget the title, but it contained the line —

The centaur crashes through the undergrowth.

Formerly he had entertained a warm admiration for Rupert Brooke, but Brooke was already dead and beyond the reach of encouragement, while the other poets of *Georgian Poetry* of whom he thought well — J. C. Squire,[4] to whom he refers

[4] See Charteris's *Life and Letters of Sir Edmund Gosse.*

in one of his letters as "that peach of a man," and Drinkwater
— were older than he liked young poets to be. So his poetic
favorites at the time of which I write were undoubtedly
Robert Nichols and Siegfried Sassoon. To the work of the
first of these I have heard Gosse give unstinted praise, in
which were mingled the names of Keats [5] and Shelley. With
Sassoon, the friendship was very genuine and of long standing,
because in addition to Gosse's enthusiastic liking for much of
his poetry, the elder man had been an intimate and lifelong
friend of Sassoon's uncle, Sir Hamo Thornycroft. . . . But
there were also those of whom he disapproved, who must not,
indeed, be mentioned in his presence, without a momentary
displacing of the aura and an interference with its regular
radiations. Of these, the ringleader was Ezra Pound, "that
preposterous American filibuster and Provençal charlatan," as
I once heard Gosse call him. At the same time, he was courteous, and his standard of politeness was old-fashioned and very
strict. Above all, no one must speak slightingly of his friends
in his presence or render anything but the respect which
eminence demands to the eminent. He was, in fact, a disciplinarian, and one of the last who could "administer a rebuke."
For so cautious a man, he was sometimes curiously unafraid
of committing himself: in a long letter to Sir Edward Marsh,
who, because Gosse had expressed his fondness for E. M.
Forster's earlier books, had sent him *Howard's End*, he descended in most injudicious thunder upon that delightful
novel. Let me quote one passage:

I hope you will not be vexed with me for speaking so plainly,
because I know that you have influence with the author of this

[5] He saw a resemblance, physically as well as in their poetic gifts. "Robert
Nichols is a very remarkable young man, with a face that in profile has a
striking resemblance to that of Keats as Severn recalled it some years after
Keats' death. He is distractingly violent, mercurial and excessive, but most
attractive in his flaming zeal and pale vehemence." (Extract from a letter to
Dr. Sim, dated March 20, 1918, from Sir Edmund Gosse.) See *Life and
Letters of Sir Edmund Gosse*, p. 423.

unhappy book. . . . I cannot help hoping that you may be induced to say something which will redeem him from the slough
of affectation and false sentiment into which he has fallen.

If I were asked to point to a passage which combined all that
prose fiction should not be — lurid sentimentality, preposterous
morals, turgid and sickly style — I do not think I could point to
anything worse than the closing chapters of *Howard's End*.[6]

In the company of the young poets I have mentioned
earlier his manner at times relaxed, for though his attitude in
general was of an unrelenting vigilance, a willingness to fly to
arms at the first sign of battle, he felt sure both of their talent
and of their friendship. Indeed the combativeness of his nature
seemed to make his amiability all the more amiable, in the same
way that it rendered his very occasional compliments, steeped
in vinegar though they always were, seem more memorable
than those of others. Thus I always look back with pleasure
to a certain Sunday afternoon. When I had first met Gosse at
luncheon, he had commanded me to go to tea with him the
following Sunday — or any Sunday, when he and Mrs. Gosse
were always at home. Gradually we came often to be present
at these gatherings. One Sunday in autumn, my sister, my
brother and I were just leaving his house. We were unde-
feated, but thoroughly mauled, and glad to go home and lick
our wounds. Gosse, with his usual beautiful manners, saw us
down to the door himself, and then called after us into the
blue dusk, "Good-by, you delightful but deleterious trio!"
and waved after us a dapper hand.

I noticed that I have not so far mentioned his hands, always
so characteristic; the fingers were rather pointed, sharp, and
the nails fine, as they should be. He did not gesticulate with
his hands when he talked, unless, for example, he were telling
one something that Swinburne had said to him, when he would
flutter his hands up and down, in the manner of the great
poet. Gosse's own hands, though shapely, were, in this re-

[6] See *Life and Letters of Sir Edmund Gosse*, p. 324.

sembling those of so many literary men, singularly useless
except when holding a pen. But this fact in no way prevented
him from making experiments with such things as cameras;
experiments which were from the outset plainly doomed.
Thus Dr. Philip Gosse has related to me how his father bought
one of the first Kodaks, a long narrow box with an opening at
one end, which the operator had to point at the object he
desired to photograph, then pulling a cord, but being obliged
to wait until the full number of exposures could be developed
before knowing the result. This camera Gosse took down
to the country, to the farmhouse where the Hamo Thorny-
crofts, Mrs. Gosse, her young family, and their extremely
correct, middle-aged Scottish governess, were spending their
summer holidays. . . . One day, at breakfast, the first set of
prints arrived, each on a separate card. Amid intense excitement, they were examined; until, suddenly, a chill fell on those
assembled — for there, in the middle of the tennis lawn, was
Hamo Thornycroft, with the governess seated on his lap!
She instantly gave notice and left immediately, refusing to accept the explanation — that Gosse, as was to have been antici-
pated, had forgotten, as he often did, to wind up the film
between taking two snapshots.

Gosse's tongue, by its occasional urbanity no less than by
its frequent poignancy, more than compensated for his hands:
people came to hear him talk, not to see the photographs he
had taken. It was because his conversation, spiced with its
own particular quality, was so delightful, that many sub-
mitted to the claims implicit in his general *ambiance* — for
that reason, and because, also, of the comparative respect in
which great men were still held. Debunking, that most decadent and degrading of literary arts, had barely begun. The
giants of the Victorian Age were esteemed, while at the same
time a new curiosity had begun to manifest itself concerning
them. As the years went by, this man who had known Swinburne so intimately, who had constituted himself his apostle

and prophet, came to possess a special interest. After Swinburne's death, he was the repository of all his secrets. And in this connection, I may say that his dislike of Watts-Dunton was not due to any sense of rivalry, in him so strong, but to his conviction that Watts-Dunton had harmed Swinburne, as well as deprived English poetry of further glories. I think Gosse knew more about Swinburne and his temperament than any man living — there are hints of it in Sir Evan Charteris's *Life and Letters of Sir Edmund Gosse*. And undoubtedly what he found out after Swinburne's death, from the poet's letters, came as a tremendous shock to him. But what does he mean exactly when he refers in a letter to Swinburne's *fear* of Watts-Dunton? It must mean something, but he never explains it. . . . He told me once that he was sure the whole world would come round to his view of the way in which Watts-Dunton had behaved. When I asked him what would effect the change, he replied that he thought that when it transpired that they had made identical wills, each leaving everything to the other, but that Swinburne at the time was possessed of money and Watts-Dunton of nothing, this would produce a great alteration in the public mind.

To revert, however, to his status, there had been other friends besides Swinburne; he had, as we have seen, known Tennyson, and, more intimately, Dante Gabriel Rossetti, Ford Madox Brown and William Morris, as well as many lesser followers of theirs, such as the fantastic character, Théophile Marziale, the poet (and a descendant of the interesting Venetian painter Marco Marziale, a contemporary of Titian's). He had known Browning, too, and had been one of Stevenson's supporters and greatest friends; Henry James, moribund when I met Gosse, had visited him often; and then there was Thomas Hardy, who, though still very much alive, ranked by his greatness as long dead.

We can even examine Gosse as a young man through the eyes of at least one of the eminent dead. . . . Robert Louis

Stevenson was fond of him, and as a symptom of it we find that he invented for him a pet name: for he often addressed him as Weg. Colvin, in a note to the *Letters of R. L. Stevenson*, states that this was partly due to the fact that Gosse in those days used to sign himself E. W. G. (later it became E. G. only), and that Stevenson chose to pretend to forget the order of the initials, partly in friendly derision of a passing fit of lameness, which called up the memory of Silas Wegg, the immortal literary gentleman *"with* a wooden leg" of *Our Mutual Friend*. But it seems to me, reading the letters and the references in them to Gosse, that there is a special tone of cordiality which R.L.S. did not manifest to all his friends, and which was perhaps founded in a sense of gratitude; for the last letter he ever wrote, dated Vailima, Samoa, December 1, 1894, was addressed to Gosse — in acknowledgement of the dedication to him, in his Samoan character of Tusitala, of Gosse's book of poems, *In Russet and Silver* — and it contains the following passage:

. . . Let me tell you a story or remind you of a story . . . between '76 and '78 I mentioned to you in my usual autobiographical and inconsiderate manner that I was hard up. You said promptly that you had a balance at your bankers, and could make it convenient to have a cheque, and I accepted and got the money — how much was it? — twenty or perhaps thirty pounds? . . . The same evening, or the next day, I fell in conversation with a denizen of the Savile Club. . . . To him I mentioned that you had given me a loan, remarking easily that of course it didn't matter to you. Whereupon he read me a lecture, and told me how it really stood with you financially. . . .

At the time of which he is writing, Stevenson was between twenty-six and twenty-eight, and it may well be that the kindness shown him so spontaneously warmed his heart.

Usually, however, as we all know by experience, the lending of money leads to the ending of friendships: and it may of course be merely that Stevenson liked Gosse and his company.

Thus, in a letter to Henley, headed Braemar, 1881, Stevenson writes of Gosse:

. . . The poet was very gay and pleasant. He told me much. He is simply the most active young man in England, and one of the most intelligent. "He shall o'er Europe, shall o'er earth extend." [7] He is now extending over adjacent parts of Scotland.

In another letter, he gives the key to the persons, such as Henley, J. A. Symonds and Gosse, who appear in his *Talk and Talkers*.[8] Gosse appears in the character of Purcel, then, and the following passage gives us his talk as it appeared, when he was a young man, to R.L.S.

. . . He [Purcel] is no debater, but appears in conversation as occasion rises, in two distinct characters, one of which I admire and fear, the other love. In the first, he is radiantly civil and rather silent, sits on a high, courtly hill top, and from that vantage ground drops you his remarks like favours. He seems not to share in our sublunary contentions; he wears no sign of interest; when on a sudden there falls in a crystal of wit, so polished that the dull do not perceive it, but so right that the sensitive are silenced. . . . I prefer my Purcel in his second character, when he unbends into a strain of graceful gossip, singing like the fireside kettle. In these moods he has an elegant homeliness that rings of the true Queen Anne.

No one would have dared to call Gosse "Weg" in the days when I met him: not even R.L.S., I imagine, had he been alive. But many eminent poets and writers had felt a warm friendship for him, had confided their hopes and their fears in him, even though, no doubt, in doing so they had clung to the familiar Victorian form of address, when the use of even Christian names among friends was unusual. (In evidence of this, one has only to recall — though he belonged to a later

[7] From Landor's *Gebir*. His line refers to Napoleon.
[8] Two papers which were published in *Memories and Portraits* (Chatto & Windus.)

date — how Sherlock Holmes, after years and years of friendship, addressed Dr. Watson as "Watson.")

How far Gosse was conscious of the special collector's interest attaching to him as the sole representative of many great men now dead, and therefore esteemed by the world, I am not aware: but, I should hazard, to the fullest extent, for he himself evinced the keenest possible curiosity in links with the past. He was fond, for example, of recalling how he had found Gainsborough at only four removes. . . . I forget the exact articulation of the chain, but I think it was that Gainsborough's housemaid had gone, after his death, as housekeeper, into the service of a family with whom Gosse's parents were acquainted. Similarly, I remember his interest when I told him that while I was descended from Arabella Churchill, being of the ninth generation, I could span the two and a half centuries in four removes, for one of my grandmothers as a young girl had known Miss Mary Berry very well, and Miss Berry had been a great friend of Horace Walpole's, and he, as a small boy, had seen a funny old lady come into Downing Street, had asked his father who she was, and had been told that it was Mrs. Godfrey, the former Arabella Churchill. All such ramifications and traditions enchanted him.

Only through him, then, was it still possible for younger men to catch a glimpse of the Victorian giants, while — which made his anecdotes extremely fascinating — in *his* voice, as he related what they had said, you could for the moment catch the very echo of *their* voices speaking. And his sense of the ludicrous — and that I think is what he possessed more than humor or wit — played even round such semisacred subjects as Swinburne or Rossetti, though it never led to the listener belittling them in his mind. Their greatness was implicit.

Let me relate three of such stories that Gosse told me.

His voice, as I have said, mirrored those of whom he talked.

When he read poems, of his own or others, his diction was invariably that of Swinburne, upon whom, consciously or unconsciously through love and enthusiasm, he had modeled it. It can be imagined. then, that his deliberate imitations, with the fluttering of the hands that I have already mentioned, were excellent, and he often told me a story (which appears in Charteris's book) relating to Swinburne in which, as he talked, you could almost see the poet, as well as hear his tones.

Swinburne had been offended by some remarks that Emerson was alleged to have made to a journalist about *Poems and Ballads*, a book which Swinburne had sent him just after it was published. Swinburne wrote to him asking if it were true that he had said these things, but no answer reached him. One day Gosse and Swinburne were sitting in the Green Park, talking, and it transpired that Swinburne had written Emerson a second letter. Knowing the poet's fiery temperament, Gosse was anxious.

"I hope you said nothing rash?"

"No, no."

"But what did you say?"

"I kept my temper, I preserved my equanimity."

"What exactly were the words you used?"

At this, Swinburne swung, chanting as it were, into the chorus with an obvious relish.

"I merely wrote, 'You are a wrinkled and toothless baboon, who, first hoisted into notoriety on the shoulders of Carlyle, now spits and splutters from a filthier platform of your own finding and fouling!' "

The second story concerns Dante Gabriel Rossetti (whose brother was considered by the elect to be the least gifted — to put it at its highest — of his family) and William Morris.

Morris had sent D. G. Rossetti a copy of *Sigurd the Volsung* when it appeared. As time went by, and no letter of thanks or appreciation arrived from him, Morris grew more

and more annoyed. Eventually, one morning he charged —
he was a very burly man — into Rossetti's studio and at once
broached the subject with a typical directness.

"Evidently," he boomed at his friend, who was painting,
"you do not like my book, or you would have written to me
about it."

"To tell you the truth, Topsy," the other confessed with
nonchalance, "I must own that I find it difficult to take much
interest in a man whose father was a dragon."

Morris at once brought the conversation down to a more
human level by roaring out, "I don't see it's any odder than
having a brother who's an idiot!" and rushed out of the
room.

The other story concerns this brother, in the 'seventies,
when the words "Italian Anarchists" bore for the British
bourgeois mind the same significance as "Russian Bolsheviks"
carried fifty years later. Bombs were their medium, and hardly
a day passed, it seemed, on the Continent without an ex-
plosive removal of some popular monarch or grand duke, or
the mysterious and pointless blowing-up of a crowded ar-
cade. Moreover, at the particular moment to which this story
refers, some of these miscreants, still wearing their ideolog-
ical livery of flowing black cloth and sombrero, were said
to have found a refuge in England, and to be planning an
outrage in London.

One winter evening, then, Gosse boarded a crowded omnibus outside that notorious haunt of foreigners, the Café
Royal. The horses went staggering on through the clear
yellow fog of those days, through the yellow snow of the
great city, that fell in large flakes past the yellow plaster of
Nash's dingy but graceful façades. On an evening such as
this people preferred being inside the creaking, jolting vehicle
to riding on top; they dreaded, even, the moment of leaving
its shelter when they arrived at their destination. In consequence, it was so crowded that Gosse had to stand. As he

looked about him, he saw W. M. Rossetti, whom he knew well, attired in the huge black cloak and the large black hat which he always affected sitting a little way off with his daughter. Remembering that a paragraph had lately appeared in the papers stating that Rossetti had turned atheist, Gosse, with an adroit directness which he adopted instead of the feline, oblique approach natural to him, bent across one or two passengers and called:

"Mr. Rossetti! Mr. Rossetti! Is it true that you have become an atheist?"

In a slow, pompous, very clear voice that rolled out each word loud above the reverberation of the traffic, Rossetti replied:

"No, Mr. Gosse. I must differentiate. My daughter, here, is an *atheist; I* am an ANARCHIST!"

At this moment the bus stopped, and the occupants of the seats, panic-stricken by the conjunction of his cloak, Italian name and self-confessed creed of destruction, dashed for shelter, and Gosse was able to travel home in comfort.

His home was then in Delamere Terrace, but when I first met him he was living in Hanover Terrace, to which he had moved in 1901. For several decades his tea parties on Sunday afternoons in these two houses had constituted a feature of London literary life. This second house, No. 17, was situated in a typical Nash layout, and the front doors of all the houses in the terrace were placed in the shelter of a plaster colonnade with Doric pillars. To this you mounted by flights of steps that served every three or four front doors, so that you were obliged to walk for a little under the colonnade, while often the mingled pleasure and trepidation that you felt at the thought of the hour or so in front of you — for the visit would be certain to prove both treat and ordeal — caused you to mount an earlier flight and wander along in its shade, pretending to yourself that you were not sure which was the house, or, at least, even if you ascended the right steps, to linger a

little and admire from this higher level the framed and ordered arrangement of domes and cupolas and arcades showing above the trees, or the nearer perspective of rich plaster
volutes, vases, statues, the clustered columns and caryatids.
When practice had made you skillful, it was possible to while
away many minutes in this kind of preoccupied concentration before you were finally committed to the correct door.
Even then, there was the knocker to contemplate before you
raised it. This, I should judge, recalling it after fifteen years,
was fashioned of copper or bronze by one of the Pre-Raphaelite artificers, and represented either a mermaid wilting into
a kind of prophecy of *L'Art Nouveau,* or else a young lady
entangled with a dolphin — I cannot be sure which.[9] At last
you knocked, and with a scrupulous promptitude Parker —
the celebrated parlormaid of whom I shall have more to say
in a moment — opened the door, and you heard it shut behind
you.

Parker showed you upstairs to the drawing room. Outside
it were various personal relics, things that had belonged to
Swinburne, Rossetti, Ford Madox Brown and Stevenson, or
were presents from them, but though often the visitor longed
to examine them, he was never given time, for Parker had
opened the door and proclaimed — *proclaimed* is the right
word — your presence. The drawing room lay before you. It
was not, perhaps, exactly pretty, for it was too crowded, but
it had a sort of glint about it, a threading of gold from picture frames and furniture and objects, and offered a charming
air of detailed late-Victorian domesticity. Moreover, it faced
Regent's Park and, as you entered, you obtained a lovely
vista, green and watery, of pool and weeping willow and
stretches of grass, and distant depths of shadow between the
taller, further trees. The tea table stood, as a rule, between

[9] Dr. Philip Gosse informs me that it was intended in the first place as an
Art Nouveau ash tray before being hammered into a door knocker, and had
been presented to his father by a female admirer.

the windows, and Mrs. Gosse sat with her back to them, between them, with a glistening silver tea equipment in front
of her. Gosse would be sitting facing the window, glaring
back at the light with his blue eyes, or looking down from
time to time, as he stroked with a rhythmic motion his black
and white cat, Buchanan. (Buchanan was an important member of the household, and had adopted Gosse a year or two
before. Though a common, he was a proud cat and would
never consent to come up to tea unless called or carried by
his master in person. Moreover, to secure his continued attendance, he had to be bribed with a saucer of milk, first
poured out by Mrs. Gosse, and then served to him by her
in a kneeling position.) Behind Gosse, in the other part of
the room — which he used also as a study — stood, rank on
rank, the tall bookcases of his remarkable library.

Mrs. Gosse, a most kind, charming and courteous woman,
understood perfectly her husband's character, comprehended
his fiery nature, his nervous irritability, no doubt aggravated
by a half century's hard work and also by the many vexa-
tions and jealousies inseparable from a literary career — incidents exemplified at their worst by the Churton Collins
episode. She tried to pad the corners for him, so that neither
he nor others should be hurt. Even her voice carried a suggestion of kindness and humor, and its tones seemed further
calculated to assure the visitor that she was in full control,
knew her job, and would rescue him in time, should the little
tiger spring too eagerly, too fiercely. She found great amusement in the ludicrous and inconsequent side of life, and I remember the pleasure with which she told me of her husband's
recent correspondence with a neighbor who owned a noisy
parrot. This bird was continually disturbing Gosse when he
was at work, so finally he sent round a note to the lady, asking
her to check the garrulity of her pet. He was dumbfounded
by the reply, for she wrote saying that she had "always understood that he was an eminent literary gentleman," and was

surprised that he should pay attention to what a poor parrot said.

Mrs. Gosse exercised her influence over her husband in the quietest way possible, and I am sure can never have quarreled with him, or said more than a remonstrative "Edmund! Edmund!" Indeed I recall an afternoon during the 1914–1918 war, when Gosse had been dancing with more than his accustomed sprightliness on the graves of all those present, when one of the guests, Miss Haldane, a sister of Lord Haldane, and a woman of massive frame and intellect, suddenly — and without any connection with what was being said, for her mind was running entirely on the current food shortage — threw a boulder into this corybantic display by inquiring in the most serious tone:

"Nellie, do you ever give Edmund *beans?*"

"Never, my dear; I have never even *tried* to give him beans."

And I am sure she spoke the truth.

She saw his weaknesses, notwithstanding, no less keenly than she appraised his vritues. Yet rarely, very rarely, did she allow a remark to escape her that showed it. During tea, however, one Sunday afternoon in autumn, I happened to be present when Gosse complained of a cold. He was still, I think, librarian of the House of Lords — a position to which he had been appointed in 1904 — or at any rate had been there again, for he remarked, "I must have caught it in those drafty corridors of the House of Lords"; whereupon Mrs. Gosse observed, in her gentle, almost unctuous voice:

"Edmund is so fortunate. He always catches *his* colds in the drafty corridors of the House of Lords, whereas I and my daughters catch ours on the tops of omnibuses or in tube stations."

Indeed, in general Mrs. Gosse was so far from sharing her husband's idealized vision of the House of Lords that she would refuse to accompany him on the visits he so much enjoyed paying to great houses. On arrival, therefore, he would immediately dart upstairs to his room, where a huge fire would already be juggling its golden coronets in the fireplace, by which he would sit and write the first of his daily letters to his wife, on heavily coroneted notepaper. But she liked best to be surrounded by her family, and was happiest in her own home.

There, though Gosse, Mrs. Gosse, their daughters, Miss Sylvia — that admirable artist — and Miss Tessa, each of them possessed enough personality to furnish a whole house, and all did in fact make their own contribution to the atmosphere, it was Parker who set the tone. And so it is essential to try, if one wishes to convey to the reader something of the feeling of this establishment, to say a little of her too, because her tactful, determined, benign and yet rather disembodied influence was omnipresent throughout its precincts. Her sense, I should say, in all social matters was infallible. Though, I think, she probably entered with enthusiasm into all Gosse's likes and dislikes, she never showed her own by the flick of an apron string, and revered him as much as he venerated her, (Once, for example, he told my sister and myself how Ezra Pound had come to see him, and had dared to ridicule to him the Rossettis. Gosse described how he had reproved him in the words, "Sir, you are uneducated!" and he had then, in relating the incident, added, as a final and fatal exposition of the American poet's character, "And when he arrived, he presumed to *push past Parker*.")

Tall, thin, unobtrusive, Parker carried the art of being impersonal beyond the range of impersonality, until it became individual again. Nevertheless she had plainly studied Gosse's feelings for many years. She was, indeed, a parlormaid of genius. And it was as herald that she found the highest medium of her art. When she announced the names of guests at tea, she seemed to be both hieratic and the djinn of the tea caddy. Her voice, formal and precise as the ritual voice of an Emperor of China in earlier times, was yet infinitely significant. Perfect in elocution, her plain and unemotional tones were calculated to convey with the greatest accuracy and the strictest economy of means, even to the casual stranger — a bibliophile, let us say, fresh from the open spaces of Kansas City or Greenwich Village, and strange as would be a Martian visitor to this enclosed world — the exact degree to which the latest arrival in the drawing room was famous or unknown, the real range of his talent or of his prestige, as well as the prevalent opinion, both within Hanover Terrace and outside it, of his brains, his character and his productions.

Thus with each word that fell from her she helped to chart unknown social seas. If, then, it would be an exaggeration to call her voice musical, as it would be equally so, perhaps, to describe that of a great *Flamenco* singer, she possessed a similar technical perfection, the instrument being to the highest degree expressive.

"The Marquis of Carabas!"

for instance, bore with it, for all the apparent dryness of style, a conviction of long and noble descent, vistas of pleached alleys, and peacocks and gazebos, and was quite different from

"Lord Haldane!"

the sound of which carried, from her mouth, a ponderous and stately thunder all its own, whole volumes of philosophy and scientific reading, many councils of state and elucidations of pure reason (looking back, it seems to me that her tones prophesied, even, that he could be uncle to a future stalwart of the Left Wing, Mrs. Mitchison, and to the scientific Professor).

"Mr. Siegfried Sassoon!"

brought with it the sound of a poet kicking in vain against a horse box, together with a suggestion of irregular political opinions;

"Mr. Robert Nichols!"

the most delicate lyricism, and hopes like the tender green of young leaves, while my own name swung into the sedate afternoon sunlight of that Victorian drawing room like a young bull entering an arena — or, perhaps, a china shop. . . . But Parker was always kind to me — and so, quite often, was my host.

Typical as Gosse could be at his tea parties, it was at his dinner parties that he was at his best. But here, again, though Mrs. Gosse and her daughters were responsible for so much of the charm of these occasions, it was Parker who set the tone, formal or festive; you could tell as you arrived. The menus were lengthy, the food solid and well cooked, without any taint of aristocratic flummery, for in this direction Gosse allowed no nonsense to obscure his middle-class origin or way of living. For example, he always carved the chief dish — a goose or turkey — himself. The atmosphere of these entertainments was unlike anything to be found elsewhere at the time. There would be ten or twelve people, and the number would be sure to include, besides the essential leaven of a title or two, George Moore or Robert Ross, perhaps Max and Lady Beerbohm, if they were in London, or Logan Pearsall Smith, and a few younger writers, but, above all, such persons as I have named who understood Gosse, and with whom he could play his own inimitable games in his own manner — and the rules prevailing at these differed from the ones governing the tea parties, or so it always seemed to me. They must be men who would observe and score up each point and counterpoint, each scratch and paw and pat and compliment and rebuff. . . . And, before I leave the subject of these dinner parties, I must relate how, the first time I went to dine at Hanover Terrace, I heard Parker make the strangest announcement that, I think, can ever have fallen from her lips. There was an air raid in progress when I arrived, the first big air raid — or so it seemed — of the 1914 war. We waited in the drawing room for my sister, who was late, to the sound of the falling bombs and of maroons. Suddenly Parker entered and announced crisply:

"Miss Sitwell has telephoned. She sends her compliments, but says she refuses to be an Aunt Sally for the Germans, so she is not coming to dinner."

The Gosses were enchanted with this message, which shows that his formality of manners yet allowed him to make exceptions. He was a charming host; yet as a guest, or rather as a prospective guest, he was intimidating, and to the young especially. For him, one had to make every preparation, take every precaution, and the nervousness that was engendered in the end made one do the wrong thing. At the same time, when the rather dreaded moment came, and the door opened, he appeared always to be in an intensely amiable mood, eager, even surprised, to be entertained, and inclined to give quarter, for he really liked the society of young people, and was anxious to know how they lived and in what directions they differed from his own contemporaries at the same age. . . . But this was, as a rule, exactly what the young, if they were his hosts, were, consciously and subconsciously, determined to prevent him from finding out.

On several occasions he dined with my brother and me, and I notice in a letter, published in the *Life and Letters of Sir Edmund Gosse*, a reference to his having dined with me one night, towards the end of the First World War, when I was Captain of the King's Guard at St. James's Palace. I remember little of it. I do, however, recall very clearly the first time Gosse came to dine with my brother and me in the house we then had in Swan Walk. There was, indeed, a good deal for us to fear beforehand, when one came to think of this night approaching nearer and nearer: for, if the Victorian and Edwardian ages were dead anywhere in London, their corpses were buried under this particular door. Grosse disapproved of all of the art of the day, except the semi-academic, but our walls were crowded with pictures by modern artists, Percy Wyndham Lewis, Roberts, Paul and John Nash, Nevinson, Gertler, Fry, Nina Hamnett and Severini, and drawings by Gaudier-Brzeska, Picasso, Modigliani and Sickert. Nor were the decorations by any means Pre-Raphaelite, for they included various masks and fetishes from Dahomey and Ashanti and the South Seas, mingled with Victorian objects displayed for qualities other than those which the Victorians themselves admired in them.

When the evening came — the first of January, 1918 — I remember Mr. and Mrs. Gosse entering the drawing room somewhat with the air of a procession. Gosse was wearing a white bow tie, white waistcoat and an evening coat and carried in his hands a little case containing five or six thin volumes.

"I have brought you," he said, "a gift. The new complete edition of Swinburne which I have edited."

At this moment my brother Sacheverell dashed nervously into the conversation with the remark:

"How delightful to have them at last in a cheap edition!"

Gosse gave him a piercing look of disfavor and distrust, and then emphatically pronounced the words —

"NOT SO CHEAP AS ALL THAT!"

Indeed he took offense with a hair-trigger-like ease and delicacy, though, also, he soon forgot it. When, therefore, he had assured himself that no disrespect had been intended, he became again his most delightful self, high-spirited and full of humor of his own kind. It was, I remember, upon that night that he related the following adventure of a young friend of his. This small boy, aged three, who had just cut a new tooth, was inordinately proud of it and anxious to put it to a use. One fine morning he was taken out for a walk in

Hyde Park by his nurse, and presently passed an old gentleman asleep in a chair.

"What is that old gentleman doing?" the child inquired.

"Hush, dear, he's asleep."

"Then I know what I'll do," the ingenious child replied;
"I'll bite him with my tooth!" and before the nurse could
stop him had planted it firmly in the old gentleman's calf.
. . . But even that child, it transpired, was eventual heir to
a dukedom.

It cannot, I apprehend, be denied that Gosse was a snob;
a vice which it is now fashionable to condemn overmuch. He
possessed the romantic, late-Victorian temperament, and liked
the minor Elizabethan dramatists, cathedrals, dukes, ruins,
echoes and ghosts. Nor, perhaps is it inapposite to recall in
this connection that his mother — who had died when he was
only eight years of age — had come from Boston, and that
through her, to whom titles no doubt were exotic because
strange and a link with antiquity, may have been transmitted
an interest in them, as well as a Bostonian appreciation of
culture. Be these conjectures as they may, to Gosse a title
was something "that took him out of himself" — that process
which, though it sounds so painful an extraction, is always
said to benefit the person who undergoes it. The very sound
of a historic title raised him above the level of current commercial squalor. There were, he had always known, realms of
light existing somewhere overhead, an earthly heaven, as it
were, which only a few mundane elect were privileged to
enter. To a participance, ex officio, in this glory, he gained
access with the librarianship of the House of Lords.

There he could sit, under the splendor of all the Kings
of England, while the bearers of titles that had been hitherto
familiar to him from the pages of Shakespeare's plays moved
dimly through the gilded twilight, Bedford and Beaufort,
Warwick, Westmorland and Suffolk, Norfolk and Somerset
and Northumberland, Stanley, Hastings, and Harcourt. But

though his love of titles was, in a sense, literary, and in no way detracted from — if indeed actually it did not add to — his passionate comprehension of literature before his own day, it did on the other hand sometimes a little impede his proper valuing of contemporary work. While as with most of the modern poets — and this was the splendid thing about him, poetry was so close to his heart — to whose verse he drew attention, his enthusiasm, whether or not mistaken, was founded upon genuine literary principles, and governed by standards which, if not infallible, were yet to be respected, nevertheless he liked to play for safety, and titles spelled safety. A book of poems by the widow of a former Viceroy of India or the younger son of a marquis would be sure to obtain favorable mention in the press, and the chorus would inevitably be led by Gosse. Even the younger son of a baron (nor need the barony be more than a year or two old) would win approval on his own terms. If, in addition, the author was not a real writer at all, he would be yet the more dearly cherished; for in England the amateur has ever been Emperor. His little diplomatic jokes and sayings would be repeated and rubbed up. . . . Yet Gosse liked above every other a title combined with real administrative ability and eminence. Lord Curzon and Lord Haldane, of such was his kingdom of heaven composed, for no dukedom, even, however high-sounding and traditional, could obscure for him native idiocy, and one of the most attractive points in his character was his detestation of fools.

The librarianship of the House of Lords offered him, indeed, exquisite pleasure, for its halls were the haunts of ponderous proconsuls and witty Cabinet Ministers. Moreover, it afforded him a regular income and sufficient leisure, besides the formerly visionary friendship of the great. And for those whose pursuits did not include literature, it provided him with a valuable label. "Who is that — that chap over there?" "That's Gosse, you know, the librarian of the House of Lords,

feller who writes books." Even this information did not sufficiently enlighten everyone, however, for I was in the Marlborough Club when a naval officer who was washing his
hands in the next basin to Gosse turned to him and remarked,
"Hullo, Gosse! I didn't know you were an author, but I
see you've just brought out a book called *The Pirates' Who's
Who;* [10] some jolly good notices you've had, too!"

As he grew older, however, he expected people to know
who he was, and if they did not, trouble was likely to ensue.
. . . It must have been in the middle of the 'twenties that
I motored over from my father's house in Scarborough to
have luncheon with the Gosses, who were staying in a large
hotel in Whitby. Gosse always entered into what he was
doing with his whole heart. On holiday, for example, he was
more on holiday — more, I mean, in holiday spirits, holiday
clothes, and seemed to have read more guidebooks to the
particular district he was visiting, and certainly to have acquired more genuine knowledge of it in a shorter time — than
anyone I have ever known. . . . It began by being rather
a stormy day, for that morning it had become apparent that
neither the manager of the hotel nor his wife had ever heard
of the name *Gosse.* The bearer of it was by no means inclined to take this lying down, but was determined to strike
a blow for English culture. That I was still Liberal candidate for the division, and that his remarks might cost me a
vote or two, he did not care in the least. Maneuvering us to
a table in the lounge, just beneath the mahogany box in
which the untutored couple disported themselves, inking
figures into the accounts and stamping papers, Gosse took
up the best tactical position, and declaimed in a loud, determined voice:

"I have never had the fortune to visit this part before,
Osbert. The country round is interesting, but oh, what an
Uncultured Lot inhabit it and this town! I assure you, they

[10] A delightful book by his son, Dr. Philip Gosse.

know nothing, nothing. They have never even opened a book. They might be black savages in the Congo! Even the Eskimos are better educated — but dear Lady Normanby has been most kind, so we don't feel quite lost, and as if we were in a foreign country!"

When he had carried out this rather ineffectual punitive expedition, his mood then changed, and in consequence I spent an enchanting afternoon, during which he told me the following story of two meetings with C. M. Doughty: the first had taken place some years earlier at the House of Lords, where Doughty had called on Gosse.

"A strange man, a very strange fellow, indeed," Gosse observed. "My friends who knew him had all agreed in telling me what a privilige it was to meet him. He was different from everyone else, they told me — a recluse, austere, unaffected, a man of the greatest integrity, who lived only for his art and asked nothing of the world, because he desired no rewards for himself. . . .

"When he called on me in my room, he began a conversation by saying rather loudly:

" 'Mr. Gosse! I have wanted for so long to ask you a question; have *you* read anything after the time of Spenser?'

" 'Yes, indeed, I have; but have not you, Mr. Doughty?'

" 'No, never, Mr. Gosse.'

"So I replied, 'Then it must have cut you off from a great deal.'

"A few minutes' silence followed, and then he said to me in quite a different voice, in, oh, such a *vehement* whisper:

" 'Excuse me, Mr. Gosse, but can you get me the O.M.?' "

The second occasion on which he met Doughty had been at Cambridge in 1920, when they were both being awarded honorary degrees. Gosse had first of all been entertained to luncheon by the appropriate authorities: but Doughty had been too infirm to attend the meal, so Gosse only met him in the procession, from which Doughty, clad in his robes and mortarboard, had, soon after leaving the Senate House, slipped away, exclaiming sonorously as he did so, "A truce to this foolery!" Gosse could see Sir Sydney Cockerell waiting for his friend down a side alley.

It was upon this same afternoon, too, that Gosse told me how Yeats had described to him an unusual adventure. The poet, it appeared, had been walking down Bond Street when he met a friend, whom he liked, but whose conduct he could not approve, and who on this occasion was accompanied by an uncommon spiritual extension of his personality, for after they had spoken Yeats noticed that behind the sinner trailed six small *green* elephants; to those in the psychic know, a sure symbol of moral obliquity.

Gosse, confronting the psychic with the matter-of-fact, had said to Yeats, "Well, I don't think it's fair to let a thing like that put you against a man!"

There can be no doubt that Gosse was wonderful company. The charm of his talk increased rather than diminished with age; for, unlike the majority of old people, it seemed as though with the passing of the years his spirits rose and he became more gay — and more quick to anger. And this emphasizing of high points in his character found a reflection in his appearance. Sir Edmund — he had been knighted in 1925 — was beginning to lose the sight of one eye, and so he was obliged to wear a green shade over it to protect it from the light. This afforded him a tactical advantage, because though he saw at all times at least twice as much with his one good eye as anyone else did with two, nobody suspected it. And it imparted to him something of the rakish air of a pirate chief — crafty but indomitable. You could perceive that he sailed the seas under his own flag. Moreover, he never lost an amazingly youthful gusto for ruse and stratagem, even when unnecessary; an expression of high spirits comparable to the use of conceits by the Elizabethan poets, and this, added to his choice of words, and his own typical point of view, made his company a delight. The symptoms of old age he showed, or chose to show, the forgetting and mixing up of people's names and achievements, the humiliating abbreviations to which he subjected their Christian names, the inquiries after persons who were strangers to them, or after some imaginary illness from which they had never suffered; all these, I am sure, were but new tricks he had added to his repertory, new weapons for his armory, and were assumed, as surely as that whisper that he sometimes now adopted, in order to persuade people that he was growing feeble. Actually, this whisper was so beautifully produced that each syllable was louder, more resonant and more spontaneous than if it had been spoken by any voice of ordinary power. What could be more natural than that, gradually, all others in the room should become quiet, and listen to what he said?

No account of Gosse, then, should omit the sheer quality of fun which he possessed in the highest degree, and which his presence never failed to impart to any occasion or gathering, large or small. Yet it is precisely this attribute which I have seen most seldom, if ever, mentioned in descriptions of him. . . . Even André Gide, with his deep comprehension of character, and a man who was, in addition, an old friend of the English writer, seems to have failed to grasp it, and in his account [11] of an incident that occurred in Paris in 1916 appears to have thought that he had embarrassed Gosse: whereas, on the contrary, it is probable that Gosse was playing one of his elaborate and elusive games with the French author, and *wished* to leave him with this feeling. . . . The episode is in any case not without humor. . . . Gosse had arrived in Paris on September 19th, 1916, where he stayed, as the guest of the French Government, on the third floor of the Hôtel Crillon, in a fine suite of three rooms. He had warned Gide by letter of his approaching arrival, and accord-

[11] See *The Journals of André Gide*, Vol. II, 1914–1927. (Secker & Warburg.)

ingly the next day Gide went to see him, and stayed to
luncheon. Gide proceeds to give an excellent account of the
eminent critic as he found him, telling us that he looked
older, "slightly shrivelled, thinned out in spots," and that his
movements seemed to owe more to mind than to heart. He
concludes the paragraph by remarking that Gosse, perhaps,
distrusted himself more than he distrusted Gide: but herein
I think he was mistaken.

Gide then goes on to describe other points in the meeting:
which was effusive. On first seeing each other again the two
eminent authors joined their hands for some time. Then Gide
sat down. No sooner had he done this than Sir Edmund, after
a very brief silence, which Gide thought that the other maintained in order to give the appearance of recovering his
breath, and as if "suddenly yielding to an irresistible impulse
(yet it was a trifle put on)," called out:

"Ah, dear friend, let us embrace once more."

Gide accordingly rose from his chair and rushing at Gosse
planted on each of his cheeks a sounding kiss, as any Frenchman would in reply to such an appeal. When this occurred,
Gosse gave a little jump, and made a slight grimace, which he
at once concealed — or, perhaps, pretended to conceal. From
these symptoms Gide recognized, he tells us, that Gosse was
resolved to remain master of the situation, and to suggest to
the French novelist that by taking seriously the French idiom
employed by an Englishman, he was proving himself to be
foolish: because to an Englishman a heartfelt handshake always means more than can any kiss. . . . To me, however,
it seems not to have been done with the motive, as Gide
presumes, of making a good story, indicating how carefully a
foreigner should use his phrases, but to have constituted, on
the other hand, a very perfect instance of that cat-and-mouse
technique which Gosse had devised at the outset of his career
and continued to improve throughout his lifetime: in short,
he wished Gide to come a modified cropper, and to be left in

consequence with a slight and rankling sense of inferiority in
social experience and usage: in which design he evidently
succeeded.

If, then, Gosse were in the room, you never knew quite
what might not happen, never could foretell in what direction
the little tiger would pounce: and through this feeling of
nervousness, of waiting for something to occur, came a
pleasant sensation of liveliness, of almost agreeable apprehension, which produced a sparkle in the surrounding air. You
enjoyed every moment as though it were your — or somebody else's — last. And this capacity of his, so difficult to
summon up for the reader, was accompanied by a superb skill
in the tactics and strategy of battle; which he conducted in a
manner highly individual. To this more subtle form of personal encounter he brought the strength of a great boxer and
the virtuosity of an expert fencer. Feint and counterfeint, followed sometimes by a sudden bang, it constituted a whole
system, devised by one man through the course of a lifetime,
and permeated by his personal quality.

Let us take two instances of this technique. . . . A rivalry
had long endured between Gosse and Sir Sidney Colvin, the
Keeper of the Prints and Drawings at the British Museum.
Each of the two men regarded the other as in the nature of
a runner-up; because they possessed competing proprietary
claims to the whole body of English poetry, but especially to
Keats, on whom they had separately written a book, and to
Stevenson, an intimate friend of both of them. In this last
direction, however, it could not be denied that Colvin led,
for, in addition, Lady Colvin had, before her second marriage,
been Stevenson's friend and confidante, and his series of
letters to her formed the best and most vivid picture of his
life.[12] . . . It was, then, at some special Stevenson celebration, long after his death, that the organizers had asked both
Gosse and Colvin to speak, without informing either of them

[12] See *Great Morning!*, pp. 33–35.

that the other was to be present. On arrival, they could hardly believe what their eyes told them, and remained glaring at each other from seats on either side of the chairman during his introductory address. After that was finished, Sir Sidney was called on, and made a long and detailed oration: during which Gosse ceased to glare, and, instead, fidgeted, smiled and waved his hand lightly at various members of the audience with whom he was acquainted. When, in his turn, called on next to speak, he rose at his most sprightly, and said:

"Ladies and gentlemen, I came here with a few platitudes prepared for your edification, for I had not been aware that Sir Sidney was to speak to you this afternoon. But, sure enough, he has delivered them all, so I shall say nothing."

He then sat down.

I was privileged to witness, and be a part victim of, his special technique at the Marlborough Club one summer day. I entered, and saw Gosse sitting alone, in a corner, brightly lit from a skylight, near the empty fireplace. He had placed himself with his back to the wall, and was wearing over one eye the green shade to which I have alluded, and which, somehow, it was impossible not to associate with coming trouble; as though it were a sign of battle, comparable to a pirate brazenly running up the Jolly Roger before opening fire. He looked intently at me, with a rather gloomy expression, but seemed not to identify me in any way, so I passed on and took a table further down the room. I noticed, just beyond, E. F. Benson, who was not a member of this club but was being entertained to luncheon by a friend. Later, I was in the morning room opposite, having coffee, when Benson and his host came to sit very near me, and we exchanged greetings. Gosse now came in, and at once approached me, as though he could see only myself in the whole room, though previously he had not known who I was. That, and something delicate in his tread, in the actual manner in which he placed his feet down on the carpet, warned me that he was at his games. Still he kept his gaze fixed on me, seeing no one else, and then he spoke.

"Was that Fred Benson I saw in the dining room?" he inquired in his stage-elephant whisper; "was it really? . . . If so, he looks much older, oh *so* much *older*, than when I saw him last. . . . But then, I recollect, his father died at the same age."

During these few seconds I had tugged unavailingly at his sleeve, and had said, "Be careful! Be careful! He's just near you."

Gosse paid no attention, and continued unflinchingly but irrelevantly, and in a louder voice:

"Quite a nice chap, I'm told, if you get to know him. But how can one do that? One never sees him anywhere. . . . And besides, I could never get on with a man who sees *spooks!*"

It has remained impossible for me fully to grasp the allusion in this last remark, for Gosse himself was interested in ghosts, and had shown me more than once a photograph he had taken, by chance, of a specter at Ightham Mote, a monk with a rope round his neck. But if *I* did not understand, I could see that Benson did. The shaft had gone home, but he said nothing to make his presence officially known, and Gosse went over to the window and sat down in a comfortable arm-chair to read a paper, only occasionally letting his roving but empty eye sweep the room.

Almost the last time I met Sir Edmund and enjoyed an afternoon's outing with him was one summer towards the end of his life. On the afternoon to which I refer, he was gay, lively and formidable as ever. I had encountered him by chance at the Marlborough, but he seemed to be expecting me, and proposed that we should at once set out for the Hawthornden Prize giving, due at 3:30 in the Aeolian Hall in Bond Street. I had forgotten even that it was to take place

that day, but when thus exhorted to accompany him, fell in
with the suggestion. Of course, I smelled a rat, and realized
that the cat was on its trail: but I knew that the afternoon
would prove to be an experience, and my curiosity also urged
me on. Looking back, I can see clearly enough that he must
have fallen out with the members of the Committee of the
Hawthornden Prize (though certainly he had been on very
good terms with them not long before, and had presented
the prize on one occasion himself), and that his peculiar and
accurate knowledge of contemporary shades of literary feeling made him realize fully the effect that his entrance with
me at this function would create. I was far from *persona grata*
in the bird-loving poetical circles of those days, when a damp
and draggled thrush still signified what Karl Marx came to
mean to the new generation, only a year or two away over
the horizon of the decade. I had publicly mocked the ceremony, and not long before had written, in the guise of a
tipster, to Beachcomber of the *Daily Express*, signing myself
"The Major," and prophesying the winner — in fact, I gave a
"double," the winner for that year and the next. My predic-
tion was published in the paper, and being based on a neat
calculation of political and poetical pros and cons, had proved
correct, and this had placed the Committee in an awkward
position, since the tip had appeared in the journal ten days
before the award had been made, and it was one of the rules
that the Committee should not finally choose the recipient
until the very day of announcing his name and giving him the
prize. That being so, the Committee had to send one of its
members forward on the platform to explain his surprise at
the exactitude of "The Major's" forecast. ("I can't think
how he did it," the member had kept on saying, rather
weakly, in a bat's voice. . . .) Of course, it had not come
out that it was my doing, but I was suspect, and it had not
added to my popularity among that little band. But further,
a year or two before, I had published *Triple Fugue*, in which

the title story described a literary prize giving and a professor, said openly by some to resemble Sir Edmund. (I never knew his own view of this, but he often mentioned the book in an unconstrained way, saying how much he had enjoyed reading it.) And, in addition, it was thought that my literary opinions would be too advanced for Sir Edmund, whose most daring boundary was *Georgian Poetry*. . . . All these factors admittedly, however, rendered it the more unlikely that we should attend the presentation together, and he had concluded that our entrance would strike terror into the hearts of the common enemy — and so, undoubtedly, it did!

The members of the audience were chattering in the foyers and corridors when we arrived. As we passed, voices were hushed, and the smooth prize-giving faces wilted, the lovelocks of the critics grayed and became more dank as we looked at them, and lankier. Sir Edmund for the most part maintained — for one eye was covered by the shade — a straight, unseeing eye that gazed in front of him and looked, X-ray-like, through those on whom it happened, in the direct line of vision, to fasten; but like a searchlight, it would, from time to time, sweep round or turn and play upon those near him. Soon a dangerous recognition would dawn in it, a smile, in the eye itself, would be stoked up with manifest artificiality, and this would be followed by a momentary but perilous effusiveness that plainly led nowhere, even if he did not make it clear that he thought he was addressing the wrong person.

Having thus stalked to our seats, we remained in the position, about four rows from the front, which he had chosen. He looked grave and preoccupied, and surveyed the audience with apparent surprise. He said nothing, though many an ear was tilted to catch the sound. Only when the doors had been shut and the speeches had begun, he occasionally gave vent to a very menacing clearing of the throat. . . . Still he said nothing, nothing — until a high-pitched nervous twitter and wordless lisping, together with cries of "It's darling Bobbie!" from the serried old ladies, told us that a well-known patron of the poetry of the time was speaking. The words lacked momentum. They soared like listless sparrows over the audience. Suddenly however, one sentence stood out. "Above all, the winner of this year's prize shows *promise*, shows *promise*" (louder). Then Sir Edmund, clothing himself in the full weight of his years, and looking for once every moment of his seventy-seven, turned to me with a ferocious but infantine geniality, and said, with that mastery of elocution which made it reach every head in the hall:

"Ossie!" (a name by which nobody else has ever called me) "Ossie! Do you consider that *I* show promise?"

CHAPTER III

Ronald Firbank

ONALD FIRBANK! The name immediately conjures up, to those who know his work, the titles of his various novels. How enticingly, how ably they beckon to one: *Vainglory, Valmouth, The Flower Beneath the Foot, Caprice, Santal* and *Prancing Nigger!* . . . But I must leave them in order to attempt to pin down upon a sheet of paper that unrivaled butterfly, their author — a butterfly, indeed, which perhaps he alone of authors could have tackled successfully — and to record a little of him before it is forgotten; a little of a shy, charming, sad, comic and altogether unusual personality.

It was, as I have related in *Great Morning!* during the early months of 1912 that I found myself in the Army, attached to a cavalry regiment. Even when I was allowed to take refuge for a few hours in London, the black cloud of Aldershot hung ever over me like the specter of the Judgment Day over the evildoer. In consequence, I strove to make the most of every minute, luxuriating in the new magic of *L'Oiseau de Feu*, and other ballets and Russian operas, in the kaleidoscopic inconsequence of the Futurist Exhibition at the Sackville Galleries, or in the new vista of strangeness and epochal beauty to be divined in the second Post-Impressionist Show in Grafton Street. No detail of these pleasures, or of the appearance of other members of the audience or public whom I saw, escaped me, with the keen, sensitive edge of my nineteen years. And always I noticed in gallery, opera house or theater — so that afterwards, when back at Aldershot, pondering over those few though vivid, now intolerably distant hours of happiness, his image would come back to me and set me wondering — the lonely, stooping, rather absurd figure of a man some ten years older than myself. With a thin frame, long head and a large aquiline, somewhat chinless face, the cheekbones prominent and rather highly colored, showing that he was ill, he had something of the air, if one can imagine such a combination, of a witty and decadent Red Indian. And onto this stock had been grafted, too, a touch of priest, and even of curate. I have never seen anyone who in the least resembled him in looks, except, as I have mentioned,[1] the late Alban Berg. This stranger haunted the background of my favorite scenes for me, just as those of Greco's pictures are frequented by a gaunt and spectral saint. The eyes of my phantom, I noticed, were full of wit, though he spoke never a word, being always alone. In the intervals he would stand at the bar, occasionally gulping down a drink, as though with difficulty, nervous and ill at ease, his long hands clutching the lapels of his coat, examining the correctness of his tie, smoothing his hair, or fluttering round him apprehensively. Rather ill and unhealthy, one judged him to be; but certainly, I decided, his silence differed in kind from that of my brother officers. Often I would wonder who he might be, and why so much alone; for it was before I began myself to understand all the cruel and humiliating mysteries of the nervous system.

Times changed, and with them my regiment; now I was stationed in London. And whenever I went, let us say, to the first performance of Scriabin's *Prometheus*, to a concert of Gabriel Fauré's music conducted by the old composer himself, or to the first night of the *Rosenkavalier*, would I see at it this curious figure. But never could I discover his identity.

Then the 1914 war came, with for me two winters in the trenches, and the diminutive spiritual paradise of books, music

[1] *Laughter in the Next Room*, p. 206.

and conversation into which I had recently found my way (in spite of constant drill and dull bouts of Pirbright, Purfleet and such places) was utterly smashed and broken. Thus one did not see him for several years: for there were no longer many concerts in London at which — even if one could be present at them — to see this silent specter. Indeed, music was under suspicion as a German agent, and even someone so civilized and cultivated as Ethel Smyth, in a bout of patriotism, said to my friend Violet Gordon Woodhouse, "Don't play Bach. . . . It's playing the German game."

One Sunday towards the end of the First World War, my sister opened a weekly review and read a short criticism by Gerald Gould of a novel called *Vainglory*. The critic owned manfully that he could make nothing of it, but fortunately quoted a short passage in which a mother describes a quarrel with her child's nurse. This passage so greatly amused Edith that she read it aloud to me, and to this day the quotation remains in my memory, almost word for word. Enchanted, we bought the book and all else that issued from the same pointed, absurd, yet indeed magic pen.

Here was to be found a new if minute world, which existed by its own pulse of time and exhibited its own standards of behavior. Strange, fresh tides of rhythm played and lapped round its breathless shores, on which figures that, however etiolate, were sufficiently substantial for the reader never to be able to forget them, moved to their own measure and were left striking the most unexpected attitudes against the mauve and lime-green horizon. Each book, as it appeared, was a new revelation of style, and of a wit that rippled the surface of every page without ever breaking it. The virtuosity of the author was able to net any situation, however crazy or occasionally even obscene, and let it loose in the realms of a harmless reality. Just as in the autumn the silver cobwebs lightly cover the trees with a thin mist of impalpable beauty, so a similar highly stylized but intangible loveliness hung over every page, while wit ran in, round and underneath each word. But the chief claim that is to be advanced for the author, I think, is his startling technical achievement. His dialogues are quicker and lighter than had hitherto been designed for a novel. He altered the pace of the dialogue for the novel, and already his influence can be detected in writers of more content than himself, and indeed, in the most unlikely quarters.

This novel that we read of Firbank's, then, filled us with curiosity about its author. Who was he, where did he live, we wondered. But for a while our search went unrewarded. The first information that reached us was through an old friend of ours who had known him since boyhood. She told us that Arthur Annesley Ronald Firbank, to give him his full name, was the son of the late Sir Thomas Firbank, a noted railway magnate, and of Lady Firbank, a charming and beautiful woman, who was at this time still alive. Ronald had spent his childhood at St. Julian's, near Newport, a fine house that had formerly been part of the Welsh estates of my great-uncle, the eighth Duke of Beaufort. Both the boy's parents were conventional enough, it seemed, so that the education of their son had been planned on the ordinary school-university model. But, when traveling in Egypt as a small child, he had been laid low with sunstroke and proved in consequence to be too delicate to remain at a public school for more than one "half." (Incidentally, it was the sunstroke which later saved him from the necessity of military service, for he showed my brother the certificate of his exemption.) At the age of eighteen or nineteen he had, however, been strong enough to fulfill his parents' ambitions for him by going up to Cambridge. There he became an esthete, and was particularly interested in every society connected with the drama. He had already published a first book [2] and it was at

[2] Firbank often in later years talked to me about his work, but never for one moment did he mention this book. He had always given me to under-

the time understood that he was engaged on an absolute mas-
terpiece of a second, for, like all intelligent and self-respecting
undergraduates, he held very strongly the opinion that a man
was finished at twenty-five. In due course he left Cambridge. Years fled by — years spent in drifting round Spain,
Italy, North Africa and the Near East — but nothing more
was heard of a second book until, some ten years later, suddenly, now unexpectedly, even, it swung into the literary
firmament with, for a new writer, an extraordinary mastery,
within its scope, of words and technique, and with its own
quaint but unbiased view of a mad world. His long sojourns
and travels abroad he broke, our friend told us, by visits to
London. Here he would usually take furnished rooms in the
neighborhood of Piccadilly. Since the war he was living in
the country, in England, but she was not sure where.

The next accurate information we obtained was from C. R.
W. Nevinson, who had met him at luncheon with Grant
Richards, Firbank's publisher. Nevinson had at once divined
in him an amusing character. He described his appearance to
us, I remember, and related how after the meal Firbank, rising
willowly to his feet, observed, "Now I must go to the Bank."

"But they are all shut, you won't be able to get in," objected Richards.

To which Firbank, displaying his long, unmuscular arms
and thin fingers, replied anxiously, "What! Not even with
my crowbar?"

Soon we heard that Firbank was living at Oxford, and
when, in the February after the war, I went there to see my
brother, we decided to call on him. Only now was it that I
realized who he was, this silent, nervous, absurd figure of

---

stand that *Vainglory* was his first published volume. The title is *Odette
d'Antervernes* and it was issued in 1905 by Elkin Mathews. It contains also
"A Study in Temperament" — and though the name of the author is given as
Arthur Firbank, this tale is said to be prophetic in style of the Ronald Firbank who was to come. Grant Richards later republished *Odette*, but without including in it "A Study in Temperament."

theater, concert hall and gallery, only now did I discover the identity of him upon whom I had so often pondered at Aldershot. And his past phantomhood strengthened my feeling of friendliness for him. Moreover, this hitherto soundless specter proved to be possessed of its own voice and accents, sharp and clear, with very much of its own interpretation of the world it haunted: though the voice was, indeed, more practiced and incisive on paper than in conversation. For at the time we first met him in Oxford, Ronald Firbank had, during two whole years, spoken to no one there except his charwoman and a guard on the train to London (upon this line he was, as we shall notice later, a well-known person). He felt himself totally out of place in a khaki-clad, war-mad world, where neither music nor gaiety existed, and in which one could no longer travel except about the business of death. He failed to summon up any enthusiasm whatever over the current war, protesting that for his part he had always found the Germans "most polite." In fact, in after years, *"that awful persecution"* was the phrase which it was most often his wont to use in alluding to the First World War. It had driven him to become more than ever a recluse: it had deprived him of all outside interests, until finally ennui forced him to write the book about which he had talked for so many years. These volumes were, therefore, far more truly than any others in the English language the product of the conflict. He was in the best, the least boring, sense a "war writer."

Very seldom, then, would he go out, except occasionally, and rather unexpectedly, for a bicycle ride. Or again, he might journey up to London to call on his publisher or solicitor. Firbank occupied charming rooms opposite Magdalen Tower, and we were to see there now for the first time that small collection of *objets d'art* from which he was never parted, and which we were to see so often, in so many different settings. With these few chosen belongings he standardized each temporary home, whether it was a tent in the desert, a palace in Portugal,³ a furnished flat in London, an old house in Constantinople or rooms at Oxford. In every country they provided a sufficiently personal setting for him and spread over his dwelling place an indefinable but luxurious atmosphere. Chief among these objects were two drawings by Downman, a bronze bull (would it be Greek or Renaissance?), a Félicien Rops drawing, a pencil portrait of Firbank by Albert Rutherston, a little green-bronze Egyptian figure of some bearded god or Pharaoh, standing rigidly above a miniature marble pedestal, all the latest novels, a number of the silliest illustrated weekly papers (which provided him with a constant source of amusement), several of his own published books and manuscripts bound in white vellum, a photograph of his mother wearing court dress, mounted in a large silver frame, elaborate inkpots, colored quill pens, a vast tortoise-shell crucifix, and cubes of those large, blue, rectangular postcards upon which it was his habit to write. To this collection he subsequently added a fine drawing of himself by Augustus John. There was always, too, a palm tree near him, and in some way the author's personality was able to translate it back into a tropical and interesting plant, so that here it lacked that withered, 1880-boarding-house air which usually it assumes in England. On this occasion, moreover, he had provided for our reception a veritable beacon of a fire and a profusion of orchids and peaches, a gay cornucopia that banished the dim February light creeping in through the gray windows. It was, then, in this Oxford version of his habitual setting, which staged him so appropriately, that we first heard those delightful fits of deep, hoarse, helpless and ceaseless laughter, in such contrast to the perpetual struggle of his speech. For so nervous was he that the effort required to produce his words shook his whole frame, and his voice, when at last it issued forth, was slow, muffled and low, but

³ One year, he rented a palace at Cintra, in which William Beckford once lived; a house I have often seen.

never perfectly in control. Most of his sentences in conversation he left unfinished — so that it was evocative, elusive, full of implication and allusion, more than factual. It was nearly always a little absurd, but the first ten minutes — only the first ten minutes — were an enchantment. He suffered, I believe, from a nervous affection of the throat, which prevented his swallowing food easily. To this misfortune was due the fact that he drank so much more than the little he ate. On one occasion, for example, he went to dine with a friend of ours, who in his honor had ordered a magnificent dinner, and refused to eat anything except one green pea.

As for his laughter, to which we have just referred, it would often descend on him just as he was beginning work. Usually he wrote his novels upon those huge blue postcards which we noticed piled up on his desk, writing on each wide oblong side of them, though each blank face only gave room enough for a few — perhaps ten — words, so much space did his large regular handwriting take up. Thus at the moment when he would be starting to inscribe laboriously one more word on the card in front of him, the essential ludicrousness of the situation that he was with such care elaborating would overcome him, and he would be obliged to quit work till the next day.

It was during this first acquaintance with him in a frosty and snowbound February at Oxford that Siegfried Sassoon and my brother and I gave a dinner party in Ronald Firbank's honor. Typically, our chief guest himself declined to attend the meal — no doubt because he ate so little, rather than because he was so greatly afflicted by his nerves — but he agreed to come in with the dessert, and even consented to read us a chapter from his new novel, as yet unfinished. The scene of our feast was the dining room of the Golden Cross Inn, and the memory of that unusual evening must, I think, always hover with a peculiar glow and a luculence all its own in the minds of those who were present. Apart from Sassoon, Gabriel Atkin, my brother and myself, they were mostly selected from undergraduate poets, and the guests numbered Wilfred Childe, V. de Sola Pinto and Thomas Earp — now the able art critic of the *Daily Telegraph* — among them. It was their introduction — I think in every case — to Ronald and his works: but they were prepared to be enthusiastic, and when at last the guest of honor arrived, he was given a rousing reception. The evident good will of his audience, however, by no whit lessened his agitation, which he sought to clothe with a semblance of debonair indifference. He sauntered towards our large table by the window, now shuttered, and past the curious faces of the other smaller groups of people, as if he were going for a stroll or had come in by chance, walking slowly, and looking from side to side, but never at the human beings in the room. He swung one arm, while under the other was his manuscript, typewritten, in a cover. He seldom frequented restaurants, except the Café Royal, or the Eiffel Tower in Percy Street, and here the background of low rooms, sanded floors, oak beams, roast pork and tobacco smoke — so different from the scene he provided for himself — must have made him feel still less at home in his surroundings. Moreover, it must have been the sole occasion, I believe, on which he read aloud to a gathering — though admittedly a small one, nine persons in all. Eventually he reached our table safely, and we persuaded him to sit down and drink some port. By now, the other occupants of the dining room were beginning to leave, and soon we had the place to ourselves.

Firbank sat on a chair, sideways to the audience, and at last began to read in a voice which contained in it the strangled notes of a curate's first sermon, but was warmed, from time to time — indeed, fairly frequently — by fits of genial, deep chuckling. He continued throughout to pluck wildly at his tie and feverishly to avoid the gaze of those watching him and concentrating on his words. The book, not yet named, from which he read, was *Valmouth:* and it was so individual, so highly stylized, that in spite of his bad reading, in spite of a

certain lack of consequence (indeed its exquisite inconsequence was one of its great merits), it held our rapturous attention from beginning to end — though I recall that subsequently the author complained to me about one of his own
difficulties with it:

"You have no idea how difficult it is to keep up one's interest, when writing of a heroine who is over a hundred and
twenty years of age — not that the other characters are meant
to be any younger!"

I was able subsequently to arrange for the printing of the
chapter he had read, then entitled "Fantasia in A Sharp
Minor," in *Art and Letters,* the periodical of which, as the
reader may remember, I was then one of the editors. The
publication of this fragment, I reflect, helped to bring Firbank's work to the notice of a discriminating audience, though
in the interests of truth it must be admitted that many of the
people who now constitute his greatest admirers were at the
time enraged by it beyond measure.

During the summers that were to follow in London, and
during certain winters and springs (as, for example, that April
and May when he was living in a villa that had formerly belonged to the Swiss painter Arnold Boecklin, situated outside
Florence, on the way to Fiesole, and when we would so often
meet him in the Via Tornabuoni, staggering under the load
of flowers he had bought, and craning round in a wild and
helpless way for a cab to carry him home), we saw much of
Firbank. Looking back over those years, let us face the truth;
for the strange being of whom we write is interesting enough,
as both writer and man, to deserve such treatment. Let us
admit, then, that there was about him something a little
ridiculous, which blinded fools to his other remarkable and
much more characteristic qualities, and which since his death,
as during his lifetime, has made him an easy butt. As a talker
he was most unequal; and if we are bound to say how extremely amusing he was for the first ten minutes of any meet-

ing with him (always a deliriously funny period), are we also bound to add that, after a time, conversation became difficult. Also he could be peculiarly irritating, though he himself always seemed surprised at the result of these moods, and when on occasion he had annoyed my brother and me, he would remark in a dazed manner, "Sachie is looking at me like an *angry lion!*" But if for some minutes he contrived to provoke his friends, it would not be long before he would again convulse them with laughter. Moreover, one was always surprised in talking with him, so vague and almost incoherent did he seem, at his love and knowledge of beautiful things. He was not, I think, a deeply read man, but his reading was very different from the rather blowsy pastures so well cropped by the ordinary "literary man." French novels, French poetry and eighteenth-century memoirs of every European country composed the bulk of it, and in these matters he was excessively well informed; yet often in his books there flashes out an allusion to some subject or another on which one would not have expected him to be an authority, but which this reference proves him to have mastered.

In addition, there is surely to be traced in all his books a marked love and understanding of the stage and its personalities. Just as virtuosity and style were for him the chief merits of literature, so he demanded in his favorites of the footlights absolute control, manner, and, above all, established fame: for the effect of celebrity, through a decade or so, upon the temperamental nature essential to the executant artist delighted him; and thus among those he most adored in the theater were to be numbered Pavlova, Isadora Duncan and Mrs. Patrick Campbell.

If it was his reading, as much as his own experience, which made the general sense of his books so cosmopolitan, yet it must be remembered that he had not only traveled, but had lived in various cities of Southern Europe and Northern Africa for quite considerable periods. He had spent nearly a year, for example, in Madrid, and asseverated that he had there become a mighty horseman. Moreover, he always accused a then promising young diplomat (now an author) of having stolen his charger out of jealousy of his prowess: an unlikely, indeed mythical, theft, but one which caused him to harbor the greatest resentment. It accounts for the rather unflattering portraits of young diplomats in *The Flower Beneath the Foot*, just as it explains, also, the rather unflattering portraits of eccentric writers in a certain book by a former young diplomat. Otherwise Firbank pursued no feuds and treasured hardly a single hatred, though he was apt, as he said, "to be disappointed" in his friends.

Occasionally, though, he would be angry, as, for instance, when he suddenly announced to everyone who would listen that I had said that the Firbank fortune had been founded on boot buttons — a remark of which I had never been guilty. He was enraged about this, and would sit in the Café Royal for hours practicing what he was going to say in court during the libel action which he intended to bring against me. The great moment in it, he had determined, was to be when he would lift up his hands, which were beautifully shaped, and of which he was very proud, and would say to the judge, "Look at my hands, my lord! *How* could my father have made boot buttons? Never! He made the most wonderful railways. . . ." But within three weeks we were the best of friends again.

The first impression of him in conversation must always have been surprise that so frail, vague and extraordinary a creature could ever have arranged — let alone have created — a book. But there it was: he was a born, as opposed to a self-made, writer. This is, perhaps, the greatest gift that can descend upon authors, so many of whom *will* write because they are intelligent or clever, and want to write, not because they must write. It was obvious as well, even at first sight, that Firbank's health was far from strong. But this delicacy at least was possessed of one advantage; it prevented him from being forced to waste his time in the Army. The constant callings-up and medical examinations had, though, further shattered his health, just as he in his turn must have somewhat shattered the health of the various military authorities with whom he came in contact. He told us, for example, that when, after a dozen or so examinations, the War Office finally rejected him as totally unfit for service (which anyone else could have told at a single glance), and then, in its usual muddled way, immediately called him up again, he replied through his lawyer with the threat of a suit for libel. The War Office, at a time when it governed the world, was so startled by this simple piece of individual initiative that it at once sent back to him a humble apology.

Amazing as it was that a man with apparently so tenuous a hold on life and its business should be able to write novels, it was even more astonishing that so vague, delicate and careless a person — one, in addition, who ate almost nothing and usually drank a good deal — should survive traveling alone in wild and distant countries. One would have taken him, the moment one saw him, as plainly destined to be defrauded or, if necessary, murdered, so weak and helpless did he appear, so obvious a victim for guile and violence. But his resistance towards the world was of an order more subtle than that of the average person, and it may be that swindler and murderer desisted because they felt the latent strength of his personality. Moreover, not only did his apparent helplessness fail to injure, it actually tended to protect him, both from danger and from boredom, for he was always able, by dint of it, to compel others to carry out for him the tedious things of life. Far from feeling it a moral duty, as we had been taught, to do something unpleasant every day, he conceived that it was his moral duty to find others who would on every occasion perform it by proxy. Thus, for example, there was his visit to Augustus John. It was related that, torn between his tremendous admira-

tion for the artist and his intense desire for a drawing by
him on the one hand, and his own nervousness at having to
meet him and express it on the other, he drove round to John's
studio in a taxicab, and decided, on the way, that the taxi
driver should introduce him to the great man and explain his
business. . . . Remembering this story, I wrote to John to
inquire what he remembered of the incident, and received in
reply the letter, some of which I quote below, though other
anecdotes contained in it I have, for the sake of context, incorporated elsewhere in this chapter.

Ronald Firbank came to me [he wrote] to have his portrait
drawn some while before the publication of *Vainglory*. As you
have heard, he sent his taxi-man in to prepare the way, himself
sitting in the taxi with averted face, the very picture of exquisite
confusion.

He came frequently afterwards, although always with the utmost diffidence, and I made various studies of him. When the
strain of confronting me became unbearable, he would seek refuge
in the lavatory, there to wash his hands. This manoeuvre occurred
several times at each sitting.

His mother once called and lamented the solitary life he led —
a dear old lady, to whom Ronald was, I think, quite attached.
Upon her death he for a moment, in my presence, hesitated on
the brink of some almost Dickensian sentiment, but corrected himself just in time. . . . It's amazing how sometimes he struck,
amidst his excellent persiflage, a chord of deep and heart-rending
sentiment.

All those who knew Firbank best agree that under cover of
this seeming futility in matters of the world he was a shrewd
and capable man of affairs. "He had," writes John, "in spite
of appearances a practical side to his nature, carrying always
in his trunk, as he did, a few good big blocks of Welsh anthra-
cite." And I too can record how he was always coming to me
with requests that I would witness wills, deeds, sales of land

and the like; which also emphasizes that there must have been a quite extensive business undercurrent to his life. One document, I remember, concerned his sale of a cemetery to a Welsh town, and seemed all that it could be of a morbid bargain. . . . On another occasion, I recollect his arriving at my house in a taxi, somewhat perturbed. But all he could say was, over and over again, "It's time that Laurel Learnt about Life." Then, averting his face, at an angle of 45 degrees, he stopped speaking. Eventually he fled back to the shelter of his cab. . . . I never found out who Laurel was, but I incline to think she may have been some cousin of his.

His ability as a traveler was not less marked, or more to be expected, than his talent for the affairs of life. On meeting him for the first time one would without doubt have pronounced against his journeying alone, even for such a short distance as that from London to Oxford; but here, again, he had found someone to be responsible for him on his recurrent trips. It was his custom, during the two years he lived at Oxford, to travel back to that city from London on the "Milk Train," but owing to the earliness of the hour, the difficult machinery of buying, and the unpleasantness of handling, tickets for himself, he had arranged a running account with the guard. This score he settled once every two months. As for his longer voyages, and those on which his helplessness found no answer to its appeal, at least they led to the unexpected — and it was precisely in the unexpected that he most reveled. Moreover, his seeming incompetence furthered as much as it hindered his traveling. Thus as a very young man he went to France with some Cambridge friends. Their arrival in Rheims happened to coincide with the local "Wine Week," in which celebration they all joined with the due earnestness and enthusiasm of their years. Ronald remembered little that took place after dinner — and woke up to find himself in Venice! It appeared that in those peaceful days a train touched Rheims once a fortnight, on its way to Venice, and that he had contrived to wander into the station and, with little money and no ticket, to catch this *rara avis* and remain undisturbed in it until his safe arrival at his distant but unintended destination the following day.

Rheims, however, is hardly dangerous for a visitor except in a bacchic sense, but Ronald Firbank even managed to make a considerable stay in the Negro Republic of Haiti (which, incorrect though the impression may be, does, nevertheless, sound perilous, as well as very distant, to ordinary English ears) without any untoward incident occurring. The announcement of his intention to go there was very typical. Usually he would correspond with me, in his large, regular hand, on a whole series of those enormous blue postcards already mentioned, upon which he also composed his novels. He would write on both sides of these cards, using them instead of letters, and would then place them in a large blue envelope and post them. This was his normal method. But on this occasion he sent us a simple postcard, simply posted, on which were the words: "Tomorrow I go to Haiti. They say the President is a *Perfect Dear!*"

There were occasions, nevertheless, on which surprising events occurred, events that were so like those that take place in his novels that they could only have happened to him. I have already suggested that there was something of the ecclesiastic in his appearance. After the war he spent a good deal of time in Rome; and I remember his being much alarmed because he declared that the priests had tried to kidnap him. The attempt had occurred in this manner. He had descended the steps of his hotel one evening, and had asked the concierge to call him a cab. A smart, black-painted brougham immediately drove up and he stepped into it. The door was slammed at once, and the horse set off at a quick trot, before he had time even to tread on the toes of the occupants of the carriage, for he found, to his bewilderment, that it contained two priests, who quickly pulled him down between them, saying, "You are one of us, aren't you!" Eventually, however, Ronald managed to escape.

After the war he had resumed his old method of life, the traveling and the returning to London for the season. But flying had recently come to his rescue, and now he often went by air from London to Rome or Constantinople. In one further respect his life had altered, for in these later days he would always solemnly announce his arrival in London through the social columns of *The Times* or *Morning Post*. By this time he had found many enthusiasts for his writings among painters and authors, though among the more purely intellectual of these there was to be found, joined to their admiration, a sort of contempt, wholly undeserved. This was caused, I think, by the perfection of Firbank's novels, and by their lack of striving earnestness in a time when nearly every author was determined to exhibit his inward struggles to an unwilling but awed public. His assured income may also have been a reason for envy, since it spared him the worries of forced journalism; while he, for his part, conscious of the income which separated him from most of the world, felt that many people were only nice for the sake of the meals and drinks which they could expect from him. He would reply by treating them with an almost childish haughtiness, as though he were a Tsar among authors, in itself an amusing feat from so amiable and delicate a man. Nobody who understood him could be offended, for this affectation of proud eccentricity was only equaled by the genuine kindness he displayed at other times.

During these years just after the war he was once again constantly to be seen. No theatrical or musical performance of note passed without his attending it. Now we usually found him lunching, dining or having supper at the Eiffel Tower, though formerly he had frequented one of the "Junior" political clubs, where his appearance and manner must have formed a strange contrast to that of the musty, bearded elders sitting all round him. It was always related that in his early days there, at luncheon, he had taken fright at sight of the head-waiter, and had hidden himself under the table!

The genial and talented proprietor of the Eiffel Tower Restaurant, Stulik — an Austrian by birth — was a great friend of Firbank's, and used to take a deep interest in his welfare. He was, nevertheless, continually somewhat grieved at the smallness of this customer's appetite, and I remember once, when Firbank had just arrived from Rome by air, Stulik saying to me: "Mr. Firbank is much better. He is vonderful. What an appetite he has got now! Yesterday for dinner he ate a whole slice of toast with his caviare. . . . How I lofe my customers!" Augustus John gives the ensuing graphic account of a typical afternoon spent with Ronald, starting at this restaurant. "I once presented him to the Marchesa C—— at the Eiffel Tower; and we lunched together, all three. He then proposed that we should go to his rooms in Brook Street, but on the way deposited us at Claridge's and on some vague pretext disappeared himself. The Marchesa and I were becoming rather bored (it was 'between hours'), when Ronald reappeared with an enormous bundle, which he unfolded in his rooms, displaying a magnificent bunch of highly exotic lilies which he offered with many apologies to the lady. He also showed her, but did not give her, a complete edition of his works, luxuriously bound. Naturally she was enchanted, and proposed we should all go to America together without wasting a moment. The plan was agreed to, but somehow or other never came to pass."

Often, too, Ronald was to be found at the old Café Royal, observing the odd life that centered there, the bookmakers in their bowler hats, the celebrities, the art dealers, the painters, touts, financiers and sculptors. Indeed, it inspired several passages in his novels, notably that one in *Caprice* where the daughter of a Rural Dean enters the Café for the first time. And it was the situation of it, as much as its habituals, that entertained him, since he was always impressed by the moral of the tombstone shop opposite; for just across the road there was a large plate-glass window, in which the Christian emblems and the white marble specters of weeping females, no less than the modest, plain headpieces in the same substance, gleamed all ghostly under the primrose light of arc lamps. On tablets shining like flat white fish could be read dark inscriptions expressive of morbid hopes or fears. From the door of the Café, after any riot when one or two people had been forcibly requested by the giant in charge of such procedure to leave the premises, they could be seen ricocheting across the road towards these graveyard paraphernalia, or standing swearing in return at his uniformed figure against this ominous and inevitable background. "It ought to be a warning to us all," Ronald would remark as he watched such scenes.

Yet whenever one saw him, whether it was here, at the opera, in a concert room or theater, he seemed to be alone: not least so when, as often occurred, he was the center of an appreciative crowd of friends. Even then he appeared to be solitary and by himself; a figure who, however kind and amusing, was hedged off from his fellows by his temperament, and must live in a world of his own seeing, different from that of others. His longing for friendship, which was strong in him, could seldom surmount the barriers of his own intense nervousness. It seemed to him that he must ever seek the affection of others to a greater extent than they sought his friendship. There was a pathetic instance of this unhappy outlook one day at luncheon time in the Café Royal. Firbank entered and walked up to one of his friends, Gabriel Atkin, a young painter, who was sitting at a table with a glass of sherry in front of him, and asked Atkin to give him luncheon. The young man replied that he could not do so, for he had no money; upon which Firbank took a pound note out of his pocket, pressed it into the hand of his friend and, sinking at the same time into the seat opposite, exclaimed, "How wonderful to be a guest!"

Yet his summer visits to London were really a delight to all his friends and acquaintances, for he never disappointed them. First there would be the solemn heralding of his arrival in *The Times* or *Morning Post*, and then some fresh piece of grotesque fantasy was sure to mark each occasion. One year he rented a small flat in Sloane Square, and there set out the few objects that were the assertion and extension of himself, raising aloft once more the standard of his palm tree. Accordingly, he arranged with a flower shop in the Square to send in a gardener twice a day to water and attend to it properly. Ronald was much pleased with this man, for he wore a green baize apron and had a rustic way of speaking, so that it was "just like being in the country." When, therefore, after a fortnight, he decided to move to an apartment in Piccadilly, he insisted that, no matter what the cost, the same gardener should come twice a day to water the palm tree. Further, he laid down, as a condition of his employment, that the man must walk the whole way — except in wet weather — from Sloane Square to Piccadilly and back again, and must wear his green baize apron and carry a miniature watering can, painted green to match it. The proprietor of the shop made no objection, for by this time he knew his customer, money rained in on him for orchids, and the gardener found him "very nice-spoken," while, from Firbank's point of view, it was worth it, for the peripatetic gardener added a touch of rural pageantry to the gray streets of London. I can still recall the joy it used to give me, as I sailed down the ugly desert of Sloane Street on the top of a then open motor omnibus, to see this solemn, rather self-conscious procession of one, and to realize that a familiar, fantastic sense of humor was again at play among us.

Towards the end of his life he was as much pleased with the select appreciation of his books as he was disappointed at the small range of it. He had been simple enough, perhaps, to expect for his work as large and wide an audience as that obtained by Miss Ethel M. Dell or some such book of the period as *Beau Tarzan*. He was especially gratified by the enthusiastic tone of Mr. Carl van Vechten, and would carry about his letters, in bulging pockets, together with various laudatory notices of his writings that had appeared recently in the American Press. He was also very much elated at a letter sent to him by some transatlantic cinema magnate, asking for the film rights of *Caprice*, the novel in which the heroine — the daughter, as I have said, of a Rural Dean — sets up in theatrical management, herself playing the chief part, but, after an enthusiastic first night, being still too poor to rent a bedroom, has to sleep on the stage and finally meets her death by falling into a mouse trap that she had not observed in the darkness!

At this period Ronald undoubtedly looked very ill. He knew how delicate he was, and as he sat there at the Café Royal showing one these documents, or as he lay, rather than sat, in the front row of the stalls at a theater the sable angel of death ever hung over him. Moreover, he was much given to frequenting fortunetellers, crystal gazers and givers of amulets, and the soothsayers, seeing him, prophesied evil. It may be that it was his intense relish and understanding of the silly and absurd side of modern life that made him consult them. But he was in many ways, I think, so near the things which he very beautifully skimmed and parodied that perhaps he was genuinely superstitious. Certainly he paid a large weekly salary to an Egyptian occultist to protect him from influences. Be that as it may, however, it had become his habit during the past five or six years to drive round in state at the end of each summer to say good-by to my brother and me, at the same time telling us that he knew there were but a few months more for him to live. These doleful tidings had invariably been transmitted to him either by a Syrian magician or by some wretched drunkard at the Café Royal. And he always brought with him, on these farewell visits, a glass claret jug in an openwork silver container, *circa* 1870, which he wished us to keep as a memento of him — but we always refused. Whilst talking with us of his impending decease, he would keep his taxicab waiting outside, ominously ticking out the pence and minutes, and would then leave us, taking the claret jug with him, in order to drive on and bid farewell to his other friends. So often did these final scenes occur that when in truth he came to say good-by for the last time in our house, it conveyed little, being merely part of a regular and ordinary routine. But actually my final meeting with him was in the Café Royal, then undergoing at the same moment the dual, and apparently contradictory, process of being pulled down and rebuilt. And upon that occasion, owing to a sudden impulse, I had the pleasure of telling him how exquisite a writer I judged him to be, and how much, how infinitely better than most of his contemporaries, many of whom were more highly esteemed. For Ronald suffered rather than gained from the fact that he was a true, born artist, with no propagandist ax to grind.

That winter he spent in Egypt, and then came back to Rome, where he had taken an apartment in the Palazzo Orsini for a term of years. But the change of climate from Cairo to Rome gave him a severe chill, which turned to pneumonia, and he died within a few days.

It was odd how slowly the news of his death traveled and it was several weeks before most of his friends heard of it. It was barely recorded in the press, and three weeks after it had taken place, while little or no mention was made of his books. The only friend of his in Rome at the time of his demise was Lord Berners, who saw him a day or two before the end, when he was already ill, and he has told me that Firbank entertained no suspicion that he was dying. The doctor, too, appears at first to have treated the matter lightly, as an ordinary chill. So little did the dying man himself expect a fatal termination that only a few hours before it occurred, since he was feeling very much better, he discharged his nurse.

He died at the age of thirty-nine. He never saw forty, the thought of which he so much disliked. Growing older afflicted him, and would have pained him more, though he held, with one of the characters he created, that "I suppose when there's no more room for another crow's-foot, one attains a sort of peace."

In any case, his death could not have been long averted, even if he had not contracted that fatal chill. Apparently he had been examined by a doctor before leaving England, and, though he did not inform his patient of it, lungs and heart were already then in such a bad state that it was obvious that any illness must finish fatally for him.

Through a strange mistake, typical of much that was paradoxical in his life, the Catholic Firbank was at first laid to rest not far from the spot where are interred the remains of Keats and Shelley and Trelawny; under the shadow of the pyramid of Gaius Sestius, in the Testaccio Protestant Cemetery in Rome. When, however, in the spring of 1933 I went thither to visit his grave, all sign of it had vanished. Subsequently it was explained to me by a sexton that the error had been discovered and rectified, and that the body had been moved to a Catholic burial ground. Thus about his last resting place itself there was an inconsequential no less than a tragic element. . . . But then one could always, even in his lifetime, see a miniature legend in attendance upon him, hovering round him, waiting like a bird of prey to batten on his corpse: and still, today, some persons say — and write — that Firbank never in fact died; that he is alive, wandering round and observing in remote countries. And we, who knew him, are left to wish this myth were the reality, so that again we might see that jaunty, sad and unique figure, and hear once more those sudden gusts of deep, silly laughter which so convulsed and shook his frame, or those few unexpected remarks, wrenched out of himself with so much seeming effort, and to deplore that we shall not again receive a sheaf of ridiculous postcards, with his large handwriting on them, and, above all, shall nevermore have the joy of reading a new book from his pen, a book that would be so deliciously unlike any others in the world save his own.

CHAPTER IV

Wilfred Owen

WILFRED OWEN! This is a name that has gathered a continual accretion of fire. It glows. It lives clothed in flame. . . . On the day when at last the news came that the Second World War was over, under circumstances so terrible and portentous as to overshadow any feelings of happiness; in that strange desert of a holiday created for public rejoicing in which there yet could exist no feeling of joy, certain lines drifted into my mind:

> Red lips are not so red
>   As the stained stones kissed by the English dead.
> Kindness of wooed and wooer
> Seems shame to their love pure.
> O Love, your eyes lose lure
>   When I behold eyes blinded in my stead!

For an instant, I could not remember who had written them, and then, with the shock that comes when one recognizes another of the distorted repetitions of history, I identified them, and in consequence today take up my pen to salute, across the intervening gap of over thirty years, the genius of a poet killed at the end of the First World War. So long ago: yet it was just such a summer day as this when I last saw him.

I did not know Wilfred Owen for long, hardly for more than a year, I suppose, but the friendships we possessed in common, notably with Siegfried Sassoon and Robert Ross, and the fact that we were deeply in sympathy in our views concerning the war and its conduct — a link of nonconformity that in those years bound together the disbelievers with almost the same force with which faith had knitted together the early Christians — soon matured our relationship. He was swift to seize the point and character of those with whom he came in contact, and eager, further, that glory should crown all whom he met in this world fresh to him, into which he had been introduced by Siegfried Sassoon, whose poetry he admired no less than the courage, physical and moral, and in two opposite respects, with which Sassoon had faced the war. And here we approach one of the characteristics that distinguished Owen. He manifested a tremendous capacity for admiration, for reverence; a quality which perhaps every poet, however much of a rebel he may be in other directions, must needs possess. It showed in his conduct towards contemporaries and elders no less than in his attitude towards the great who had gone before. It sounds from much of his early verse; in the last stanza, for example, of the poem he wrote in the summer of 1912, when he was nineteen, "On Seeing a Lock of Keats' Hair."

> It is a lock of Adonais' hair!
> I dare not look too long; nor try to tell
> What glories I see glistening, glistening there.
> The unanointed eye cannot perceive their spell.
> Turn ye to Adonais; his great spirit seek.
>   O hear him; he will speak!

It seems, then, only just that in return we should show reverence to, and exalt the memory of, this great poet, and those of us fortunate enough to have known him can best accomplish this by sifting our recollections of him, and by trying to describe him as he was, even superficially, how he looked, how he talked — a task all the more necessary because his surviving friends daily grow fewer. Indeed that I have not brought myself to the portraying of him before is because the cruelty of Fate, which deprived England of a poet of such stature when he was twenty-five, prevented me for many years from wishing to look back in that particular direction.

The quality of greatness that differentiates him from other war poets is in the truth both of his poetry and of his response to war. If he can be properly called a War Poet — since, greater than that, he was a Poet — he may be the only writer who answers truly to that description; the first, as he may be the last, for the very phrase *War Poet* indicates a strange twentieth-century phenomenon, the attempt to combine two incompatibles. There had been no War Poets in the Peninsular, Crimean or Boer wars. But war had suddenly become transformed by the effort of scientist and mechanician into something so infernal, so inhuman, that it was recognized that only their natural enemy, the poet, could pierce through the armor of horror with which they were encased, to the pity at the human core; only the poet could steadily contemplate the struggle at the level of tragedy. . . . The invention of the atomic bomb again changed these values: for war has once more altered its character, and an Atomic-Bomb Poet is one not to be thought of. . . . No, Owen was a *poet* — a War Poet only because the brief span of his maturity coincided with a war of hitherto unparalleled sweep, viciousness and stupidity. Alone of contemporary poets he fused, without confusing, the thoughts and emotions of war: but his compassionate heart could have been moved by other matters to the same profound and poignant expression.

His feelings about the struggle in which he was involved are stated by implication in his finest poems; they are summarized more forthrightly still in the following passage from a letter he wrote while in hospital on the Somme in the spring of 1917:

Already I have comprehended a light which never will filter into the dogma of any national church: namely, that one of Christ's essential commands was: passivity at any price! Suffer dishonour and disgrace, but never resort to arms. Be bullied, be outraged, be killed; but do not kill. It may be a chimerical and an ignominious principle, but there it is. It can only be ignored, and I think pulpit professionals are ignoring it very skilfully and successfully indeed. . . . And am I not myself a conscientious objector with a very seared conscience? . . . Christ is literally in "no man's land." There men often hear His voice: Greater love hath no man than this, that a man lay down his life for a friend. Is it spoken in English only and French? I do not believe so. Thus you see how pure Christianity will not fit in with pure patriotism.[1]

In a document found among his papers — a curious, fragmentary work of genius intended as a preface for his unpublished poems, and composed at the Front in the weeks immediately before he was killed — he writes:

> Above all I am not concerned with Poetry.
> My subject is War, and the pity of War.
> The Poetry is in the Pity.
> . . . All a poet can do to-day is warn. That is why
> the true poet to-day must be truthful.

"The Poetry is in the Pity." Yes, but it is also, in Owen's case, in the poetry. It is through the poetry of it that Pity makes her voice heard. All through his poems, even those he wrote when a boy, runs not only the same deeply flowing stream of feeling, but the same individual music, both like and unlike that of the great poets at the beginning of the previous century, of whom he was the heir. As a poet, he advanced, moreover, in both content and technique, by natural degrees from the conventional to the original, instead of beginning, as do so many writers, by being original when young and then lapsing later into the academic. His use of assonances was a profound modification of traditional English verse usage, and found its perfect expression in the most famous and the most

[1] Quoted by Mr. Edmund Blunden in his preface to *The Poems of Wilfred Owen*. (Chatto & Windus.)

moving of his poems, "Strange Meeting," as great a poem as
exists in our tongue. Let us turn then,

> Turn ye to Adonais; his great spirit seek.
> O hear him; he will speak!

What do we hear; what are the young to hear from
him? . . .

— Whatever hope is yours,
Was my life also; I went hunting wild
After the wildest beauty in the world,
Which lies not calm in eyes, or braided hair,
But mocks the steady running of the hour,
And if it grieves, grieves richlier than here.
For by my glee might many men have laughed,
And of my weeping something had been left,
Which must die now. I mean the truth untold,
The pity of war, the pity war distilled.
Now men will go content with what we spoiled.
Or, discontent, boil bloody, and be spilled.
They will be swift with swiftness of the tigress,
None will break ranks, though nations trek from progress.

The material facts of Wilfred Owen's short life are soon
told. He was born at Plas Wilmot, Oswestry, on March 18,
1893. Even in his earliest years, he loved, as we might have
presumed, the sound of words: for his mother said, "He was
always a very thoughtful, imaginative child — not very robust,
and never cared for games. As a little child his greatest
pleasure was for me to read to him, even after he could read
himself." He was educated at the Birkenhead Institute across
the river from Liverpool, to which city his family had moved.
About the age of thirteen or fourteen, he showed a passionate
desire for learning, and began to reveal the great power that
poetry exercised over him — though a poem he wrote when he
was twenty tells us that it had been at Broxton by the Hill,

where he went for a holiday when he was ten, that he first felt his boyhood fill

> With uncontainable movements; there was born
> My poethood . . .

Between his fourteenth and sixteenth years, he spent two holidays in France, a country for which he developed a great affection. In 1910, he matriculated at the London University. His early verses, written with the greatest diffidence at this time, reflect his continual reading of Keats, and the adoration he cherished for him. In 1913, a serious illness led to his seeking a more equable winter climate in France, where he accepted an engagement as tutor at Bordeaux — a post he filled for some two years. This period must have been most important in his development; he was keenly appreciative of the beauty of the mountains; and he was fortunate enough to become acquainted with Laurent Tailhade, the poet. Tailhade, it is clear from the work of both of them, exercised no direct influence upon the young man. Indeed, there is little sign in his work of any influences save those of Shakespeare, the Bible and Keats — especially Keats: and this is unexpected, because of all the poets of the English Romantic age he was the most perfect, and therefore, you would have presumed, the least likely quarry for others to work; because it is generally the great but incomplete poet who is the father of those to come. This by the way. . . . No doubt Tailhade's conversation and his knowledge of the French literary world were of the greatest interest to Owen. It was plainly a happy interval, and his poems written at this time show a light and gaiety that events were soon to deny to them forever. In July 1914, the last month of the last year of the old world, he wrote the poem beginning

> Leaves
>   Murmuring by myriads in the shimmering trees.
> Lives
>   Wakening with wonder in the Pyrenees.

Birds
    Cheerily chirping in the early day.
Bards
    Singing of summer scything thro' the hay.
Bees
    Shaking the heavy dews from bloom and frond.
Boys
    Bursting the surface of the ebony pond.
Flashes
    Of swimmers carving thro' the sparkling cold.
Fleshes
    Gleaming with wetness to the morning gold.

During this score of months he grew to understand the French way of thinking, and to learn to talk and write in French: though about this accomplishment he remained typically diffident. In token of this, we find Tailhade writing to him, in April 1915, *"Votre lettre est charmante. Cette impuissance de vous 'exprimer en français' qui vous fait hésiter, n'existe que dans votre imagination. Vous peignez avec un délicat pinceau; votre piano a les touches nécessaires pour la grâce et l'émotion."*

Owen's professional contract prevented him from returning until 1915, and in that year he came home and joined the Artists' Rifles; being gazetted later to the Manchester Regiment. He was posted to the Second Battalion on the Somme front, where sharp fighting was already in progress, in January 1917. His letters of the time present with perfect veracity and consummate skill the life of the infantry officer of those years in France and Flanders. Each war produces its own particular harvest of horrors for the soldier, and those of the 1914–1918 struggle — in addition to such flimsy but none the less abiding troubles as that which the poet notes in the words "Since I set foot on Calais quays I have not had dry feet" — were boredom, mud and, in especial, No Man's Land, the space between the enemy trenches and our own. Of this, since it is important to realize out of what suffering the full-

[107]

ness of his poetry was born, I give the following description from one of Owen's letters:

It is like the eternal place of gnashing of teeth; the Slough of Despond could be contained in one of its crater-holes; the fires of Sodom and Gomorrah could not light a candle to it — to find the way to Babylon the Fallen. It is pock-marked like a body of foulest disease, and its odour is the breath of cancer. I have not seen any dead. I have done worse. In the dank air I have *perceived* it, and in the darkness, *felt*. . . . No Man's Land under snow is like the face of the moon, chaotic, crater-ridden, uninhabitable, awful, the abode of madness. . . .

After months of hard service and almost intolerable cold — for the winter of 1916–1917 was particularly severe — Owen was taken into No. 1 General Hospital suffering from neurasthenia, and probably from concussion, the result of a fall into a cellar, of being blown up and of exhaustion. (It was from this hospital that he wrote the letter I have already quoted, dealing with Passivity.) Thence he was sent first to the Welsh Hospital at Netley, and finally to the Craiglockhart War Hospital for nervous cases, near Edinburgh — an establishment housed in a building which he compared to "a decayed hydro." Here he led an active life, lecturing and editing the hospital magazine, and took lessons in German — no doubt to prepare himself for future intercourse with the Germans, the majority of whom he held to be fellow victims of war — from Mr. Frank Nicholson, the then librarian of Edinburgh University, who gave to Mr. Edmund Blunden a most living account of him as he was at this time.[2] In it he describes how Owen took him out to tea, after one of these lessons, in a café, the only occasion on which they were alone and able to speak freely. He had on him a collection of photographs of mutilated and wounded men which he had made in order to bring home to the unimaginative the horrors that others faced for them.

[2] Published as an Appendix to *The Poems of Wilfred Owen*.

(I remember those photographs. Robert Ross, too, used to carry some of them on him, and, when an acquaintance voiced views that seemed to him stupid, overenthusiastic for war and bellicose, would take them out of his pocket, saying, "Then these will interest you!") Owen spoke of them to Nicholson, and started to raise his hand to his breast pocket to bring them out, but then suddenly realizing perhaps that his companion was not one to whom it was necessary to emphasize the horrors of war — refrained. Later on the same occasion he spoke to Nicholson — and this is important — on the problem of literary form, and how he believed that he had discovered a medium for himself through the substitution of a play of vowels for pure rhyme. (In this connection it must be remarked that quite apart from the mastery in the matter of assonances and dissonances which his work shows, and that can only be the result of long practice, many of his early poems manifest his preoccupation with this technical device.) In a letter to me, Nicholson says:

What really drew me to him so strongly was the beauty of his personality. I bear a certain grudge against myself for not having, on the occasion to which you refer, pursued the subject of his "new" poetic technique more sympathetically and more intelligently than I did. I fancy he was then more or less feeling his way toward that vowel-music which he made so peculiarly his own and used with such tremendous effect in some of his later war poems. When he spoke to me of enlarging the older traditional rhyme-range of English verse in this fashion I could only think of such freedoms as poets like Tennyson had occasionally indulged in — for example in some of the Lady of Shalott stanzas — and I failed to grasp how immensely different in character Owen's experiments were and how this device or discovery of his was to form an integral part of his technique. I was, therefore, I am afraid, less attentive to his exposition than I ought to have been. . . .

During the first weeks at Craiglockhart, it is plain that Owen was depressed. . . . On August 8th he wrote:

. . . I am a sick man in hospital, by night; a poet, for quarter of an hour after breakfast; I am whatever and whoever I see while going down to Edinburgh on the train: greengrocer, police-man, shopping lady, errand-boy, paper-boy, blind man, crippled Tommy, bank-clerk, carter, all of these in half an hour; next a German student in earnest. . . .

At this very moment of his life's lowest ebb there arrived in the same hospital a new patient, Siegfried Sassoon, whose celebrated book of poems, *The Old Huntsman*, had recently made its appearance. Owen admired the newcomer, his work and the moral courage of his pacifism — which, indeed, was in part responsible for his being in the sanatorium — equally.

The younger man summoned up his courage and called on Sassoon. He showed him some poems, and persuaded him, too, to give some of his work to the hospital magazine, which Owen was editing. *The Hydra*, as it was called, was thus privileged to publish two famous poets of the war. . . . The friendship that started in this manner gave Owen hope, and a new vision of life, so that from now onward, in the short year that opened up before him, his full stature, which grew con-tinually until the end, was revealed. Within a year, everything was changed; he now both understood his own capacity and was sure of his strength. Two years before he had written:

To be able to write as *I know how to*, study is necessary: a period of study, then of intercourse with kindred spirits, then of isolation. My heart is ready, but my brain unprepared, and my hand untrained.

But now, in November 1917, in a letter to Siegfried Sassoon, he says:

Know that . . . I held you as Keats + Christ + Elijah + my Colonel + my father-confessor + Amenophis IV in profile. What's that mathematically? . . . If you consider what the above names have severally done for me, you will know what you are doing. And you have *fixed* my Life — however short. You did not light me: I was always a mad comet; but you have fixed me. I spun round you a satellite for a month, but I shall swing out soon, a dark star in the orbit where you will blaze. . . .

For all the modesty of demeanor and manner that showed so touchingly when one met him, he possessed, as every poet must possess, his ambitions: in his own words "lesser than Macbeth's and greater, not so happy but much happier." . . . Now they were realized. On the last day of the last year he was to complete — 1917 — he wrote to his mother:

And so I have come to the true measure of man. I am not dissatisfied [with] my years. Everything has been done in bouts: Bouts of awful labour at Shrewsbury and Bordeaux; bouts of amazing pleasure in the Pyrenees, and play at Craiglockhart; bouts of religion at Dunsden; bouts of horrible danger on the Somme; bouts of poetry always; of your affection always; of sympathy for the oppressed always. I go out of this year a poet, my dear mother, as which I did not enter it. I am held peer by the Georgians; I am a poet's poet. I am started. The tugs have left me; I feel the great swelling of the open sea taking my galleon. . . .

(Alas, he sailed the open sea for only a few more months — eight, to be precise — but in that time produced imperishable poems.) Again in the following May, he wrote to his mother:

I've been busy this evening with my terrific poem (at present) called "The Deranged."[3] This poem the Editor of the *Burlington Magazine* . . . old More Adey, I say, solemnly prohibited me from sending to the *English Review*, on the grounds that "the *English Review* should not be encouraged"!!! Five years ago this would, as you suggest, have turned my head — but nowadays my head turns only in shame away from these first flickers of the limelight. For I am old already for a poet, and so little is yet achieved.

[3] "Mental Cases."

And I want *no* limelight, and celebrity is the last infirmity I desire.

Fame is the recognition of one's peers. I have already more than their recognition. . . .

Though to Siegfried Sassoon belongs the glory of having discovered Wilfred Owen, and of having helped him and launched him, it was through Robert Ross once again that I first heard of the new poet.[4] The reader of this volume will remark for himself how many of the friends described in it I first met through the good offices of Robert Ross. Of Robbie, as his intimates called him, it need only be said here that to the very end of his days this kind and perceptive being, who had known all the celebrated authors of his epoch, had guarded and preserved, in spite of the disillusionment that the years had brought him in other directions, a youthful excitement about poetry. Round him he collected the young poets, and he did more to gain them recognition than did any of his contemporaries. Various poets of my generation, notably Sassoon, Robert Graves, Wilfred Owen, Robert Nichols, and my sister and brother and myself, had reason to be grateful to him. To several of us he acted as impresario, reaping no benefit for himself thereby. He got our poems published, encouraged the notice of them in the press and by the public, introduced us to older and more eminent writers who he thought would be likely to be interested in our work, and to be of use to us. Thus, as I have mentioned in *Laughter in the Next Room*, it was he, for example, who drew Massingham's attention to my work, with the result that the then editor of the *Nation* had

[4] I find in a letter from Siegfried Sassoon to me headed 25th R.W.F., July 3rd, but with the year omitted, a reference to Owen. "Have you met Wilfred Owen, my little friend, whose verses were in the *Nation* recently. He is so nice and shy and fervent about poetry, which he is quite good at, and will do *very well* some day." This letter was presumably written on July 3, *1918*, for only two poems of Wilfred Owen's were published in the *Nation*, the first, "The Miners," on January 26, 1918; the second, "Futility," on June 15, 1918.

begun to publish, in 1917, various poems of mine which appeared under the signature "Miles." I give this as an instance, for in this sort of way Robbie rendered innumerable services and kindnesses to young authors, and to young poets especially. It is impossible to overrate his eagerness to promote the interests of young writers in whom he believed or to exaggerate the trouble he took, the tact he expended upon the matter. With him friendship was a solvent, which broke down casual enmities and united every friend to every other. Nor, so long as he lived, were there any quarrels, at any rate in this body, though he possessed several foes of the most bitter sort, chiefly, of course, as the result of his innumerable acts of generosity in the past. In a feud, he who lives longest has the final and most convincing word. Lord Alfred Douglas, Robbie's most virulent enemy, though unfortunate in all else, was fortunate in living long enough to be the last surviving member of Oscar Wilde's circle, and thus to be able to leave for others, who had not known Ross, a distorted presentation of his character, and to show him as an unprincipled and injurious friend to the fallen writer, whereas in reality he was a martyr to this friendship, which, by the sorrows, worries and troubles it brought him, shortened and ruined his life.

He had no foes, however, among the young. His wit, for which he was justly celebrated, was apt to die with the day that gave it birth, being of the type that, most exquisite of ephemerids, is so true and pointed as to depend for its value on the currents, trends and feeling almost of a particular week. A few *mots* survive, to hibernate in the mind, and come out again on an early summer day: and these, no matter if you disagree with the opinion they express, are brilliant. (Such a one was the epitaph he designed for his tomb. . . . When asked one evening by a friend what he would choose to be written on his own gravestone, he replied that, at the end of so stormy a career, the appropriate inscription would be,

"Here lies one whose name is writ in hot water.") And his tact — even when, as in the example I give, it was mock-heroic — his manner, and his voice with its slight transatlantic roll of the *r*, left over from a Canadian childhood, all exercised a powerful charm and a mollifying effect. He took me, in this instance, to luncheon with a hostess of the time, who was said to have a Negro strain in her. Inadvertently, I remarked about somebody, during the course of luncheon, "His energy is said to be due to black blood." Robbie kicked my foot under the table, and remarked in an innocent voice that was at once re-proving to me and calming to others, "Not *black* blood, Osbert: Senegalese! Senegalese!"

This account of him, I am aware, affords the reader only the slightest impression of his kindness, wit, humor, and, in especial, of the warmth of his whole personality, an attribute that dies with the person who has it, being quite impossible to convey. Nor, I fear, does it carry either the *sound*, as he talked, of his rather purring voice, or give a clear idea of the particular *quality* of his conversation, the intoxicatingly sub-versive element in it, provocative in the extreme in its refusal to accept other people's rags and tags of ideas. An implicit attack on authority — nearly always an ingredient of wit, though not necessarily of humor — combined in him with its opposite, a curious, sincere, but in a certain degree mock-deferential care for the surviving Victorian conventions. (I recollect his saying of a collusive and cuckolded husband, "I don't like the angle at which he wears his horns: he should wear them as if he didn't know they were there!") In his rooms on the first floor of 40 Half-Moon Street — a lodging house of which the landlady, Miss Burton, had been his mother's maid — there congregated nearly every night after dinner friends old and new, for it was known that Robbie liked to stay up late talking. You would find many writers, journalists, editors, connoisseurs and usually one or two rela-tives — his elder brother, Alec Ross, or his nephew Sir Squire

Sprigge (then editor of the *Lancet*). Tancred Borenius was often there too, and many who were concerned with the fine arts, for Robbie had been formerly art editor of the *Morning Post,* had for several years owned a gallery in Bury Street, and was now on the advisory board of several galleries and museums. His rooms possessed the same genial glow that we have noticed about his personality; papered a dull gold, they contained fine eighteenth-century bookcases enclosing many valuable volumes signed and given by the authors, several pieces of mahogany furniture, a typical and exquisite painted *cassone* front, and the panel by Giovanni di Paolo of Saint Fabian and Saint Sebastian, now in the National Gallery.[5] There was also hanging on the wall a picture by Richard Wilson — an artist for whose fame Robbie had done much — and a particularly striking and romantic seventeenth-century portrait of a young man in a periwig — presumably a sculptor, for he was holding a statuette. On the big table, among the books and papers, would be several large boxes of Egyptian cigarettes — which our host would scarcely ever stop smoking — and tins of biscuits, figs and Turkish delight, lying hospitably open, with a bottle of brandy and glasses.

Among the other friends one would usually meet at Robbie's, one in particular I must mention, for his name occurs in Owen's letter to his mother from which I quote [6] — More Adey. By origin a squire from Gloucestershire, he had played some part in the literary life of the 'nineties, and had latterly been for several years editor of the *Burlington Magazine*. I greatly liked this intensely fantastic character. In appearance, at the time I met him, he resembled, I see now, a water-

[5] To which Robert Ross left it in his will. I saw this picture again yesterday, after twenty-eight years. — The Gallery was crowded, and two men were looking at it — one said to the other with a strong sense of rebuke latent in his cockney accent, "It's not *suited* to English taste. . . ." I recorded this remark as it would so much have delighted the former owner of the picture.

[6] P. 111 *ante*.

color drawing of Lenin as he would have been rendered through the etherealized vision and by the etiolative hand of Burne-Jones: a small figure, with a bearded face of pale complexion and minutely lined. How much he knew of art I shall never be aware, for he scarcely ever mentioned a picture in front of me, but talked always of war and politics. In politics, he took, as the misleading phrase goes, an advanced view, and though thoroughly innocuous, so kind that he would not injure even someone he much disliked, and so ineffective as to be incapable of hunting a midge, it pleased him to dramatize himself to himself as a dangerous anarchist. In this imposture he was entirely successful. I remember his taking me round to show me some new rooms he had found — or rather, that others had been obliged to find for him — on the ground floor of a house in Burlington Gardens, and his remarking to me in all seriousness, pointing in the direction of the street:

"This place has great advantages. It's convenient for the police. Whenever they want to know where I am, they can just send someone round the corner from Vine Street to look through the window. It saves us all a lot of trouble."

When I first met him, I recollect he was absorbed in framing a question that he was intent on persuading a friend, who was a member of Parliament, to ask in the House of Commons. More was very antiwar in his attitude, and also resented being unable to go abroad. The question he had designed was to be addressed to the Secretary of State for the Home Department, and ran:

"Can a British subject voluntarily denaturalize himself, and be then in consequence compulsorily deported?"

Though Robbie was intensely sociable, and so frequently in More Adey's company, More often used to make him irritable: for example, he never knew what time it was, and after working late at the office of the *Burlington*, would arrive round at 40 Half-Moon Street at 2 A.M. thinking it was

7 P.M. and sit there, expecting to be taken out to dinner. Though Robbie liked sitting up late, he did not like sitting up as late as that, but it would be impossible to move More without hurting his feelings. . . . More Adey was also persuaded in his own mind that Gold Flake cigarettes — in those days cheap as postage stamps, and more easily procurable — could only be obtained through the good offices of poor Miss Burton, to whom he would repair in shopping hours or whom he would rouse at night, begging her to secure a packet for him — though if the shops were open, all he had to do was to go to the tobacconist next door and buy one.

Plainly Owen had met Adey; but not in the evening in question. . . . The younger men who would be found at Robbie's were usually writers and often poets, and he would often ask me to come and meet them. I was not surprised, therefore, when, in September 1917, he telephoned to me and invited me to come round to his rooms in Half-Moon Street the next evening after dinner. He said it was very important, and when I inquired why, he told me that a newly discovered poet called Wilfred Owen, a friend whom Siegfried had met at Craiglockhart, was dining with him at the Reform, and that he wanted me to meet him. He gave promise of being a remarkable poet, Robert Ross added, and he asked me especially "not to frighten him" — oddly enough, a thing I have often been asked — for he was the most diffident and sensitive of men.

Accordingly, I went round at the hour named, and there, in the comfortable warmth of Robbie's sitting room, I saw a young officer of about my age — he was three months younger than myself — of sturdy, medium build, and wearing a khaki uniform. His face was rather broad, and I think its most unusual characteristics were the width of eyes and forehead, and the tawny, rather sanguine skin, which proclaimed, as against the message of his eyes — deep in color, and dark in their meaning — a love of life and a poet's enjoyment of air and light. His features were mobile but determined, and his hair short and of a soft brown. His whole appearance, in spite of what he had been through, gave the impression of being somewhat young for his age, and, though he seemed perfectly sure of himself, it was easy to perceive that by nature he was shy. He had the easy supple good manners of the sensitive, and was eager and receptive, quick to see a point and smile. His voice — what does his voice sound like across the years? A soft modulation, even-toned, but with a warmth in it (I almost hear it now), a well-proportioned voice that signified a sense of justice and of compassion. With his contemporaries he talked with ease. Only in the presence of such literary nabobs of the period as Wells and Bennett could he scarcely bring himself to speak; and this silence, apart from being rooted in his natural modesty and good manners, was due, I think, to the immense esteem in which he held literature and those who practiced the profession of author. His residence in France may have deepened this attitude of respect, and almost awe, which had in it nothing of the Englishman's casual approach to books. To him they were all-important, while poetry was the very crown of life, and constituted its meaning.

At the first meeting, he was inclined to be shy of me, although, as I have said, he was at ease with his own contemporaries, conscious of their esteem: but I had already had a different, and perhaps a larger, experience of the world. His shyness in my presence, however, soon wore off, for we possessed in common a delight in the company of our friends, a love of books, and a hatred of modern war and of those who did not feel its burden. Moreover, we shared the unspeakable experiences of the infantry officer of the time and an enormous pity for those engaged in this vile warfare. We both knew the look he had described: ". . . the very strange look on all faces in that camp; an incomprehensible look, which a man will never see in England, though wars should be in England; nor can it be seen in any battle. . . . It was not despair, or terror, it was more terrible than terror, for it was a blindfold look, and without expression, like a dead rabbit's. It will never be painted, and no actor will ever seize it. And to describe it, I think I must go back and be with them. . . ."

His visits to London from Scarborough, whither he had been posted on leaving Craiglockhart at the end of October, 1917, were infrequent. Scarborough was a town I had known intimately since childhood, and to which, a year later, I was to return to stand as parliamentary candidate; and when Owen and I met in London, I would — for I had not been in the North for two or three years past — ask him about the place, what damage the bombardment had done, and what the life in it was like in wartime conditions. He resided there in a hotel where the 5th (Reserve) Battalion of the Manchester Regiment was quartered, so Mr. Blunden tells us: though I always understood that he had been stationed in the large red cavalry barracks, outside the town, at Burniston, and his letter to me, which I give below, is addressed from there. Scarborough was a place for which he had formed no liking, and in a letter he wrote the following year he says:

. . . But this morning at 8:20 we heard a boat torpedoed in the bay, about a mile out, they say who saw it. I think only ten lives were saved. I wish the Boche would have the pluck to come right in and make a clean sweep of the pleasure boats, and the promenaders on the Spa, and all the . . . Leeds and Bradford war profiteers now reading *John Bull* on Scarborough sands.

In July 1918 Wilfred Owen wrote me the letter which I interpolate here as a good example of his style as letter writer. I had sent him an epigram I had composed on Clemenceau, at the time French Premier. Whenever catastrophe threatened to overwhelm the Allied cause, as frequently it did in 1917 and '18, and whatever the extent of human suffering involved, inevitably in the English papers some such reassuring sentence as this would appear: "On being informed of these happenings Monsieur Clemenceau announced that he was fully satisfied." . . . "Ill Winds," as the epigram was called, remained unpublished.

It ran:

> Up on the Cross, in ugly agony,
> The Son of Man hung dying — and the roar
> Of earthquakes rent the solemn sky
> Already thundering its wrath, and tore
> The dead from out their tombs. . . . Then Jesus died —
> But Monsieur Clemenceau is fully satisfied!

I give this poem — which I have found recently — and the foregoing facts only to explain the reference in the letter that follows:

Dear Osbert Sitwell,

I rehearsed your very fine Epigram upon our Mess President — rather a friend of mine. He did not immediately recognise Jesus. The rest of the Mess would not of course know the name of Monsieur Clemenceau. (To my mind this would be no indication of any man's ignorance of affairs.) May I send "Ill Winds" to a French youth who might translate and circulate it where it would be appreciated?

Always hoping to find an hour in which to copy out and generally denebulise a few poems acceptable to you either as Editor or — may I not say — friend — I have delayed this letter so long. Tonight there is only time for a tedious brief speech with you before the mind wakes up for its only amusement these days — dreams.

For 14 hours yesterday I was at work — teaching Christ to lift his cross by numbers, and how to adjust his crown; and not to imagine he thirst till after the last halt; I attended his Supper to see that there were no complaints; and inspected his feet that they should be worthy of the nails. I see to it that he is dumb and stands at attention before his accusers. With a piece of silver I buy him every day, and with maps I make him familiar with the topography of Golgotha.

Last week I broke out of Camp to order *Wheels*, 1917. Light-foots refused to stock copies. I persisted so long that the Young Lady loudly declared she knew all along that I was "Osbert himself." This caused a consternation throughout the crowded shop; but I got the last laugh by — "No, Madam; the book is by a friend of mine, Miss Sitwell."

Smith's people would not order a single copy without deposit!

Is the 1918 vol. designed to go on the caterpillar wheels of Siegfried's Music Hall Tank? If so I might help with the ammunition. Would you like some short War Poems, or what? Please give me a final date for submitting them to you.

I very much look forward to meeting you again, and if it be in Scarborough the pleasure will be that of all snatched joys. I am incarcerated more strictly than you imagine. Westborough is now a weekly ambition. The Spa is beyond my hopes. This is the beginning of decadence. As is proved by my Father's message on hearing I was G. S.: "gratified to know you are normal again." — Very sympathetically yours, W. E. S. OWEN.

A little later he sent me the poems of which he spoke; among them his magnificent "Mental Cases":

> Who are these? Why sit they here in twilight?
> Wherefore rock they, purgatorial shadows. . . .

The others are "Disabled," "Parable of the Old Men and the Young," "The Last Laugh," "The Last Word," "Soldiers' Dreams," "Arms and the Boy," and an early poem, untitled, beginning,

> Long ages past, in Egypt thou wert worshipped
> And thou wert wrought from ivory and beryl.

"The Last Laugh" and "The Last Word" are very similar versions of the same unpublished poem, and are not among the first rank of his work. The early poem and "Soldiers' Dreams" also remain unpublished. . . . And each of the rest presents variations from the published text. But this was not unusual with Owen, for many manuscript versions exist of nearly all his poems. The version I possess of "Mental Cases" offers an interesting alternative three lines for the four that appear as the end of the poem in the book. The published version runs:

> — Thus their hands are plucking at each other;
> Picking at the rope-knouts of their scourging;
> Snatching after us who smote them, brother,
> Pawing us who dealt them war and madness.

whereas in my copy it is:

> Thus their fingers pick and pluck each other,
> Picking the hard scourge that scourged them, brother,
> Plucking us who dealt them war and madness.

The reference in the letter to me as an editor can hardly refer, as I thought it did, to *Art and Letters*, a periodical of which I subsequently became one of the editors, but must be an allusion to *Wheels* — to which later in the letter he makes specific reference (mentioning the cover, by Roberts) — the celebrated annual miscellany of contemporary poetry founded and edited by my sister, whom unfortunately Owen never met. She played a part in the subsequent life of his poems, however, doing much of the work of editing the volume of his poems which was the first to be issued. Moreover, it was in *Wheels* (1919), dedicated to his memory, that Owen's poems, notably his chief and most moving work, "Strange Meeting," first appeared. (The others included were "The Show," "A Terre," "The Sentry," "Disabled," "The Dead-Beat" and "The Chances.")

The last time I saw Wilfred Owen was on an afternoon of full summer, a Saturday in July, 1918. He had let me know that he was coming to London, and I had been able to arrange to take him and Siegfried Sassoon to hear Violet Gordon Woodhouse play the harpsichord and clavichord, and she made the afternoon stand out as an oasis in the desert of war. For over two hours she played Bach, Mozart and the early English composers to us, as only she could play them. Wilfred Owen felt deeply the appeal of music, as will be seen from a letter he wrote to his mother in 1914 speculating on the course of a future that was, alas, to be so short:

I certainly believe I could make a better musician than many who profess to be, and are accepted as such. Mark, I do not for a moment call myself a musician, nor do I suspect I ever shall be, but there! I love music, with such *strength* that I have to conceal the passion for fear it be thought weakness. . . .

It can be imagined, then, with what rapture he heard this exquisite music rendered as it should be; he was dazed with happiness at the fire and audacity of the player.

After hearing Mrs. Gordon Woodhouse, Owen, Siegfried Sassoon and I went back to my house in Swan Walk — or rather we first sat in the Physic Garden opposite, under the mulberry trees. (This privilege we were only accorded through my friendship with my neighbor, the guardian; for visitors, except members of the Apothecaries' Society, are not really allowed within the precincts.) We walked across to the house for tea — including, I remember, bowls of raspberries — and then returned to sit in the Garden. It was the ideal of a summer afternoon: various shrubs, late-flowering magnolias and the like, were in blossom, there was a shimmer and flutter in the upper leaves, and a perfection of contentment and peacefulness, unusual in the tense atmosphere of a hot day in London, especially during a war, breathed over the scene. So listlessly happy was Owen that he could not bring himself to leave the Garden to go to the station and catch the train he had arranged to take.

That afternoon, so untouched by premonition, was yet full of lamentable fate. Those persons who, thinking he was not yet fit for foreign service, were seeking to find him a post at home, suddenly desisted. Had they continued, Wilfred Owen might well be alive today: but within a week, he was ordered to attend for medical inspection, and knew that he was going out to France again. "I am glad," he wrote. "That is I am much gladder to be going out again than afraid. I shall be better able to cry my outcry, playing my part. . . ." A little more than a month later, he embarked once more for France. He rejoined his old battalion, and after winning the Military Cross in October, he was killed in an attempt to cross the Sambre Canal, on November the 4th, a week before the Armistice was proclaimed.

It was some weeks before his friends heard of his death: he had disappeared into the gray mists of those autumnal regions which had swallowed so many young lives — but never one that could be a greater loss to England than this. His death occurred many years ago now, but it is only a short period since one of his friends wrote to me: "I have found many letters lately of Wilfred Owen's, and looking back over the time since the last war, I see how much easier all our lives would have been if he had lived. . . ." These words bear true witness, both to his influence on his friends and to their feeling for him.

CHAPTER V

Gabriele D'Annunzio

GABRIELE D'ANNUNZIO! the sound still carries with it a political as well as an esthetic echo: yet who today remembers him as the Regent of Carnaro, and who, it may be, reads now the great poet who purified the Italian language, and wrote novels and plays which obtained a world-wide renown? Yet, in addition, D'Annunzio had long been a figure of universal fame, of a kind that scarcely attaches itself to anyone in this age. Indeed, it is difficult to find any just comparison for him, or prototype, except Byron. Like Byron, he had become famous at a very early age — in his own case, in his teens — with his poems. The two men were alike in the shock their books created, in their force of character and in their interests: though a great fire shone, too, in the oratory of D'Annunzio — a gift denied to Byron. But Byron's personality wielded as powerful an influence as D'Annunzio's, and each left his mark on the world forever, even though his books were for a time not read. Both poets in the end turned men of action and eventually sought refuge, after lives of dissipation, in political adventure. Both men provided innumerable scandals for the boudoir and drawing room: since, again like Byron, D'Annunzio, though he lacked the earlier writer's personal beauty and aristocratic background, was the hero of love affairs that were most eagerly discussed in the worlds of art and fashion. Even those who had never read a line by him were interested. To be able to give details of his quarrel with Duse conferred on him or her who announced them a flattering quality of "being in the know." If the truth was obscure, then stories, of the most improbable kind, were invented for the consumption of the inmates of the salons of America and Europe. . . . Even today I can recall hearing one of them related: D'Annunzio, it was said, was spending the end of a love affair, and a long Italian autumn, in a decaying castle in the hills. The place was enormous, the scenery appropriate, but as the season dragged into winter, a bitter dullness invested the castle, no less than the love affair it sheltered, until again the surrounding world of neighbors and peasants was fluttered by the news that a lady in a white cloak rode into the courtyard at midnight and ensuing midnights on a white horse — or should I write white palfrey? — the explanation of this singularly tall story being that the lady in the flowing cloak was D'Annunzio, who had thus clothed himself in order to reawaken interest and induce those who beheld the phantom to believe that a new love was beginning. Such anecdotes were swallowed easily, for undoubtedly an element of sensationalism existed in him, as in various other artists. Inherent even in the name he invented for himself and used — Gabriele D'Annunzio — which attaches itself so easily to the titles of the Archangels of Italian Culture, is something of this quality, as well as of the same free indulgence in obvious flights of poetry, the same fondness for the old poetic symbols, which is to be found equally in, for example, his assumption of the pomegranate as his personal emblem, and in the imagery of his books.

This sketch, then, though it too deals with the man more than with his work, must yet differ from the other portraits in this volume: for it attempts to paint an atmosphere and a place, and to record a singular episode in European history, as well as to give a necessarily rather fragmentary impression of a great writer. More than that it cannot be, because my contact with him was so brief, whereas his companions in these pages I knew well. But at least, though our acquaintance was so slight, I visited him in his, as it proved, temporary dominion, and that, too, colors the portrait. . . . One misses so many opportunities, from caution, foresight or the desire for a peaceful life, in consequence leaving modern history and its extraordinary episodes to be described either by those specialists who have developed a nose for news, but no hand with which to write it, or by the hapless beings who write letters signed "Onlooker" or "Eyewitness." The very excuse that these last advance on their behalf is in reality the accusation against them. They chanced, they aver, to have been on the spot when such and such a thing occurred. In short, like Casabianca on the burning deck, they obtusely remained behind when all their more intuitive and sensitive companions had already sought safety. And what do they tell us, subsequently, of what they beheld? Not long ago, for example, I met an officer who had been present at the great catastrophe of the Quetta earthquake. He had been engaged in something he thought to be sport — would it have been pig-sticking? — and at the time had been standing on a hill above the town.

"How extraordinary!" I remarked. "What a tremendous spectacle and experience it must have been! . . . Tell me, what did you see?"

With an air of concentration, he thought for some time, and then, with an outward gesture of his hands, replied:

"Well, first of all, the city was there, and then, the next moment, it sort of wasn't, don't you know?"

Of such are the graphic descriptions usually to be obtained from those accidentally present at events, and the episode of Fiume seemed to deserve more sympathetic, or at any rate professional, study than it would obtain from someone casually stranded there at the time of the poet's escapade. Already there had been great misrepresentation, and it is important to analyze here the causes. Partly they were political, and owing no doubt to a very wise sense of fear of direct political action, as well as to the less wise democratic fear of action of any sort, partly they were due to the fact that D'Annunzio was a great poet. The English-speaking peoples, in spite of poetry being essentially their art, have rarely admired poets as individuals: there has been, at any rate of recent centuries, a small and highly specialized audience for contemporary poetry and a popular dislike of it, and of those who write or are likely to write it. . . . In case I should be accused of exaggeration, I must here hurriedly interpose a story of the school days of one famous poet, to which I had listened a few months before I went to Fiume. . . . I had sat next, at luncheon, to an old gentleman who owned to eighty-six years, and a fine impressive machine he looked, as he told me how much he had enjoyed his long life. "If a man — or a schoolboy for that matter —," he continued, "does not get on well, it's his own fault. I well remember, when I first went to Eton, the head boy called us together, and pointing to a little fellow with a mass of curly red hair, said, 'If ever you see that boy, kick him — and if you are too far off to kick him, throw a stone.' . . . He was a fellow named Swinburne," he added. "He used to write poetry for a time, I believe, but I don't know what became of him."

A poet, then, of D'Annunzio's type, with his intensely Latin approach to life, will be necessarily more unpopular in Anglo-Saxon countries than even Shelley or Swinburne. Also, usually, there is less chance of kicking him. But D'Annunzio's usurpation of Fiume provided just such a rare opportunity. The press imputed to him not only an imperialistic outlook but a love of money, of power, of sensationalism: in fact whether rightly or wrongly, he was arraigned for those very faults he shared with his accusers. But the real crime he committed in their eyes, but which was seldom mentioned, was that he appeared to be a great artist and as such would naturally be unpopular with the leaders of commercial states, and their businessmen. Only occasionally did the truth peep out in such a heading as "Fresh Attempts on Life of Crazy

Poet" — for, in this similar to Lenin, Trotsky, and later to Hitler and his lieutenants, D'Annunzio had been time and time again triumphantly consigned to the asylum or, more effectively still, assassinated in the columns of the world press. No Power, one should have known, "would tolerate for an instant" the vicinity of a ruling poet; whatever might have been the artistic possibilities of his venture, they were killed, though the political and subversive ones were driven back to survive in a more acerbated form in their own country, for a time to conquer, and everywhere for many years to constitute a challenge to the established order that had been responsible for D'Annunzio's defeat: for Fascism was the child of Fiume.

Yet, though D'Annunzio was a poet, one would have expected the world public, or at any rate the Allied public of the 1914–1918 war, to have venerated him. By his reputation as a man of genius, and by his altogether exceptional powers of oratory and appeal, he had brought Italy into the war on the side of the Allies. At least, then, those who admired and enjoyed the war should have admired D'Annunzio; no less for the great personal bravery he showed in the struggle, and for the inspiration his courage afforded to his countrymen, than for his success in political persuasion. But having incurred this heavy moral liability, D'Annunzio was soon made to feel that he had brought the Italians into the conflict under false pretenses, because, albeit secret treaties between England, France, and Italy guaranteed the Italians certain territories if the Allies won, these conditions, entered into without the knowledge of President Wilson, were never recognized by him, or carried out. And it was D'Annunzio's consequent feeling of being accountable for this failure, his belief that Italy had come out of the war on a par with the defeated nations, that made him risk his life once again at Fiume. Thus, to the Italian people, who know no fear of poetry, D'Annunzio remained not only the man who had done more for their language than any writer since Dante, and the patriot who had alone stood out against what they considered the futilities of the Peace Conference, but — it was a popular claim in Italy — he was supposed, by his seizure of Fiume, to have been the cause of the fall of President Wilson: to whom, in a speech, he had characteristically referred as "that coldhearted maniac who sought to crucify Italy with nails torn from the German Chancellor of the Scrap of Paper."

It was at the end of November, 1920, on the shores of the Neopolitan Bay, that the idea of Fiume first laid hold on us. My brother suddenly remarked to me, as we stood on a terrace overlooking the sea, mountains and islands:

"We never saw Lenin seize power in Petrograd: let us now go to Fiume to see D'Annunzio. It may be the beginning of something else."

Immediately I realized with what truth he spoke; for here was a small state seized and ruled over by a poet, and who could tell but that it might develop into an ideal land where the arts would flourish once more on Italian soil (D'Annunzio was wont to claim that Fiume was "Italian by right of landscape," and so it was, belonging clearly, as we were to see, to the same order as Naples or Genoa) as they have so often blossomed before? It might even offer an alternative or escape from the Scylla and Charybdis of modern life, Slum-Bolshevism or Democratic Bungalow-Rash — morbid states of the soul that are of no help to the artist.

Whatever, then, may be thought of the results of the Fiume adventure, my brother was right: the moment, the man, the place were of importance. Though he spoke when the last month of the year was so close, as we looked from the terrace, the sun still streamed over the flat roofs, highly colored tiled domes, feathery palm trees and built-up hills, and glittered on the blue-green waters with an unequaled brilliance and sparkle. All difficulties became minimized under this parade. My father with his ceaseless drive to remodel our careers, and his cautionary refrain of "Oh, I *shouldn't* do that!" as if something appalling lurked in the execution of any plan of ours, seemed in our imagination for once to be quite tractable: to journey for a night or two to Venice, and then proceed to the small principality D'Annunzio had established for himself, seemed in itself a small and easy matter. The icy fingers that already held Northern Italy in their grip were not to be conjured up in the imagination; while such things as passports became totally negligible, mere whims of a genial international bureaucracy, under the rays of the late but glowing sun. I at once telegraphed to my friend Massingham, asking if I might write for the *Nation*, of which he was editor, an account of D'Annunzio's Fiume, and obtained permission to represent the journal. My brother and I then decided to invite Orioli, the Florentine bookseller, to accompany us, for he was an entertaining and appreciative companion, and his knowledge of the ways of his countrymen, and their language, might prove invaluable. Soon we set off.

We met in Venice; from there, all night long, we sat in a railway compartment, talking and smoking. Orioli, with his emphatically accentuated and fluent foreigner's English, and with his rather lisping gift of vivid phrase, told us, I remember, of his childhood in Romagna, and of how, later, working as a young Italian without means in a shop at Cambridge, he had educated himself by borrowing cap and gown from various undergraduates whose hair he cut, and attending, thus clad, and without making any payment, those lectures he thought would be of use to him. He spoke, too, of his methods of avoiding creditors in those early days — for he realized, when he started his bookshop, that he must have a good suit in order to present a respectable appearance, but he could not pay for it for many years. All these stories he told with an abundance of amusing and well-observed detail.

. . . . So, with such tales of private enterprise, the night wore on, and, indeed, the day following, for the trains in North Italy were still in a chaotic condition after the war, and we arrived in Trieste in the evening, just as dusk had fallen. The harsh north wind with the Greek name blew along the stony streets of the city, and roared in the piazzas. The electric light failed — perhaps, for such was then its way, as a fresh tribute to the anarchist Malatesta — and the fur-capped, flat-faced Slavonic peasants from outlying villages huddled together in clumps, speaking outlandish tongues, within the barren shelter of the great drafty station. No one there, least of all guard or porter, seemed to know when the train would start for Fiume. Italian officers, *Arditi*, Wolves of Tuscany, gesticulated in groups outside an obsolete train. Cloaks, daggers and the feathers of eagles proclaimed rather melodramatically that the Roman legions were assembling once more under a new Caesar, while, further, the flowing black ties of the *Arditi* indicated that the new Caesar was a poet. Through the pervading braggadocio atmosphere, through the noisy, vapid chatter, there flickered like a flame an unmistakable enthusiasm, not often at that time to be encountered.

At last the groups broke up, and the individuals who composed them settled noisily into their chosen places in the antiquated train. There was no light in carriages or corridors, but as the train jolted higher into the hills, the snow outside threw a ghostly, almost green illumination on the faces within. Even at this distance, the influence of D'Annunzio was omnipresent and his name scarcely ever left the conversation. First the somewhat Jugoslav lady in the corner, with eyebrows that even in this pallid obscurity could be seen to meet and intertwine, complained that the cause of Fiume had become a Massacre of the Innocents, a Children's Crusade. And indeed the officer who sat next me confessed that he was smuggling into the Regency the two enthusiasts of sixteen years of age who accompanied him. They had tried to become legionaries a year before, but on the score of their youth had been turned back by the Italian troops at the border. Both lads were evidently caught in the magic net of D'Annunzio's words, and their pockets were heavy with his speeches, prayers and threats, which, at great labor to themselves, they had copied out in a round but flowing hand. They vowed that if they could not get through to Fiume on the train, they would walk there, over the frozen mountains — and thousands of boys, they declared, would do the same from all over Italy: for Gabriele D'Annunzio remained until his death the idol of young Italy. Even the lady with the eyebrows admitted that, when the Regent rode out through the stony countryside, the people, whether Italian or Croat, would strew the ground with flowers.

We began to approach the rather elusive frontier of an unacknowledged principality. To enter Fiume was by no means easy. The Allies, and the Italian Government in particular, did not wish to encourage their nationals to visit the city: while the Regency was also, for its part, strongly opposed to receiving foreigners in a time when there was a shortage of food and necessities. Journalists especially were disliked — and as such I was appearing — because some, who had been received with kindness, had on their return home published attacks of a personal nature on those who had entertained them. Thus it was that, after we had journeyed for some five hours, my own troubles began. . . . The soldier at the border could not read easily, but he could, and did, with some trouble to himself, at last decipher uneasily a name on my passport. . . . Alas, it was not my name, as it happened, but that of the Foreign Secretary who had signed the document. At first the Italian was obviously not sure where he had heard it before, but then, as his eye lighted on the motto under Lord Curzon's coat of arms, *Let Curzon holde what Curzon helde*, and he repeated it in broken Eng-

lish, turning it on his tongue, he received suddenly the full
impact of the astonishing plot he had by chance uncovered.
Here, he concluded, was Lord Curzon, the chief instrument
of English democracy, trying to sneak into the Regency,
without informing any of the ministers or officials. He gave
a bellow of rage and informed me that I was *not* allowed to
proceed on my journey. . . . It was only after moments
seemed to have turned to hours that, with the help of Orioli's
natural eloquence, and the aid of a Tuscan Wolf with whom
luckily a flask of wine had been shared on the cold journey,
finally I was permitted my own identity and released.

Eventually we arrived at Fiume. Below us lay the giant
warehouses and docks, in plain disproportion to the size of
the town. In the harbor was congregated D'Annunzio's by
no means negligible fleet. Some of the vessels had been captured by the poet's pirates, others — like the *Dante*, which
had deserted to him from the Italian Navy — by his phrases.
The leviathan outline of this great ship loomed up into the
cold darkness, and its lights, and those of the smaller boats
round it, flickered threateningly. Otherwise all was dark,
and it was difficult to comprehend the conformation of the
port until the next day. . . . Then the sun sparkled and it
was possible to appreciate the disposition of the place, with
its clustered houses and its bay, a spur of hills sinking into the
opalescence of the far seas, and the quivering misty outlines
of the islands. The cold, which was intense, crystallized each
sound into a greater precision. But the human element was
here of more interest than the form of hills or the incidence
of climate. Outside our hotel was the chief Piazza, where the
Governor had placed two flagstaffs, the idea of which derived from his beloved Venice. And in the Piazza at all hours
of morning and afternoon loitered a crowd as fantastic as any
— even when one recalls the tumblers and clowns, Turks and
Oriental merchants in turbans — ever sheltered by the bubble domes of St. Mark's. The general animation and noisy

vitality seemed to herald a new land, a new system. We gazed and listened in amazement. Every man here seemed to wear a uniform designed by himself: some had beards, and had shaved their heads completely, so as to resemble the Commander himself, who was now bald; others had cultivated huge tufts of hair, half a foot long, waving out from their foreheads, and wore, balanced on the very back of the skull, a black fez. Cloaks, feathers and flowing black ties were universal, and every man — and few women were to be seen — carried the "Roman dagger." Suddenly, as some messenger arrived — it might be an emissary of the Regent himself — on a very palpitating motor bicycle, a stir would pass through the throng so full of swagger and of youth — and yet, as I write this, I recall that, included in the gathering, as if to prove that youth was not universal or eternal, were two Garibaldian veterans with red waistcoats and white hair. But even they seemed to possess some paradoxical secret, and behaved in a manner that gave the lie to their years. For instance, I recall that as, a few days later, we left Fiume, we observed them making a meal of oysters, crayfish shaped like scarlet aircraft, and cherry brandy, the staple but somewhat exotic foods of this land of youth.

D'Annunzio had detailed, to take us round, as guide, an officer who was gay, enthusiastic, pleasure loving. London in particular — London, which was then truly a city of life and pleasure — London, which he had never visited, was the object of his almost passionate longing. He — for, in his Italian way, he was, though perhaps not consciously to the full extent, a Futurist — dreamt of the tubes and motorbuses and the great stores, the cars in lines, the delicious traffic blocks scented by petrol fumes, the music halls. And the buildings must be beautiful too, he averred. But none finer, I replied, than those to be admired in Italian cities. "*Ma*," he replied in a voice infused with astonishment, "*il Palazzo di Cristallo.*" He had fought in Poland, and during that time had met many English officers, of whom, however, he retained a singular memory, for he remarked, "*Molto gentili: ma sempre mangiano* jam, jam, jam."

Our new friend had been ordered to show us the town, the people, the army, and the night life of Fiume. . . . The army could be divided roughly into three categories. The biggest consisted of Italian romantic patriots, spiritual grandchildren of Garibaldi, gathered together by the glamour of the Regent's name and words: next was the smaller brand of Futurists, who, whilst disapproving of D'Annunzio as a writer, acclaimed his deeds of bravery and applauded a leader who took no heed of yesterday or for tomorrow; and finally, closely allied to the Futurists, came a little gang of professional fighters, who preferred war at any price to peace. These three divisions it is possible to illustrate for the reader by extreme cases. To the first belonged an officer we met who was a close friend of D'Annunzio's, and a poet himself, and who refused all pay for his services; to the second, Keller the Futurist, a fine-looking bearded giant who somewhat resembled the Augustus John of those years, and had expressed his Futurism in a famous gesture, since he had set out in an aircraft from Fiume for Rome, where he pelted the venerable Giolitti's Ministry with beetroot; to the third, a man like a tiger, with medals instead of stripes, whose very appearance constituted a danger signal. This last individual, by birth a Sardinian, had been in prison for murder at the outbreak of the war, but had specifically been released, it was rumored, on condition that he promised to devote himself to slaying the enemy. Subsequently he was said to have taken prisoner thirty Austrians in the war, and to have strangled them with his own hands. Yet he was so extremely shocked — as by the way were my brother and I — at the contemporary doings of the Black-and-Tans in Ireland that, in a night club to which we were conducted, he smashed as a protest, immediately behind our heads, the champagne bottle he had just emptied.

Thus, as we walked up the hill to the Palace the following morning, we reflected how, by the singular magic of his personality, D'Annunzio had succeeded in uniting for a time those who loved the past of Italy with those who hated it. Some had been drawn to his cause by the fervor of his words, and by the glamour of ancient and decayed cities such as Torcello, Ravenna or Mantua, while others, who agreed with Marinetti in thinking Venice a city of dead fish and rotting palaces, inhabited by waiters and touts, saw in the policy of the Regent the means of making Italy into a new Roman Empire, mighty in arms, a dangerous and insolent power with skyscrapers and an efficient train service — ideals, as it turned out, afterwards inherited and finally for a time achieved by Mussolini. The hill was steep and we walked up it slowly to the Palace, built in the well-known Renaissance-elephantoid style that is the dream of every Municipal Council the world over — for it had formerly been the Town Hall. Everything was large and square — but in fact not quite large enough. You entered a large square hall, with pillars supporting a square gallery. D'Annunzio's love of the exotic had caused this apartment to be filled with hundreds of pale plaster flowerpots of every size, but all incised with Byzantine patterns or Celtic trellis, and containing palms and succulents. Soldiers lounged among the greenery, and typists rushed furiously through swing doors. In the square gallery, and leading out of the side situated nearest the sea, were the rooms of the poet, always closely guarded: because he would often remain for eighteen hours at a time shut up in his apartment, and during these periods of thought he would take no food and must on no account be disturbed. Today, as it happened, one of these stretches of work had begun, and in consequence, since no one knew when he would return to life, we were forced to pass two days of an incredible monotony, broken solely by a lecture on the political situation of the Regency of Carnaro, which was delivered to us by the Foreign Minister. This gentleman held the unique distinction of being the only bore in Fiume: a fact proclaimed by all who knew him, but which we were destined to find out for ourselves. In looks, he belonged to the small mustachioed, tactical-authority type and, while my brother and I balanced tall frames in agonized positions over diminutive maps, he laid down the law in that flowery French, reinforced with a twang like a guitar, which is the official language of so many Italians and Spaniards. . . . At last, just as the lecture ended, we were informed that the poet would receive us the next day.

At five o'clock the following evening we were, accordingly, conducted to D'Annunzio's study. Our sole interview with him lasted only three quarters of an hour, but it would be impossible soon to forget it. As we entered, I recall a Portuguese journalist was just being shown out, reiterating fulsomely in Italian as he stepped backward out of the presence: "The Portuguese nation regards you as the Christ of the Latin World — the Christ of the Latin World — the . . ." When he had gone, in the ensuing silence, the repetition of the words could still be heard from the next room, and then gradually died away. . . . The study was fairly large, and contained little furniture. Its walls were almost entirely covered with banners. On the inner side, supported by brackets, stood stiffly two gilded saints from Florence, their calm, wide-open eyes gazing out over the deepening shades of the Fiumian sea. Near the fireplace, on one of the tables, rose the shape of a vast fifteenth-century bell, made by the famous bell-maker of Arbe, and presented to D'Annunzio by the people of that island. At the central desk sat the Commander himself, with his pomegranate in front of him, behind inkstand and pens.

Often, as I have before emphasized, an analogy in appearance will summon up more effectively for the reader the look of a man than can the most elaborate and precise description. What can one say? That D'Annunzio was small, lightly

made, dressed in gray uniform, had a face of rather Arab cast
— he came from the southeast of Italy — and streaky mustache
and embryo beard. But if I write that — as was the case — the
first thing that struck one was that he bore a distinct resemblance to Igor Stravinsky, the admirers of that great
genius can picture D'Annunzio more easily. The poet wore
many ribbons and on his left shoulder carried the Italian Gold
Medal for valor, the equivalent of our Victoria Cross. Though
he was completely and grotesquely bald, though only his
left eye remained — for he had lost the other in the war —
though he was nervous and exhausted, yet at the end of a
few seconds the extraordinary charm he possessed, which had
enabled him on many occasions to change mobs of enemies
into furious partisans, had exercised itself on us. . . . He
began to speak. The first words he addressed to us were,
"Well, what new poets are there in England?" (Not, you
will notice, "What new generals are there?" or "Who plays
for Woolwich Arsenal?") Then he went on to talk of our
country, and of his fervent admiration for Shelley, whose
death he himself had tried to imitate at the age of fifteen in the
Bay of Castellammare. In his discourse there was not a little
to northern ears of absurdity, but through it ran the hyp-
notic thread of his eloquence. He switched soon from poetry
to sport, and talked of English greyhounds — which after
poetry, he considered evidently the greatest national specialty
— "running wild over the moors of Devonshire." He proceeded to tell us of the strange conversations which he held
with the people. A silent crowd would begin to collect, and
then swell quickly outside the Palace. He would go out onto
the balcony and demand what it was they wanted. A voice
would answer, and thus would gradually build itself up a
system of direct intercourse between the people and their
ruler. This he claimed to be the first example of such inter-
play since Greek times. He told us, too, of Fiume and of his
intense loneliness there, of how he, who had always loved

books and music, had remained in his city for fifteen months, surrounded solely by peasants and soldiers, while the Italian Government, relying on his roving temperament, tried to "bore him out." He spoke of the enthusiasm of his legionaries, and declared how difficult it was to keep them at peace: weary of waiting for battle, they would fight one another in some sham contest, and it was by no means unusual for there to be serious casualties from bombs and bullet wounds. Soon after his proclamation, for instance, of the Fiumian Constitution, in which he had announced that music was to be the "Religious and Social Institution of the Regency of Carnaro," he had invited an eminent Italian conductor to bring his orchestra over from Trieste and give a series of concerts, and had provided for him a fight for the orchestra to witness. Four thousand troops, among whom were the two Garibaldian veterans whom we had seen — one aged seventy-eight and the other eighty-four — had taken part in the contest, and one hundred men had been seriously injured by bombs. The members of the orchestra, which had been playing during the quieter intervals, fired by a sudden access of enthusiasm, dropped their instruments, and charged and captured the trenches. Five of them were badly hurt in the struggle.

This new principality seemed full of paradox and of hope, as well as of a certain menace: but the Muse of History had decreed that it should fall within a few weeks of our visit. Giolitti showed his native cunning and unrivaled experience by the way in which he brought matters to a head. D'Annunzio had always relied on the fact that feeling in Italy was so strongly in his favor that no Italian Government would dare openly to oppose him, still less to use its forces against him: but the crafty old politician contrived that the whole affair should be over before the Italian people could be aware that it had begun. He waited until the night before Christmas Eve, so that he could be sure that no newspapers would appear for three days, and then sent the fleet to Fiume, with instructions to bombard the place to pieces if the poet remained there. There seemed only one thing for D'Annunzio to do, to leave before the inhabitants were exposed to the fulfillment of this threat. . . . When the news of the fall of Fiume spread, on the morning after Boxing Day, shops and theaters in all parts of Italy were closed as a sign of popular mourning: but it was too late for public opinion to exercise any force — if ever it can in modern conditions.

This rather pitiful end of the poet's adventure was hailed with relief by the press. It was supposed to finish "an awkward incident": while the poet himself — for whom no word had been good enough when his eloquence had so largely helped to persuade Italy to enter the war — was now abused and insulted. In some instances, this frail little genius, who had flown over Vienna during the war, as well as over the most perilous of battlefields and over the Austrian fleet, of which he had destroyed two battleships, was now accused of cowardice in leaving Fiume: a charge that he could afford to spurn. . . . In some cases the writers who attacked him showed hitherto unsuspected powers of imagination. Thus one journalist, in an article published in an English daily paper, headed *Chorus Girls and Champagne*, declared that one could tell from "the glassy glitter of D'Annunzio's snake-like eye" that he was addicted to cocaine! This compelled me — for D'Annunzio had not many champions at that moment — to write a reply, in which I pointed out that this "glassy glitter" was not to be attributed to the drug habit, but to the fact that one of the poet's eyes was, in fact, made of glass, since he had lost his own in the war, so recently over, while fighting on behalf of the Allied peoples, among whom the proprietor of the paper in which the libel appeared, and the writer of it, were numbered.

The poet has long been dead, and is today neither insulted daily nor praised. Together with the majority of the great army of the dead, he is out of fashion. Yet truly, though I have here written an impression of an episode in his life, it is his writings, more than his actions, which are of interest, as must always be the case with an author. His novels, so tremendous in their power of evoking emotion, and in their poetic eloquence and rhetoric — books such as *Il Fuoco, Le Vergini Delle Rocce, Il Piacere,* plays like *La Città Morta* — are there for us to reawaken and revive by our interest. In them is to be found often an overwhelming force of imagery, and sometimes a certain quality of lushness — though this does not apply to his poems — that might be cloying, were not its sweetness also contaminated and reduced by the morbidity prevalent at the end of the old century. . . . The public always clamors for a message in poetry or prose: seldom is it more angry than when it gets one. But what words can picture its rage when a poet, having for years preached his message, proceeds, as did Tolstoy and D'Annunzio, for example, to translate it into action? Tolstoy, abandoning wealth and family, and finally running off to die in the snow at a wayside railway station, in an attempt to hide from those he had abandoned to their worldly fate, was accused of insincerity; so was D'Annunzio. He had for years preached the importance of being a leader of men, the importance of staying for years immured in the dark strength of your travertine palace, impervious to the light and clamor of the democratic days outside, of waiting for your moment to emerge, armed in the full panoply of your strength, then to act swiftly and with decision. He followed his own advice. For a time he led and acted swiftly. Today his politics belong to the past, so derided by the Futurists who supported his actions, where his written words, which they criticized, belong to the present and the future, and are still there for us to read, their meaning moving and flickering through the immortal phrases, in the same way that a salamander, in part obscured by the smoke of a great fire, might be seen to glow.

CHAPTER VI

Ada Leverson

DA LEVERSON! The name still lingers in the minds of older readers as that of a wit. By the early years of the century, her several novels were very popular with a small circle. At their best, they seem the forerunners of Ronald Firbank, and are inhabited by an exquisite and even morbid absurdity. All her work was, as she wished it to be, light, but lightest and brightest of all was the preface she contributed to a collection of letters to her from Oscar Wilde.[1] This little essay is full of wit and of feeling. Even more than her books,[2] her personality, however, deserves a tribute, and I write of her here, not only for those reasons, or because, from 1920 until her death in August 1936, she was so loyal and devoted a friend to me, but also because through her instrumentality I met several of those who had been figures in her epoch, and so by being introduced to her and some of her contemporaries after this fashion, the reader may be able to catch for himself, as he reads, a momentary glimpse, here and there, of the fine flower of Willis's Rooms ("Remember Pomegranates at Willis's 8 o'clock Friday," Wilde had telegraphed to her in January 1894): persons now as shadowy, yet showy, and

[1] *Letters to the Sphinx from Oscar Wilde and Reminiscences of the Author* by Ada Leverson, and with a note of explanation by Robert Ross. Issued by Duckworth, in an edition limited to 275 copies, of which 250 were for sale in 1930. Reprinted in *The New Savoy*, 1946.

[2] In addition to the above there were the following: *The Twelfth Hour*, 1907; *Love's Shadow*, 1908; *The Limit*, 1911; *Tenterhooks*, 1912; *Bird of Paradise*, 1914; *Love at Second Sight*, 1916; and a Preface to *Whom You Should Marry* (an American book on Astrology), 1915.

as remote from us — though some of them, while I write, are still living — as would be a Roman Emperor.

When I was a boy of fourteen or fifteen, I had by chance come to know Ada Leverson by sight, as in due time I shall relate: but when, finally, some thirteen or fourteen years after, I met her at the house of her sister Mrs. Sydney Schiff, a different, an unrecognizably different, person stood before me. She seemed already to have become an old lady, though she did not purposely affect this as a style. The reasons for such a change were many. She had experienced affliction, and now suffered many disabilities in her present life, as compared with that of her young days. Chief of her sorrows, she had lost her only son when he was a small boy. Many of her friends, too, were dead, and the principal had been notoriously disgraced before he died. In her recollections of him, she tells us — to descend to lesser but still important matters — that in the middle 'nineties wealth was beginning to be scarce, and that when "two capitalists were heard one June night singing in a wood near Esher, Oscar Wilde wrote to *The Times* immediately." But if riches were scarce — which is hardly our view of the position as it was then — she had, all the same, been the wife of a rich man: but his fortune had much of it gone many years before, and the loss of wealth as an item in the scale of adversity can only be estimated by those who have experienced it. Lavish by disposition, generous in everything, she had been obliged to curb herself. Further, she had grown distressingly deaf, and her fear of talking in consequence too loud made her use her naturally soft voice so softly that it was often, indeed almost always, difficult in the extreme to catch what she said. Her friends who were alive were scattered: some of them had gone to live in Italy or France, and in her mind, and in the climate of it, she still dwelt with them, and with those who were dead. Thus, directly we met, she had begun to talk to me with great warmth of Robert Ross. And I recall how he, for his part, had often spoken to me of Sphinx, as he referred to her, and as I soon came to call her (she had been christened "the Sphinx" by Oscar Wilde), with affection. Indeed he had often said that he would ask us to meet, but owing to circumstances I had never seen her since I was a boy, until that day, some fifteen months after his death.

Certainly she had altered. . . . She usually wore now in the daytime a flowing black cloak, and a black hat with a rather wide brim, shading well her eyes which were blue and often suffused with smiles. Though the lines of her face were serious, her general and natural expression was a smile, not caused by any wish to mock, but by some absurdity she had detected in the world at large. To a Sphinx, it is true, she bore some resemblance, in the shape of head and the molding of her features. She was rather pale, but her lips were brilliantly made up, and her hair was still golden — as golden as it had been in 1906 when, so Marcel Boulestin tells us in his autobiography,[3] he had met her at Paris Plage. He goes on to relate how, when she had been accused of using peroxide, she had indignantly denied it, adding that she "only darkened her hair a little at the roots." In the evening, if there were a party and she went to it, she wore her hair curled all over her head, and then, with her emphatic profile, she had something of the look of Sarah Bernhardt. On such occasions she entered a room, though she was of small stature and stooped in the manner of all those whose life is devoured by books, either in the reading or in the writing of them, with an indubitable air of distinction. She was both self-possessed and timid, and when she found herself among many people, she would evince an almost touching pleasure at sight of a friend.

Though even at this late period of her life she had been abroad so little, her outlook was yet cosmopolitan. She read French and German with ease. She had several brothers, and

[3] *Myself, My Two Countries*. (Cassell, 1936.)

in addition to Mrs. Sydney Schiff, another sister living, Mrs. Seligman (in whose possession at her death in 1935 were found more than seven hundred letters from Puccini, while many more had disappeared,[4] for it was the composer's wont to consult her on many matters). Mrs. Beddington, their mother, who lived to be a very old lady, had possessed a great love of music. Paderewski used to play to her, and her devotion to the great executant was intense. Though she had nine children before she was thirty, she remained herself a passionate pianist, and was resolute in keeping up her practicing. Her daughter Violet has told me how surprised she was, after hearing her mother playing the piano the whole morning, to be told by her in the evening, "I have scarcely touched the piano today." She was as loyal to her friends as were her daughters, and would decline to credit ill to anyone she liked or thought talented. At the time of the Wilde trials she used to say, "I do not understand anything about it, but I do not believe a word against him. He is a most charming and delightful man. . . ." Though this was Sphinx's background, and though her home ever to a certain extent had been an abode of the arts, yet I gathered it had also been severe in an old-fashioned way. Out of this strictness had come the gracefully light and frivolous touch which imparted to her novels their essence, and to her talk an enchanting personal extravagance. Her conversation was artificial, in several senses elusive, chaotic and often captivatingly absurd. It was the things she said rather than those she wrote, or even those she did, of which I must tell. Her life had been full of incident, but with one tremendous exception, in which she set an example of courage and selfless and unquestioning devotion (that is another story, to which I revert at a later page), mostly of conversational incident: and this, and the continual obligation it imposes upon the author to report the things she said, renders it a difficult character to write, and must make it tend a

[4] See *Puccini Among Friends*, by Vincent Seligman. (Macmillan, 1938.)

little to resemble one of those Elizabethan books with some such title as "The Merry Quips and Jests of Mrs. Ada Leverson." Moreover, she remained caught in the glittering web of her own puns and allusions; and these, often because of their very virtue, the firmness with which they were rooted in the moment of their creating, are difficult to present many years later.

How well I recall that talk in the low voice which one was always compelled to ask her to raise: otherwise there was this steady flow of inchoate and uncapturable conversation, which only ceased to make way for a silent, shaking laughter. Horace Walpole in one of his letters describes Madame du Deffand as "an old, blind debauchee of wit" — but to be a "deaf debauchee of wit" would have been a fate infinitely more cruel and ironic for the person who suffered it — and that is what Ada Leverson had become. Sometimes her ears caught nothing that was said, sometimes, it seemed to me, as much as those of the ordinary person or more. Shouting never reached her, except as a sound that was painful and humiliating, but whispers might be understood. Doubtless, however, other factors, besides her fear of roaring like a lion without herself being conscious of it, were responsible for the pitch of her voice. Naturally low, the expression of a diffident and gentle disposition, it was the true vehicle of her personality. And she told me, some years after I first met her — and it proves, I think, that she had always been inclined to speak in this manner — that on the first occasion she had sat next Henry James at dinner, she had not been able to resist putting to him certain questions about his books, for she had been a lifelong admirer of them, and that, at last, after he had answered some of these murmured inquiries, he had turned his melancholy gaze upon her, and had said to her, "Can it be — it must be — that you are that embodiment of the incorporeal, that elusive yet ineluctable being to whom through the generations novelists have so unavailingly made invocation; in short, the

Gentle Reader? I have often wondered in what guise you would appear or, as it were, what incarnation you would assume."

It would, notwithstanding, be a mistake to think of this quality I have stressed as pervading the whole of her character. To the contrary, one of the traits she showed, and which no doubt she retained from more lively days, was a certain impatience or arrogance. Quite sure of herself, she did not in the least mind what impression people in whom she took no interest formed of her; she paid no attention to bores or those whom she thought stupid, unless for some reason or other they, in their very folly, amused her. She craved passionately, however, the good opinion, and the society, of those whom she liked.

After our first meeting we soon — indeed, almost immediately — became friends. I saw her nearly every day, and if, through some cause or other, I was prevented from keeping an appointment with her, I would be sure to receive the next morning fourteen, fifteen, sometimes twenty, pages of gossip, flattery and reproach, in a hand as illegible as her voice was inaudible. Every word had become simplified into a single letter, a hieroglyph, but now and then a meaning would flash out from a collection of these symbols, by their grouping or order, and, casting illumination on a person or scene, would make one wish it had been possible to decipher the rest: but it would have constituted a whole day's work! She as it were adopted me and soon formed, so far as I was concerned, a welcome addition to our company abroad, in Sicily or Italy, where we used to spend the winter. The rest of the party would invariably consist of William Walton and of my brother, while sometimes, for a shorter period, my sister would join us. It was a condition of Sphinx's coming to us that she should act, so far as was within her power, on the motto I had devised for her: *Silence and Self-Help;* for she had grown a little vague, reliant on others, and with my brother and myself in the middle of writing long books, and William at work all day at his music, it would have been difficult to give her all the attention she required, or the amount of time she would willingly have absorbed in muted conversation. It was typical of her tolerant humor and lack of personal vanity that she took up with enthusiasm the axiom invented for her. No one enjoyed its ridiculous directness more than she did herself, and as she began to look for some object she had just lost, she would shake with her gentle, silent laughter.

Wherever she was, she dressed very quietly, for she held that no woman should indulge in fussy details of adornment in her clothes, or wear any color but black after the age of fifty — an age to which she admitted. In common with other less gifted members of her sex, she remained, though, sensitive on that score. Thus, when going abroad, she took care that her passport should suppress the real facts, or if it revealed them would explain what absurd mistakes the officials made. Even at that, and on this question upon which she felt so deeply, she could make a joke, and I remember, a good many years later, when some of us were teasing her about the attentions paid her by an old gentleman staying in the same hotel at Amalfi, she observed, with perhaps just a trace of irritation latent in her tones:

"Well, never mind! For better or worse, I've passed the Age of Consent."

In this same delicate matter I recall, from a much earlier occasion, soon after we had met, that I told her how my father had begun a chapter in a book of local antiquarian interest, which he was writing, with the tactless words: "It was a fine morning in 1257, and Mistress Ada Leverson was gazing out of her casement." For a moment she looked nettled, and then complained:

"My dear boy, I wish he wouldn't do it! People will think I'm older than I really am."

Eventually my mother persuaded my father to alter the

name and modify the offending sentence: though he was loth
to do so, maintaining to the last that *Leverson* was a constantly
recurring local patronymic in the early records of the Ecking-
ton Parish Register. But though he altered what he had written,
I do not think that Sphinx ever quite forgave him, and I
remember that when, not long afterwards, he moved from
the London hotel in which usually he stayed into Batt's Hotel
in Albemarle Street, she observed to me airily, "I see your
father's changed belfries. . . ." The truth is that each disapproved of the artificiality of the kind of artificial existence
led by the other: but neither of them could have adopted a
different mode of life. With the ways of spending her hours,
as with people, she made no compromise; she liked or she
disliked. And it was the quickness — if she could hear — and
the audacity of her wit, often thinly wrapped in sugar, that
distinguished it from that of other people.

From the faraway 'twenties, an age of saxophones and
strident pleasures, that soft voice comes back to me, laden
with honey that yet contains hidden in it a sting. . . . At a
party, I remember her looking at a highly colored and pro-
gressive young woman of the period, who was notorious for
straying, sometimes unwantedly, into the courts of love. Her
father was a former American clergyman, who some ten years
before had voluntarily abandoned his sacred calling to work in
Wall Street, where he had made a fortune. Sphinx contemplated the behavior of his daughter at that moment, and then
asked:

"Didn't someone tell me her father unfrocked himself?"

"Yes, I believe he did."

"Well, *that* must be where she gets it from!" On another
evening, elsewhere, watching the same young woman, she
remarked to my sister:

"My dear, I've always preferred a plain Bread-and-Butter
Miss to a *Tartine!*"

In a very different connection I have always remembered

a tea party at my sister's, when Sphinx was introduced for the first time to our dear friend Arthur Waley. He took a seat by her side, but remained silent, thinking of other things, when Sphinx, who was in mischievous mood that afternoon, broke the ice by turning to him and saying suddenly: "I suppose *you* often go to *The Mikado*, Mr. Waley?"

Most of all, I recollect another snatch of conversation. Here I must go back in time. . . . About 1910, a very popular, rich and good-looking young man — he was still under age — who was just starting work in the family concern, one of international ramifications, became involved with a married woman, much older than himself. It was well known that this was not her first escapade, but that on the contrary she had already been mixed up in several affairs of the same sort, from which in the end she always emerged richer than she went in; while her husband also appeared to benefit financially from these transactions. The relatives of the rich hero or victim, as the reader likes to regard him, when news of the scandal reached them, determined to put an end to it, especially because they feared that divorce and remarriage might be in this instance the woman's aim. Accordingly they transferred him to the Argentine, where there existed an important branch of the business: but she followed him. They found out and moved him to their office in St. Petersburg: undeterred, she entrained for Russia. When she arrived, Clotilde and Terence traveled about together in Poland for several months; until eventually, by means of some fresh ruse or other, they were separated. . . . Years later, when he had already been long married to a girl his parents considered suitable, Terence took it into his head to speak of his old love to Sphinx, who had known her. He still, it was evident, liked to talk of her.

"I always feel I behaved badly to Clotilde when she came to Russia," he confessed.

"Why?"

"Well, what I refer to happened actually in Poland," he

continued. "One spring morning we were sitting in a field, when suddenly, out of a wood at the side, a bear came lumbering towards us! Almost before I knew what was happening, I had run away, leaving Clotilde behind. The bear . . ."

"Don't say another word, Terence," Sphinx cut him short. "I know exactly what happened next. The bear hugged Clotilde, and she blackmailed him, poor brute!"

I recall, too, another very different occasion, when a conventional young woman, lately married, came to call on Sphinx. The bride, in almost too enthusiastically social and domestic mood, chattered a lot of her husband and his relations. Sphinx bore it with a certain grace, until at last she began to grow restive. Still the flow continued. "I had such an interesting talk with Tom's aunt, Lady Norah," the visitor went on, referring to a well-known hostess of the time. "She explained to me how to *manage* a party. If, for example, things aren't going well after dinner, you start a paper game, or one of those games when you ask questions — you know . . ."

"Of course I know, my dear. . . . 'Would you rather be a bigger fool than you look, or look a bigger fool than you are?' Men love it!"

Much of her day, wherever she might be, was now spent in solitude, for her daughter had recently married. But Sphinx's life, though her circumstances had so greatly altered, remained as artificial as ever it had been. She spent a large part of her time in reading — especially in the morning; mostly she read Flaubert and his contemporaries, and Proust, and many other French writers. As a rule, when I, or any other friend of hers, went to see her of an afternoon in the hotel in London in which she usually made her home in the summer, we would be sure to find her in the corner of a vast public room, a little figure in black, sitting on a large sofa, a black satin bag and a paper-bound French book by her side, quite alone, but shaking with quiet irrepressible laughter. This laughter was at many things, at incidents which had occurred, and at incidents which had not occurred, at things people had said or that, in fact, they had not said, but which had been suggested to her by the marriage of her deafness to her wit. On one afternoon, I remember, she was laughing at the memory of a party the evening before: what desperation could the guests have been suffering within themselves that would have been sufficient to make them abandon their own homes, and drive them out thus, on the blackest and coldest night of the year, to a gathering of which they could entertain so few, and yet such deceptive, hopes? For, in the intervals of these sessions of silent laughter, she contrived to see a good deal of the world, and in particular of the young of the 'twenties. They amused her. She liked to live in the time she lived in, and the ways of thinking, the manners and social outlook of each decade interested her: for she was — or thought, or perhaps pretended, she was — bored with the late 'eighties and early 'nineties whereto she so evidently belonged. There may have been more truth, however, than I allow in her claim, for in some directions she was very modern-minded: and since the young were always eager to question her about the earlier period, it was difficult for her to escape from it. Moreover, if her wit belonged to a decade, it was also highly idiosyncratic. Yet it seemed to me that instinctively she bent the shape of incidents that occurred to the model of the ideally absurd image which she had retained from the 'nineties. Of it, every book she wrote — indeed, every line of every letter — though individual to a high degree, was redolent. Wilde had enjoyed her ephemeral writings of that moment, slight sketches which had been scattered through the pages of *Punch* and *Black-and-White* and other periodicals, for she had not at that time begun to write novels, and one day when obliged, in her drawing room, to ask for materials in order to record more permanently an improvisation, he had remarked to her, "You have all the equipment of a writer, my dear Sphinx, except pen, ink and paper."

If she was living in a flat which she had taken for the summer, instead of staying in a hotel, she would invariably, when one went to see her, pour a whole bottle of scent over her visitor before he had time to stop her. The perfume was always Chanel, *Numéro Cinq*, and she would explain her action by saying, "There are so few really *clever* women. I buy more of this than I need, for I think a clever woman ought to be supported." . . . I disliked being dipped in this way as if I were a sheep, and tried to avoid it by protesting that the perfume afflicted me with hay fever. But Sphinx was very fond of scent herself, and used to tell me how her friend Aubrey Beardsley had once written to her, the day before he was giving a party, saying, "Will you come an hour earlier than the others, and help me to scent the flowers?" When she arrived, as requested, she found her young host engaged in spraying bowls of gardenias and tuberoses with opoponax, and as she entered, he handed her a spray of frangipane for the stephanotis.

"Though not affected myself, I like other people to be," she would say, and she would quote Aubrey Beardsley's observation to her one day, "Really I believe I'm so affected, even my lungs are affected," and described too, how, when he was leaving the Brompton Oratory on a particularly golden morning, he had startled the rest of the devout flock by exclaiming, as he looked up at the sky, "What a *dear* day!" Sphinx used often, indeed, to lecture my brother and me on our odious inadequacy in this respect. For defense, I used to urge that such a trait was usually hereditary, and seldom ran in families such as mine: but she would retort, "Well, you ought to *try* and think out some affectations, even if it doesn't come easy to you! People expect it. It's not *natural* for a writer to be natural, that's what I say!"

Sphinx had first met Wilde, she told me, through an anonymous parody she had written of *Dorian Gray*. This skit had attracted his attention, and had amused him. He had written to the author, who had suggested a meeting, and when this took place Wilde had been amazed to find it was a woman who entered the room. Before long, she had become one of his intimate circle; he often dined with her and her husband at their house, 2 Courtfield Gardens, or they would have supper together at Willis's. But it is plain from his letters to her that her talent for caricature in words had rendered his friends a little suspicious of her, so that when the anonymous *The Green Carnation* [5] came out in 1894, some of them at first hazarded that it was by her hand. She possessed many letters and telegrams from Wilde, and always maintained that he stood head and shoulders above all his contemporaries in respect of being a master of the wire as a literary medium. It was her intention to edit and bring out a book entitled *The Collected Telegrams of Oscar Wilde.* . . . She used to tell many stories of him. One I remember, because she gave it as an instance both of his kindness and of his use of the mock-pompous to make nonsense, by saying something that sounded right when said, but in reality meant nothing. They had gone together to a concert of his own songs given by Isidore de Lara, [6] whose execrable music, good looks and manner of sing-

[5] A novel by Robert Hichens, long out of print, but lately republished. In it were characters who were said to resemble in their conversation Oscar Wilde and Lord Alfred Douglas.

[6] Isidore de Lara, though slightly exotic, as his name suggests, is typical enough of his time to deserve a long footnote. He was born in London, his patronymic being Cohen. As a young man, he had been extremely handsome in a luxuriant Eastern, but by no means effeminate, way. He and his songs must have made their first success in the 'eighties, and — in spite of the solitary exception which gave birth to these lines — he remained for many years a popular draw with a fashionable audience, as always unable to resist the particular combination of good looks with bad music. In fact he possessed an appeal comparable at the time, though much smaller in range, to that of a modern film star, and hundreds of somewhat superannuated bobby-soxers — as they would now be termed — used in the tranquillity of middle age to recollect with fond pleasure the occasions on which they had seen him, or had trilled his sebaceous, odorous songs after dinner, under the palm trees and over the sociables of the drawing room. But from the writing of these songs Lara had marched ambitiously on to the composition of operas couched in the debased French idiom of the day. In all, he completed eight,

ing had already irresistibly appealed for some years to the fashionable public. But on this occasion, for some reason or other, the hall was nearly empty. Failure hovered with sable

of which *Amy Robsart*, produced in 1893, was the first; *Messalina*, in 1899, the most successful; and *Les Trois Mousquetaires*, in 1921, the last. These works possessed their faults — indeed, little else; but at least they could be performed, while many more worthy could not be given at all. They were given in Russia, Germany, Italy, England and North Africa: while in France, especially in Monte Carlo, Nice, Cannes and Paris, they were quite often to be heard. The composer spent much of his time in France, though he often returned to London, notably in the 1914–1918 war.

In those years, when first I met him, he was a rather heavy man, still with curling, raven hair, the air of an aging but yet Byronic matinee idol, but with also a special touch of crocodile-skin distinction. To talk to, he was kindly, intelligent and on the side of the arts (for he genuinely believed himself to be a musician), though bitterly opposed to their more modern and sincere manifestations. In society, his manner became somewhat exuberant; he liked to strike an attitude and create an impression. So, he would stand in front of a chimneypiece, and in a deep voice that startled a drawing room like the sudden baying of a hound, would bring out, smack, one of Wilde's more meaningless epigrams, such as — and I still recall the sensation it made — "*I* am in love with *love!*" In 1916 or 1917 I was present, too, at a concert he organized at Claridge's on behalf of war charities, and I was amazed at the enthusiasm and immensely touched by the loyalty of a whole bevy of former young girls of the 'eighties, now changed in contour, over rotund or meager, who had disentangled themselves from the duties of chaperonage or disinterred themselves from a round of country pursuits to come here to worship once more at the shrine of thirty years before. When the saurian old image treated them to a few of his own syrupy songs in a hoarse voice, rapture and adoration shone in their eyes.

Even as late as the 'twenties of the century, Isidore de Lara could still be seen sometimes of a fine spring or summer morning, when the gentle gold of the industrial haze lay lightly on the rich beds of tulips, carnations or begonias, so neatly potted out, cycling round Hyde Park, clad in the style of his younger days, and accompanied, on a machine at his side, by a rather bulky devotee — always the same one — even then exhaling charm at an advanced age and wearing the otherwise extinct feminine costume, wide cap or straw hat, blouse, coat and rather voluminous skirt that had been designed for the new sport at its inception. . . . Towards the end of his life — he died in 1930 — Lara interested himself greatly in one of the always current schemes to extract money out of those who hate opera in order to provide it for those who like it. He was wont to grow angry with persons whom he approached for the cause but who refused to subscribe; and though one or two of his own operas were down on the list to be performed, his anger no doubt arose from altruistic as much as from selfish motives. My sister reminds me that many years ago I complained to her: "It's hard; if you don't subscribe, you get brimstone from Lara, and if you do, you'll get treacle."

wings over the composer's head, and it made Sphinx, who liked him, feel unhappy at the idea of having to go up at the end to congratulate him. She could not think of anything to say, yet it was impossible to slink out without a personal greeting. But Wilde made it easy for her. Approaching Lara with a tremendous air of patronage, he puffed out his chest, and said portentously, emphasizing certain words very heavily, "Isidore de Lara. *Your* greatest *failure* will always be *greater* than *my* greatest *success*. For there will invariably be present *Mrs. Leverson* and *myself!*"

No doubt, in the first place, Sphinx's resourceful and insouciant wit had appealed to Wilde. She had just the personality, the absence of conventional outlook, just the stylishness, that he liked at the time. How greatly, for example, he would have enjoyed — though in fact it belongs to a subsequent year — the story of the Caribou, as related to me once in Sphinx's presence by Arthur Humphreys, the bibliophil and former head of Hatchard's bookshop. . . . Every Sunday there was a large family luncheon party at No. 3 Deanery Street — to which Sphinx moved in 1896. The hostess, however, found it somewhat tedious, for she disliked the thick, intimate atmosphere created by the same elderly relatives, many of them from the country, who clustered round the table, and the conventional, stolid, prosperous gloom they distilled; which made her regret the hours she might be spending with her own more lively and enlivening friends. Sphinx's husband, Ernest Leverson, whom she thus faced once a week down a long Galsworthian table, I never met: but I have always understood that he had a sporting and pleasure-loving disposition. He liked to talk, in especial, of his exploits in shooting and hunting: but this form of conversation bored Sphinx profoundly. One Sunday, when about twelve or fourteen people were present — the only young person there being his small daughter, then a very young child — Ernest Leverson began again to talk about big game. This time, Sphinx knew that she could not stand it a moment longer — the effect had been no doubt cumulative, and all round the table the relatives were talking of matters parochial, discussing the last sermon, or some obsolete play. Something must be done.

Now, in an otherwise heavy silence, his voice rang out: "I feel like going out after the caribou again this winter!"

Sphinx, who quickly deduced from the blank faces round her that no one else in the room was quite sure what a caribou was, at once rebuked him in a voice of shocked reproof and entreaty.

"Oh, Ernest, *Ernest!* Leaving *me* out of it altogether, is that a subject to choose to speak of, in front of your little girl?"

There was a silence: her husband looked taken aback, and the guests began to talk feverishly. But when the women had left the dining room, they crowded round her with such remarks as, "Ada, dear child, we're glad you've made your protest at last!" and "Ernest sometimes goes too far: you were right to pull him up."

If Wilde first liked Sphinx for the things she said, she had provided him later with very solid reasons, both for gratitude and for affection. He had sent her a ticket for a box for the first night of *The Importance of Being Earnest,* on the fourteenth of February, 1895. She took to it Aubrey Beardsley and his sister Mabel, and other friends of hers and the author's. This was Wilde's supreme moment of success, and his last great outing. Within a few weeks it was followed by the terrible climax and nadir of his life. On April the fifth he was arrested. Who else among his friends would have done for him what Ada Leverson did then? In her book [7] she mentions it almost casually. The disagreement of the jury after the first trial, which ended on May the first, had left Wilde free for some three weeks, but since in London people talked of nothing but this scandal, and since the papers at home, and even

[7] See p. 143, note 1.

abroad, were full of it, naturally enough the hotels and clubs refused to receive him. Even friends who, not so many days before, had almost fought with each other for the honor and pleasure of his company now knew him no longer.

He was [the author tells us] like a hunted stag, with no place to find refuge. . . . He seemed so unhappy with his family at this time that we asked him to stay with us, feeling that he would be more at ease with friends than with relatives . . . we called all the servants together, parlourmaid, housemaid, cook, kitchen-maid, and our old nurse, Mrs. Field, who acted as my maid. We told them who was coming, offering them a month's wages if they wished to leave at once. Each servant in turn refused. . . .

Sphinx then went to fetch Wilde in a pillbox brougham. Since her little boy was in the country, the nursery in Court-field Gardens stood empty, and Wilde was secreted there, among the dappled rocking horses and golliwogs. In this singular retreat he remained, receiving his few loyal friends, while the rest of the world raged at him, and wondered where he could be. To avoid causing his host and hostess embarrass-ment, he observed certain rules. Breakfast, luncheon and tea he had in the nursery: from which he did not emerge until six o'clock, when he came down elaborately dressed for din-ner, with a flower in his buttonhole. He would then talk to Sphinx for a couple of hours in the drawing room: but he was very careful never to discuss his trouble before her, but in-stead treated enchantingly, she says, of many subjects, of books, of art, of the effect of absinthe drinking and of taking of drugs, or else he would improvise prose poems, or relate incidents from his life. . . . So he stayed, until the morning he left the house for his second trial, which opened on May 22, 1895.

After that, she did not see him for two years: but, on his release, she and her husband went to meet him in Bloomsbury, at the house of the Reverend Stuart Headlam. It was very early, on a cold May morning, and five or six friends had gathered in the drawing room, furnished in the esthetic style — the kind of room which Wilde had done so much to popularize some fifteen years before, but of which he had long ago tired, though this apartment with its pictures by Rossetti and Burne-Jones was beautiful enough in its way. Those who were waiting felt intensely nervous: they suffered, she says, "from the English fear of showing our feelings, and at the same time the human fear of not showing our feelings." But Wilde on his entry had quickly dispersed these nervous apprehensions. "He came in talking, laughing, smoking a cigarette, with waved hair and a flower in his buttonhole. . . . His first words were, 'Sphinx, how marvellous of you to know exactly the right hat to wear at seven o'clock in the morning to meet a friend who has been away. You can't have got up! You must have sat up.' " (Sphinx, in her account of this occasion, remarks also how much better he looked; and Robert Ross, I remember, told me the same thing, but added that the governor of the prison had said to him, "He looks well: but like all men unused to manual labor who receive a sentence of this kind, he will be dead within two years.") He wrote to her the next day, a letter from Dieppe, in which he said:

DEAR SPHINX,

I was so charmed with seeing you yesterday morning that I must write a line to tell you how sweet and good it was of you to be the very first to greet me. When I think that Sphinxes are minions of the moon, and that you got up early before dawn, I am filled with wonder and joy. . . .

During the 'nineties, though she may not have been happy, Sphinx was at least a well-known and scintillant figure in the perpetual contemporary battle between the Philistines and the esthetes or lotus-eaters. Of this joyous struggle, one of the chief and latest-developed weapons used against the dunder-headed mob was the *Yellow Book*. Wilde had written of this magazine in a letter in which he asked Sphinx if she had seen it, "It is horrid, and not yellow at all," [8] yet it cannot be denied that its index remains a key to the period, and that the names inscribed in it retain for later generations a certain glamour, as might those on a battle roll. We may note, therefore, in this connection that a sketch or short story by her was published — together with a delightful portrait drawing by Sickert, entitled "Mrs. Ernest Leverson" — in Volume V,[9] and a further story in Volume VIII.[10]

It was not easy now to connect this old lady dressed in black with the earlier and more modish incarnation — as difficult, in fact, as it was to link either of these with the figure of the middle period — of whom I retained an image in my memory. When I was a boy on holiday from Eton, my mother and father would sometimes take me and my brother and sister to stay in London for a month at Christmas. Usually we stopped at the same hotel in Mayfair (where also my brother and I would spend a night or two on our way back to school). It provided a convenient, comfortable and economical retreat for the more innocent of county families, and other persons more sophisticated. The food was good and the place was not noisy: indeed the proprietor, who hailed from the confines of the old Austrian Empire, made rather a point of its quietness. We were still in the lightheaded, if full-bodied, heyday of Edwardian hedonism, and at the apogee of restaurant music (upon which I have long intended to write an essay, but with which I must deal here and more briefly). In a thousand luxurious restaurants, towards the end of the meal, the strains of "Sole Mio" and of kindred songs, and of "Le Chant Hindou" from *Zadko*, would insinuate above the *Pêches Melba* a kind of glad sorrow, following on satiety and overabundance, a nostalgic resignation, an admission that, though it was nice

---

[8] See p. 143, note 1.
[9] "Suggestion," in the *Yellow Book* for April 1895.
[10] "The Quest for Sorrow," in the *Yellow Book* for January 1896.

to be comfortable and rich, yet the herds assembled round the troughs felt a romantic yearning for wilder fields, for pastures that, if not new, would at least be different, for gypsy ways of life under palms, in groves of orange and almond, in the ideal climate of the more tender and tense moments of musical comedy. There were also from Vienna the drinking songs, and the more robustly sentimental waltzes, which arrived, fresh every few months, from the pens of Lehár, Leo Fall or Oscar Straus: while before long the plaintive repetition, rather like a plover's call, of "The Volga Boat Song" and the simple, melodious archness, dressed *à la Pompadour*, of "In the Shadows" would be added to the repertory. But the proprietor of our hotel did not wish, I suppose, to go to the expense of providing a band for luncheon and dinner, and so deprived us of these delights. Instead, he countered with romantic stuff of another kind, for he issued a small pamphlet about the hotel, containing a printed picture of the dining room, infinitely exaggerated in size, so that compared with reality it became like one of the enormous models of insects in the Natural History Museum when contrasted with the original, and carrying underneath it one sentence of such magical lilt that it still lingers in the recesses of my mind, wherefrom many famous poems I learned at that time have totally vanished: "Here no blatant band-strains mar the hum of well-bred voices."

My father, as the reader of other volumes of this work will be aware, liked to come down to dinner early, and would sit by himself, so that by the time my mother arrived with the rest of the family, he would be drinking his coffee, and exhaling an air of the strongest moral and physical disapprobation, no more of us than of the other diners who ate on, serenely unconscious. But far later, so that I apprehend hers would have been the heaviest black mark scored in the whole evening — so late, indeed, that the aristocratic murmuring of which the management boasted had already a little begun to die down in the restaurant, one half of which was covered in green arcaded lattice of an Edwardian Louis XV style, while from one or two key points were suspended gilded baskets of rich artificial flowers — a youngish woman, seeming to me rather tall, rather angular, dressed often in white, with golden hair and with a face of striking pallor, would, with a somewhat abstracted manner, take her place at a table in the center of the room. Usually she would be accompanied by a child, her daughter, and by several friends. It would have been impossible not to wonder who she was, because, as a person, she possessed a distinctive style, an atmosphere, and seemed to move in a world of her own — it was certainly not my mother's — and not to see or wish to see outside it. Therefore, in the course of time, my mother inquired who she might be, and in return, after a sly glance over his shoulder to see whom we meant, the headwaiter informed us that she was a writer, who had very recently brought out a new novel. (This I recollect particularly, for, since my meeting at the age of four with Augustus Hare,[11] I had never encountered again an author, and still expected a person of this trade in some fashion to be different from any other.) Her name was Ada Leverson. . . . It was scarcely possible now, eleven or twelve years later, to fit these persons together.

Of her, as she then was, we have a glimpse in the memoirs of Marcel Boulestin: where, too, he gives us an instance, not, certainly, of her high wit, but of the way in which she liked constantly to play with words; and if this specimen, isolated after this fashion, may seem trivial, yet in the climate of the time it must have been as amusing as it was typical. Boulestin, who was then secretary to Willy and Colette, first met Ada Leverson at Dieppe, where it was explained to him, he tells us, who she was — "A charming witty, amusing woman, and how faithful she had been to Oscar Wilde when he was in trouble, faithful too, in a way, to that period." They met again at

[11] See *Left Hand, Right Hand!* p. 243.

Paris Plage in the late summer of 1906, and after that he often
called on her in London, where he would meet Mabel Beardsley, Max, George Street and other writers of the period. At
Paris Plage, he had seen her dining in a hotel restaurant with
Frank Richardson, the barrister and novelist, who for two
years had led a kind of music-hall crusade against beards and
whiskers (a humorous feud revived, as some readers may remember, in the 'twenties, a few years after Richardson's death,
with cries of "Beaver!" in the streets at bearded passers-by!)
. . . The joke had now begun by its familiarity to appeal to
the English public, and had been taken up by the press. Thus
when *Colonel Newcome* was produced at His Majesty's, one
of the illustrated papers had quoted Richardson's remark about
"the Colonel's chinchilla full-set." At Paris Plage, directly
he met Boulestin, Richardson walked over to Willy, Colette
and their friends and began once again to labor his point,
cross-examining them, putting such questions as: "Do you
believe in face-fittings? . . . Do you comprehend that whiskers are funny? . . . Do all the *notaires* in France wear whiskers, or only the ones from the provinces?"

"You mustn't mind him," said Sphinx. . . . "He's got it
on the brain. The other day, without realizing it, he ordered
a whisker-and-soda." [12]

Colette was surprised at this, for she had not been aware
that the English indulged in that kind of joke — then the rage
in Paris — not quite a pun but what the French term *à peu près*.
Sphinx explained that in England its range was confined to a
few; among them Robert Ross, who wanted to write a book
the title of which was to combine a quotation, an alliteration
and a pun. (*Masques and Phases*, his book of essays, published
some years later, perhaps approximates to this ideal.)

I do not know that since these days Ada had grown — at
any rate on the surface — more serious. There was still about

[12] Four years later, Frank Richardson published a book entitled *Whiskers-
and-Soda*. (A. L. Humphreys, 1909.)

her an airy aloofness from practical worries and the wear-and-tear of everyday life. Physically, in the interval — for I remembered perfectly the earlier version — she seemed to have become a little heavier, yet to have shrunk, her face to have lost a little of its pallor, and of that look of inner concentration, while at the same time her features appeared to have accentuated themselves, and to present a more intellectual cast. (It has often struck me as singular with what curiosity I regarded at an early age those who were later to be my friends, or to interest me in some way: thus the reader may recall from an earlier page in this volume that I saw Ronald Firbank and most carefully observed him several years before I even knew who he was.)

Sphinx, I think, as she grew older, had become happier. . . . During the 'twenties, she passed every winter, or at least part of it, abroad in our company. She grew to love Italy — although it is true that she knew it only within the limited orbit of a sunny terrace or two, and of a few streets. In particular she liked the hotel at Amalfi, with its garden and stupendous view. There below, in the town from which the servants were drawn, life remained old-fashioned, with the primitive poverty of the houses of peasants and fishermen of which the place was composed, so that, to those who tended and looked after her, she must have seemed a very artful and artificial being. What can they have understood, one party of the other? For example, several of the peasant servants could not read — and Sphinx's life was consumed in reading: they spoke no English, she no Italian. But it was quickly evident that she had won their affection, and in spite of their natural southern indolence, and their inquisitiveness — which made them want to stop to talk to everyone they met on the way — they would hurry on her errands. She never walked far, but towards the evening she could often be seen trailing her cloak in the sunset, tasting the cool fragrance of the Neapolitan dusk, scented with lemon blossom and roses. Sometimes she would pause and look up longingly over her head at a tangerine, just out of reach of her grasp — rather as if, in the manner of the fabulous marauding seal or *vacca marina*, which was believed locally to dwell in a cavern below the cliffs and to come out at nightfall to scale and rob the orange trees of their precious load, she intended to climb and snatch at the fruit, for which, though her appetite was always so small, she had formed a great liking.

With us, too, she paid visits of varying length to Taormina, Syracuse, Palermo, Acireale and Rapallo. The visit to Acireale was a curious experience, and one I have described more fully elsewhere.[13] We had been staying in Catania, but were driven out by my finding a dead rat lying in funeral pomp outside my door, in a corridor full of dust and rattling wind. Reading a prospectus of a new hotel that had been opened in Acireale, with an enticing description of its charms, we decided to move there and make an experimental stay. The town, which is continually shaken down by earthquakes, had been rebuilt in a shoddy and malign baroque after the great disaster of 1693 (elsewhere in Sicily, as at Noto, the style was superb, but here, because earthquakes were so frequent, it had not seemed worth while to take trouble and all that had appeared necessary was to run up a stage setting, with a minimum of architectural work, as background for the life of the city). In the early nineteenth century, after the Napoleonic Wars, Acireale had become a fashionable resort to which English visitors went to take the waters: but gradually the fame of them had subsided, and it had sunk to constituting merely a squalid and forlorn outer suburb of Catania. Few foreigners, I think, had set foot in the town since the 'sixties. At any rate, since Wagner, Cosima and their children had spent in it the spring of 1882 — a year before the great composer's death — the place had remained forgotten by the tourist world, until a rich Sicilian Marchese, who owned a large palace here, had decided to open it as a hotel, and himself to write the prospectus.

[13] See *Discursions on Travel, Art and Life.* (Grant Richards, 1925.)

On one side of the hotel there was a view of Etna, which suggested — quite truly — that you were living almost in the crater of the mighty volcano, and on the other was a street bounded by a railway. At night, by the nearness of their noise, the trains seemed to shunt in one's bedroom, or actually under the bed. Well, now we had arrived: but we found no one else in the vast and echoing vaulted dining room. The hotel proved to be unheated and there was no sign of the large and blossoming garden that the proprietor had promised in his glowing pages. But, on the other hand, we were asked to take part in the opening ceremony, when the Bishop, in full white and gold Episcopal robes, wearing a miter, and carrying his pastoral crook, entered each room to bless it in a flurry of holy water; after which we went in procession downstairs to the dining room, where a cohort of brown-habited monks were already engaged in an orgy of swallowing ices and sweet champagne at the expense of the Marchese, to the accompaniment of the "March" from *Aïda* played on a mandolin band. It was a memorable feast, unlike any I have attended, and I think Sphinx, who in the course of the proceedings got herself sprinkled by the Bishop, enjoyed it as much as anyone present.

Many episodes, some of them exquisitely ludicrous, occurred in, and because of, her company: and there returns to me particularly the trivial but typical incident of Poor Minnie. This took place at Rapallo, in the winter of 1924–1925, when Sphinx, William Walton, my brother and I were staying at the same hotel, though we met usually only for meals. A table near by was occupied by an elderly Englishwoman, Mrs. Tiscote, and her middle-aged niece. The aunt was an almost professional aunt, and the niece a wholly professional niece. They belonged — or rather the aunt belonged — by birth to a county family, celebrated for its long tenure of an estate which had given its name in the course of the centuries to its owners. The elder lady was a disagreeable flattened woman, all profile and fringe, who showed herself ever eager to say the wrong thing in the most acidulated way; while the younger — if that differentiative term can be applied in such a connection — was outwardly dutiful, soft, docile, easily shocked and excessively stupid, though she too possessed a certain hard core of spite into which she could withdraw at times and become for those moments less obtuse. In appearance, she was a dumpy, tweed-clad, cotton-spool figure, with a round face carrying a look of Alpine simplicity, deepening at moments into cretinism, under a round hat, turned up, and revealing a skull of brachycephalic type, thinly covered with hair — in fact, the sort of niece of whom, when I was young, one, at least, was part of the resident population of every country house, and was invariably referred to by associates and relations as Poor Minnie. This Poor Minnie, now retrenching with her aunt abroad, was useful in many ways to the elder lady. She ran — or rather stumped — errands for her aunt, made new allies and new enemies for her, and voluntarily handed on her messages and accusations. Thus she registered with us the completely unjustified complaint that her aunt had seen either my brother or me, she could not be sure which, clad in a dressing gown, carrying a sponge and stealing down the passage to her bathroom to make an unauthorized use of her private bath. My brother, however, proved equal to the occasion, for, allowing no slightest sign of annoyance to escape him, he with great solemnity asked Poor Minnie — to the great delight of Sphinx, who by a lucky chance was able to catch the words — "Would you inquire from your aunt whether the man she saw was walking backwards or forwards down the passage? — that will give her the clue; if forwards, in the more ordinary way, it would be my brother; if backwards, myself, for I have a bad tear across the seat of my dressing gown."

The two ladies were most plainly interested in Sphinx, not knowing what to make of her: for they could fit her into no category within their knowledge of the world, and they sought to extract facts that would help them to come to a conclusion about it, by talking to her and asking her perpetual little questions, but all of them informed by an air of patronage. They would begin, as a rule, by inquiring how she was, in a fashion that implied that she must be suffering from some fatal malady, and then proceed to cheer up the imagined invalid by giving her accounts of knitting parties during the years wasted by the First World War, or by tales of earlier adventures in the hunting field. Precisely how much of all this Sphinx heard I do not know, but plainly she was bored, and she treated the two ladies with a levity that was her peculiar form of arrogance. This, in time, though they persevered, they came to resent. . . . One Sunday morning — it happened to be the day following that on which the aunt had beheld the spectral or astral figure of my brother or myself breaking into her bathroom — I had just taken Sphinx to the lift, with the intention of accompanying her to her floor, since she did not like to go up in it alone, when Poor Minnie arrived. I had shut the door, preparatory to pressing the button, so I now opened it and let her in. As we started to ascend, she suddenly turned and roared at my poor old friend.

"I don't know if you realize it, Mrs. Leverson, but my aunt was a THUNDERBY." (This classification was made in the same sense in which, in the pages of *Hard Times*, Mrs. Sparsit, by her father's side "a Scadgers," was wont to announce that Mr. Sparsit was, by the distaff, "a Powler.")

"Oh, how *terrible!*" replied Sphinx with a shudder. "Oughtn't we to inform the management?"

At this moment we arrived at the first floor, and it must be admitted that Poor Minnie had the last word, for as, with a rather flushed face, she got out, she turned and enunciated very clearly in a loud, hollow voice:

"I'm afraid, Mrs. Leverson, that your deafness cuts you off from a great deal."

Sphinx, however, was by this time shaking with her quiet

interior laughter, and seemed not even to notice Poor Minnie walk out of the lift.

In autumn and spring, she would often stay in Florence, and if we were at Montegufoni with my father and mother, we would go and visit her when we came into the town. The life she led there exactly suited her; the only exercise she need take was to walk, if it were fine, down the length of the Via Tornabuoni, in which she could hardly lose herself. She could obtain the new volume of Proust, the latest books of every kind, or she could cross the road to buy a tube of aspirin at Roberts', select an English newspaper, and go home to find one or two new friends waiting for her, to take her out to tea at Doney's or Giacosa's; after which they would accompany her back to the hotel, and sit in the hall in thin Italian rocking chairs, talking to her. My mother, who, though she was so different from Sphinx in tastes and outlook, had come to like her greatly and to see her point, could be counted among her new friends; and so could Ronald Firbank, tenant at the time, as I have mentioned, of Villa Boecklin at Fiesole. Occasionally he could be seen in her hotel, peeping in a rather disconsolate and helpless manner over the top of an enormous bouquet he had bought on his way here to present to her. . . . But she possessed also old friends in this city.

I have reason to be grateful to Sphinx for many things. My perseverance in my career as a writer owes much to her: for when blows, insults and no halfpence were the order of the day, when we derived from our background and condition every disadvantage that was possible without any compensating advantage, she offered my work continually the balm of her extravagant and assiduous praise, and it greatly helped me. Similarly, when in 1922 I decided to abandon all thoughts of fighting another Parliamentary election and so deviated from my family traditions she was not sure at first whether I had been wise (for poetry she did not understand, and so far she had only seen my poetry), but directly I read her the first prose, apart from reviews, that I had written — a story called "The Machine Breaks Down" — she had said to me, "I feel happy now: you were right to give up the thought of Scarborough." And it had been through her agency — for one of the paradoxes of my life at the time was that, though, as an already celebrated writer, what I said or did was news, I often encountered difficulty in getting anything published — that the *English Review* printed this story. All through those years she made it plain how much she looked forward to reading anything I was writing, and she would continually entreat to see it. She could, I am sure, perceive and understand through the medium of literature things that in life she would not have comprehended. (That, no doubt, is what Wilde meant when he wrote to her, "You are one of those who, in art, are always behind the scenes.") I am grateful to her, too, for introducing me to several friends — and, in order to convey Ada Leverson's personal atmosphere, we must first discuss and describe them a little.

Albeit she was exacting both as friend and as guest, all of them were extremely kind and affectionate to her. Through her, and in her company, I met so public a figure as Max Beerbohm, so private a one as Reginald Turner — or Reggie Turner as he was always known to his friends. Both of them were equally survivors from her own circle. When she first knew the second of these, he had been a young barrister and journalist — he wrote for the *Daily Telegraph*, to the former proprietors of which newspaper he was related — and a novelist. As a young man he had been a great friend of Wilde's, and a devoted admirer of his wit and of his writings, and he had been one of the two people who had accompanied Wilde to France when he came out of prison, and who were with him when eventually he died in Paris some two years later — Robert Ross being, in each instance, the other. Reggie's name occurs in the celebrated postscript to a letter [14] written by

[14] The same from which I have quoted on p. 160.

Wilde from Dieppe when he first arrived in France, and addressed to Ada Leverson: a postscript which manifests at its best Wilde's particular style of nonsensical wit, of absurd fun.

I am staying here as Sebastian Melmoth, not Esqre., but Monsieur Sebastian Melmoth. Reggie Turner is staying here under the name "Robert Ross," Robbie, under the name "Reginald Turner." It is better they should not use their own names!

To an earlier date, that of Oscar Wilde's prosperity, belongs the incident of which Sphinx told me — for she had been present — when one evening he had fitted the cap of prophecy to his head, and had announced to the several younger men who were round him, "Now, I'll tell each of you what you will be doing in fifteen years' time." He then took them one by one and foretold, rather fantastically, the development of their careers; until he came to Reggie, when he predicted very solemnly:

"Reggie will, of course, be living in Florence on three hundred a year."

Though at the moment this had sounded most improbable, it had worked out true, even to the figure given for his income. One cannot help but wonder what else, in that moment of precognition, Wilde may have seen. Did he perceive the reason of Reggie's retirement to Florence, which surely was that, as in the case of several other of the playwright's friends, his nervous system had been dislocated and wrecked by the tremendous shock of Wilde's catastrophe? The continual bitter disputes between Lord Alfred Douglas and Robert Ross may in part be ascribed to the same cause. Wilde's many great gifts, seen at their best in the social world, had exercised a fascination upon all of his group, the members of which had entertained for him a profound regard. For them he was unique, a person no one could emulate, and in his company they had certainly enjoyed such conversation as was never to come their way again. When, therefore, the storm broke, and the Master was pilloried and imprisoned, it can be imagined what they felt, and how difficult for them it must have been to salvage that part of their lives and to recover.

Reggie Turner, now a middle-aged man, had been settled in Florence for some years, and had not seen Sphinx since he left England. The ugliness of his appearance at first took strangers aback, yet it was not unsympathetic and even possessed a certain distinction. It was a hideousness hard to describe, because the features and the whole face were rather formless. Out of a chaos of sallow skin and wrinkles shone two quick but contemplative, amused but rather melancholy, blue eyes light in color. His voice was emphatic and attractive, and there was an undoubted charm about him, especially when he talked, for he was a most lively and amusing companion. He would often come round to spend the afternoon with Sphinx, and they would fall to speaking of old friends: of George Moore, who had at one time been a close friend of Ada's, or of Frank Harris, whom they had both known well, and who, though still alive, was apt, I noticed, to haunt like a ponderous ghost — and with a weight to which his works, one would judge, scarcely entitled him — the conversation of all those who belonged to his epoch. This constituted, I suppose, a tribute to a personality which, if untrustworthy, was nevertheless dominant.

Reggie Turner's usual way of talking was informal, and this gave an added point to the exaggerated deference and courtesy of his manner, as also to certain moments of almost ostentatious conversational formality. His jokes were often brilliant, his understanding of character most shrewd, so that one continually wondered why his novels had not been more successful. He used to complain in later years that though he had written a dozen of them, no friend of his had read a single one. . . . Just as, in paintings by the pupils of a master, you can observe certain touches that might have come from the

brush of the great man himself, so, sometimes, as I listened to
Reggie's voice, and recalled that the same tricks of manner,
the same burlesque solemnity, the same inflections and stresses,
the same lingerings and abrupt halts had been noticeable in
Robert Ross's conversation, as well as in that of others who
knew Wilde well, I would wonder whether there might not
be present in this talk some projection of the brilliance of
Wilde, some tones and tricks of speech and thought that belonged to him who in truth was apparently the greatest talker
of his age: for I had made it my business to ask several masters
of the art, including Max, whom they considered the greatest
conversationalist they had ever heard, and all — with one
exception, Sickert, who demurred, and observed that it was
easy to obtain a laugh if you carried your claque round with
you wherever you went — named Oscar Wilde. The others,
each of them, maintained that he was in this respect without
an equal, that his talk possessed a range, a poetry, a wit, a
power of fantasy lacking altogether in that of anyone else;
that, in addition, it was never a monologue, and that — a feat
Robert Ross accomplished in later days for our generation —
in his presence every man shone with an equal brilliance, and
when he left, went away with the comfortable conviction that
he himself had been the fiery and scintillant core of the talk.[15]
And if, as I surmised, those tones themselves derived from
Wilde, they went even further back: for Ada Leverson in her
book tells us that, in the matter of vocal emphasis, he had
adopted the tradition of Swinburne.

Sphinx first introduced me to Max in the spring of 1923,
when he was paying London one of his then rare visits,
during which he executed his first caricature of my brother

---

[15] As I correct this manuscript today, I notice in the newspaper that
Bernard Shaw, asked, in a symposium, whom he would most like to meet of
the dead, replied, ". . . if I craved for entertaining conversation by a first-
class raconteur, I should choose Oscar Wilde. . . ." Shaw knew him well,
and once remarked of him that Wilde could tell stories better than he could
himself.

and me; a drawing which is now in my possession.[16] In the winter of the following year I saw more of him, for we were in Rapallo, and Sphinx would sometimes take my brother and me to have luncheon with Lady Beerbohm and Max at the Villino Chiara, about a mile outside the town. I was younger then and did not count time as I do now, but I have often thought since then of the drawings and of the writings that he might have executed and that were lost to us, and to others, by our visits. (I recall in this connection the story told in a number of *Horizon* by Denton Welch, of how he and a friend had gone to tea with Sickert in his studio at Ramsgate, and of how as they left they heard him crying cheerily into the night, "And come back, when you've a little less time to spare!") On the other hand, on the credit side, we gained the conversation and, I hope, the friendship of our host, and he drew one or two caricatures of my brother and me. We would arrive usually at about 12:30 for luncheon — always the most delicious of meals, but especially if cooked by our hostess, who had among her other remarkable talents a great and unexpected gift in this direction — and often stay until after five. This was, indeed, a difficult house to leave willingly: moreover, as well as being a model of wit, distilling in conversation the rarest essence out of the most ordinary subjects, our host was, and is, a model of courtesy and patience, from whom there was much, in those long, lighthearted afternoons, passed between sea and mountain, to learn. (The sun seemed always on these days to be out, and to stand still.) He appeared for example, though most trenchant in opinion, never to allow himself to be ruffled. He would sit there, on his terrace, calmly, with a glass of red wine in one hand, observing the world with his large, round-lidded, rather frighteningly luminous round blue eyes. From this remote — as it might seem — vantage point, he saw a great deal — much more than those

---

[16] This is the caricature to which "Mr. London" referred in such scathing terms, in a chat note quoted in *Laughter in the Next Room.*

who hustled themselves about in the cities. Thus one day, when Mussolini was still a popular figure with English visitors, I recall asking Max what he had thought of the dictator, who had, not long before, passed down the road beneath the villa. "My impression," he replied, "was of a larger and darker Horatio Bottomley."

On another occasion, at the time of Thomas Hardy's death, so that it must have been early in January, 1928, I was shown up, before luncheon, to his study on the roof terrace. The papers had lately been full of the ceremonies that were to take place in Westminster Abbey in a few days' time, when the ashes of the dead great man — all but his heart — were to be interred there. As I looked at my host's writing table, I could not but observe that he had drawn on the blotting paper peculiarly vivid caricatures — executed, I thought, with real pleasure in his work — of the principal pallbearers, who, if I remember rightly, numbered among them Shaw, Galsworthy, Sir Edmund Gosse and Sir James Barrie. It seemed a waste to have done such exquisite work on such paper, and I mentioned this, and added that Barrie always seemed to be to the fore in literary obsequies. In reply Max then told me that he had attended Meredith's funeral, which had been largely organized by Barrie. "As I left," he went on, "a young woman rushed up to me, crying, 'Mr. Barrie, Mr. Barrie — you are Mr. Barrie, aren't you? — will you write something for me in my autograph book? Here it is!' . . . I know it was in poor taste; I said nothing, but when I took the volume my pen ran away with me, and I wrote, 'Ay, Lassie! It's a sad day the noo. J. M. Barrie!'"

In London, too, Sphinx introduced me to a few of her old friends — among them notably Miss Constance Beerbohm, sister to Sir Herbert Tree and Max: she possessed much of the wit for which her brothers were celebrated, and to it she added a fascinating but by no means aggressive inconsequence of her own, as well as, plainly, an inexhaustible kindness and generosity. . . . Then, a very different person, there was Mrs. Aria — Eliza Aria. Mrs. Aria, a veteran woman journalist of the lighter kind, was sister to the late Frank Danby, the well-known woman novelist of the late 'nineties and first decade of this century. Sphinx was fond of her, though she alleged — unfairly, as I thought — that Mrs. Aria tried to make the air crackle and sparkle with quirks and epigrams in a manner she imagined, from hearsay, and quite erroneously, to have been that of Wilde and his circle. Be that as it may, Mrs. Aria was often genuinely witty, and it was a pleasure for me to go to tea or luncheon with her at her flat, where she collected people drawn from the arts and especially from the stage, in which she found her chief interest. She was by no means young, but had remained astonishingly pretty, and with her headdress — a sort of black lace cap that with great success mimicked in its fall a mantilla — which she usually wore in the house, she exhaled a style and distinction of her own. Though she had suffered for many years from diabetes, I can think of no one who enjoyed life more thoroughly until the very hour of her death. "At my age," she used to say, "one has to suffer from some disease, and now that insulin has been discovered, I think diabetes is quite a good disease to have."

It was delightful, too, to talk to her alone — even more, perhaps, than when others were present — for while she had known many of the eminent in several walks of life and talked of them in a way that was never dull, I believe her to have been, too, one of the few women who *prefer* to listen, and her lively and mobile face registered by its expression an immediate appreciation of what was said. . . . She never stayed in the same home for more than a year or so, because she was adventurous and liked to move about: but, wherever she might be living, her most treasured and revered possession was a death mask of her great friend, Sir Henry Irving; a mask, noble and impressive, which invariably reposed on a cushion of blue velvet in a special recess or a small room leading out of the drawing room. I recall that one day when we were alone, in talking to me of *Before the Bombardment*, she mentioned to me the "Superb Hotel" at "Newborough" which figures in that novel, for she had identified the place in her own mind with the Grand Hotel at Scarborough, a town she knew well. She went on to tell me of an incident that had occurred in it when she had been spending a week or two there with Sir Henry Irving about eighteen months before his death. . . . One day a man who was also staying in the Grand Hotel had come up to her when she was sitting alone, and had said:

"Madam: may I speak to you for a moment? I am by profession a doctor. I see you are here with Sir Henry Irving, for whom I have a great admiration. . . . I have watched him very carefully, and I am sorry to tell you he is a *very* sick man. He shows all the symptoms of" — and here he mentioned some often fatal malady of the heart — "and if he continues to work," he went on, "he will, without a shadow of doubt, be dead within eighteen months. If, on the other hand, he retires and takes things easy, he may still live for years. He ought to be told this."

After this fashion a heavy responsibility was laid on her: that of breaking to the greatest actor of his age the news that he was a mortally stricken man, and must give up his work! . . . Mrs. Aria did not know what course to pursue. But at last she made up her mind; he should pronounce on his own case. So, one day at luncheon, she talked to him of various illnesses, and of an old friend who had been told to abandon his profession: and in the course of the conversation, she remarked, "Well, what *can* one do in a case like that? Now to take an imaginary instance, Henry: if, for example, you were told that you were suffering from some grave complaint, and that, if you continued to act, you would be dead within eighteen months, while if you retired into private life and rested, you might live for years, which would you choose?" . . . Sir Henry pondered the matter carefully, and then answered:

"I would remain on the stage, every time!"

Therefore, Mrs. Aria never mentioned to him her interview with the doctor, or what he had then told her. And one night in Bradford about eighteen months subsequently, Sir Henry collapsed at the close of his play, and died later the same evening.

It should perhaps be added that Mrs. Aria herself died in a theater in 1931, in the stalls after the second act of a new play.

As my travels in the winter grew longer and further, I came to see less of Sphinx abroad. She would willingly — for she was quite undaunted and did not consider such matters as distance — have traveled to China or elsewhere: but it was plainly too far. She continued, therefore, to spend several months in Florence every year. I would see her in London, and she would come to pay us a visit at Renishaw in the late summer. Here she could be useful as well as amusing, for we would ask her from time to time during her stay if she would be so kind as to bore my father for us — because that meant that he would go to bed earlier than even his accustomed early hour; ten o'clock, at Renishaw in August — and then we could talk as we wished, and enjoy ourselves. Nearly always the plan worked, since he found it a strain to listen to her light, inaudible conversation, when he wanted to dwell within his own mind on some really urgent matter, such as the History of the Two-Pronged Fork and Its Introduction into Medieval Europe, The River Rother and Its Part in History, or The Principles of Design in Leaden Jewelry. When treated to her jokes in the modern taste — some of them, if he had been able to hear them, altogether more "advanced" than those to which he was accustomed — he would, I apprehend, look back longingly on those ideal places in their ideal periods upon which he was an authority: Sheffield in the Revolution, Nottingham under Cromwell, Rotherham at the time of the Black Death. Meanwhile the volatile talk, and sometimes equivocal allusions, the silent laughter, continued: for Sphinx — though we must admit that she was only interested, equally, in re-creating the airy hedonistic pleasances of her own period — knew what she was doing.

Again, on one occasion, when Renishaw had been filled, as sometimes it was, with two contending groups of people, our own friends on the one hand, and those of my parents on the other, and when an ancient but recurrent guest of the second faction insisted on telling us the same very silly old chestnut which we had heard every year — and which must, indeed, have echoed in the rooms long before we were born (it had first appeared in *Punch* about 1884, and had gone ricocheting about the country houses of Great Britain ever since) — and not only on telling it to us all once, but on repeating it, separately, to my brother, my sister and myself, we at last explained to Sphinx the situation. She at once took it in hand, sacrificed herself, and maneuvered him into retelling her his moth-eaten joke. Whereupon she shook with laughter, told it straight back to him without flinching, and then, at a signal, summoned us together, and related it to the whole party *en masse*. . . . An odd, timid, haunted look came into the eyes of the aged raconteur, rather as if he were inclined to doubt the truth of his own experiences. Thus inoculated, he never afterwards within our hearing repeated the story.

As the years went on, there was little sense of flagging in Sphinx's sense of fun. She did not seem young, but she had grown no older. Thus, her death seemed to come suddenly. . . . After spending the spring in Florence, she returned to London and, in July, was struck down by illness in the hotel in which she was staying. There I saw her, and she made the bravest effort to pretend she had recovered. And, in fact, at first she rallied. Later she was moved to rooms in Clarges Street, where it was thought she would be more comfortable and could be better nursed; but she began to grow worse. I was only able to visit her once in her rooms, for I was obliged to go to Renishaw. But the last anecdote I heard of her was singularly typical and what she said was true.

A few days before she died, my friend David Horner called to inquire after her. Violet, her daughter, who was devotedly nursing her, went into the room, and returned in a moment, saying, "Mother would like to see you." Sphinx insisted, however, on making up her face before he entered, and David was kept waiting for a moment outside while she got ready. As her daughter let him in, she said, to cheer the invalid up:

"Isn't Mother wonderful! She'll soon be the same as everyone else."

With an effort, Sphinx sat bolt upright in bed, and very clearly enunciated the words —

"That, thank God, is one thing I shall never be!"

CHAPTER VII

Walter Richard Sickert

WALTER SICKERT, later *Richard Sickert*, A.R.A.! The run of these syllables summons up the representation of an entire period, covering sixty years: so many decades do they evoke that it may be difficult for some to recall when first they heard the name, or names. It is not often, I think, that one remembers clearly how and when in the first place one met with the work of a favorite artist, unless it is fixed in the memory by some occasion, such as a first visit to a great gallery, the Uffizi or the Zwinger, and the sudden amazement that in certain rooms therein takes the newcomer unawares. . . . But I recollect with vividness how, originally, I heard of Sickert and saw his work. I was still at Eton and had just arrived at Renishaw for the summer holidays, and my sister [1] — then my only link with the living arts — returned about the same time from her first grown-up visit to London, bringing with her a drawing, upon a tawny paper, of the heads, crowned with the large hats of the period, of four or five women, sitting in the back seats of a music hall. It is, indeed, in its simplicity, a memorable drawing in the way the faces are placed on the paper, and in the brooding intensity and expectation that characterize their look. Greatly impressed, I

[1] She had, it is true, first mentioned the gift to me a few days before, in a letter describing my Aunt Florence's reactions. "I want you to see the drawing Mr. Sickert has given me," my sister wrote; "Aunt Floss is such a fool about it. She doesn't think it 'pretty.' And she doesn't think it quite 'right' to draw four women watching at a music hall. Church of England Saints are the only really suitable subjects for art. She says one ought not to have any character or individuality. It is the devil trying to get hold of one."

asked who was the author of this work so new to me, and where she had acquired it, and she answered with pride that it had been given to her by a great artist called Sickert. She then proceeded to tell me how our cousin, Mrs. George Swinton, had taken her to tea with him. My sister had been shy — she is by nature shy, and further, she had been that afternoon particularly nervous, for we had both of us been very carefully brought up according to correct standards of class and period; that is to say, we had been taught to avoid the society of anyone intelligent, and to shun the creative — if such people existed, but of this, of course, one knew nothing — as though they conveyed to others some hideous infection. Fortunately it sometimes was not quite plain to our governors and masters who were intelligent and who were not, and it was thus that my sister had, to her delight, found herself in the first place staying with Mrs. George Swinton.

As I was explaining, however, my sister had this particular reason for shyness, that she was not used to the company of painters, musicians or writers. Therefore, when Elsie Swinton had remarked to Sickert, "This young woman likes 'La Vecchia'" (a fine painting, representing an old Venetian, which Sickert had recently executed, and which was then, at the moment, undergoing the usual processes of abuse and misunderstanding reserved by the press in this country for works of art of an unexpected quality, a hitherto unassessed nature), she had felt particularly stricken. Sickert had said, "Then she must either be very clever or mad," and, turning to her, had added, "Which is it?" . . . "*Mad, mad,*" she had replied in confusion, and the artist had answered, "Well, then, I must give you a drawing." . . . And a few days later, when he had come to tea with Mrs. Swinton, he had brought with him the drawing, which he himself had chosen for my sister, and now presented to her. It remains, indeed, among her most cherished possessions and, as I write, hangs downstairs by the side of another drawing of a later period.

[183   ]

Richly hatched, this shows the moment of a shabby woman
in a hat rattling sulkily at an afternoon piano in a back room
to a bearded, somnolent figure with his back against the
window. . . . I had acquired it thus. One night in the
'twenties, Sickert sat by me at dinner. I was wearing some
gold links that had been given to me by my father, who had
bought them in Naples, at the shop of a small practicing
jeweler he had found, the designer and maker of all his own
goods. These links consisted of the boldly modeled heads and
necks of two girls under large hats, and possessed an un-
usually strong flavor of 1900 and *L'Art Nouveau*. Sickert examined them with delight, suddenly taking a great liking to
them. He was determined to have them, and when finally he
said, "I'll exchange them with you for a drawing," I accepted
his offer enthusiastically, only stipulating that he should
choose for me, himself, an example of what he considered his
best work at the time.

These two drawings, then, have one thing in common:
they were selected by the artist. Beyond that, they show,
raised to the highest pitch, that exquisite precision and economy of line which constituted his particular gift and attain-
ment. Nothing is wasted and nothing can be spared. . . .
And it is on account of this that I have told the reader the
story of how these two drawings came here, for the fact that
he chose them himself manifests how much he valued in his
own work this quality which, evident in his paintings no less
than in his drawings, is chief of the several reasons why his
work lives and will continue to live. It may have been in
compensation for the strictness he practiced in his pictures
that he allowed his writings to be the exact opposite of them:
for Sickert was a prolific, a surprisingly prolific, writer.[2]
In this connection I remember being told that when, towards
the end of the 1914–1918 war, he had been asked to con-

[2] See *A Free House! Or The Artist as Craftsman*, being the writings of
Walter Richard Sickert. Edited by Osbert Sitwell. (Macmillan, 1947.)

tribute an article to the *Burlington Magazine*, he arrived at the office in person after some days, and delivered to a puzzled messenger an enormous parcel, on the label of which was written in large letters ENGLISH PROSE! THIS SIDE UP! WITH CARE! Indeed, how he could have fitted into the space of his eighty-two years the sheer amount of painting, drawing and writing and talking that he achieved is matter for wonder: you would have thought that no single lifetime would have sufficed for the talk alone. And it is with the conversational and social aspect of the artist that I am here chiefly concerned, rather than with his writings or paintings; though these, too, must come into my survey to the extent that they help us to define the man behind them.

Several writers have already described — or attempted to describe — him: and a difficult enough task it must always prove. But at least I can add my testimony, that of a professional observer — for I am a watcher of human beings, and especially of artists, as others are, for instance, bird watchers, and the movable hollow tree or hide-out in which, to further my purpose, I conceal myself is (this, by the way) the blank, and I hope bland, mask and massive frame that I have inherited. To my task, in this unlike the dealers who trade in prestige values in the arts, I bring no ax to grind — unless it be that of George Washington — only a pen to sharpen. I need not be concerned with what Walter Sickert said of Roger Fry, or Roger of Walter: both were truly remarkable and delightful men, and if Roger was the more learned, with a kind of genial, yet astonished, serenity born of wisdom, it yet cannot for an instant be in doubt which was the greater painter, the more versed in life, the greater wit — and wit is often the summary of a wisdom learned from life rather than in books. And if Sickert, who never failed to point out the genuine merits that he saw in Roger Fry's paintings — even when many followers of Fry's esthetic doctrines could not perceive them — writes sharply of Fry's championship of the Post-Impressionist giants, at the back of it there may also have been the human feeling that whereas he, Sickert, as a very young man, had already recognized the elegance and style of Whistler, the greatness of Degas and Renoir when they were in their prime, in those days Fry had paid no attention to them, having been engaged in painting in the style of Alma-Tadema, only in middle age, when the whole continent of Europe had already been converted, to become the shaggy apostle of the *dernier cri*.

To return to the portrayal of Sickert, let us first consider the type of artist to which he does *not* belong. . . . To a poet, painter or composer, albeit he may view the progress, in one direction or another, of the outside world with disinterested astonishment, and though, indeed, the life round him is of prime importance as constituting the leading raw material of all art, yet Waterloo, or the whole of a total war, should appear as of little consequence when compared with the emergence of a great new poet, painter or composer, or a discussion, even, of his merits. This devotion in chief to their own, and usually to other, arts, that all artists must necessarily share, Sickert, of course, possessed, though in front of strangers he was polite enough to disguise it. (The only difference between an artist and a lunatic is, perhaps, that the artist has the restraint or courtesy — and Sickert was equipped with the finest of fine manners — to conceal the intensity of his obsession from all except those similarly afflicted.) But in other respects the Kingdom of Art has many mansions, and their occupants need only possess in common that one essential mania.

Sickert, then, presented none of the characteristics of the painter of the abstracted, or mooning, variety. Never, I am sure, could he have emulated such a feat as that I saw Duncan Grant perform some quarter of a century ago, when, while engaged in a discussion, he fell down to the bottom of a long, steep flight of stairs. holding in one hand a candlestick with a lighted candle in it and, apparently without having noticed his tumble, and certainly without having allowed his candle to go out, continued his talk where he had left it off as soon as he regained the landing.[3] . . . Nor, as is the manner of some painters, did Sickert deliberately sacrifice the comforts of life — he often quoted with approval Sir John Gilbert's dictum, "I like to paint with my comforts about me." His life, notwithstanding, was far from luxurious. Thus I remember going to see him one day, when he had returned to London after Mrs. Christine Sickert's death.[4]

"This studio used to be a stable," he remarked, and then added, after a pause during which could be heard very plainly a sound that transcended scuffling and became plunging:

"That's not horses. It's rats!"

And on another slightly later occasion, visiting him in the same place, when I inquired why he had not been visible for some three weeks, whether it was because he had been working so hard, he replied:

"No, I had an internal abscess. I ought to have gone to hospital to be operated upon. Then you'd have read in the morning paper how Mr. Walter Sickert, after undergoing a wholly successful operation, had, during the course of a splendid night, unfortunately succumbed to heart failure."

He had not much faith, I think, in doctors, and he could not afford to take the time away from painting in which to be ill, yet he never developed that particular slow and patient attention to his health, for the sake of his art, that his contemporary Wilson Steer displayed, and of which George Moore writes in one of the books of his trilogy, describing the care with which that painter put on his overshoes in damp

[3] It is only fair to state that my friend Mr. Duncan Grant continues steadfastly to deny that this incident took place. But I was walking at his side at the time it happened.

[4] His second wife, Miss Christine Angus. Some few years later, he married Miss Thérèse Lessore, the well-known and talented painter, who died on December 10, 1945.

weather, in case he should catch cold and so lose a day's work.
Nor did he feel, as some artists have felt, a need for either
stimulants or sedatives to excite or lull his creative gifts: he
was compact of energy, slave-driven though an artist always
is. Even his art did not exhaust his vital forces. It left him
a margin, and plenty of it: hence the jokes, the quips, the
seriousness, the fun, the acting, the singing, the snatches of
old music-hall songs and even of hymn tunes, the disguises,
the beards, the dancing, the declaiming, all those things, so
characteristic of him, that persons who did not comprehend
the nature and force of this great painter might stigmatize
as posing or clowning, but which were, in reality, merely a
way of using up that superfluous energy with which he was
so fortunately — for us — endowed.

Much has been made by some writers of the fact that acting was Sickert's first profession. The painter encouraged this
view of himself, he liked to remind his friends of his days in
the theater, and to talk of Irving — in whose company he
had played, as a very young man, various small parts — and
of other famous actors. But when Sickert emphasized a special point, it was always well for anyone, novice or initiate,
to be on his guard, and though his first trade had left its relics
in his personality, though there may have been histrionic
traits every now and then in, for example, the choice of titles
for his canvases, or again, in the typical use in various of his
essays of some such phrase as "the prompt-side of the picture," nevertheless to me it seems more important to remember that, with all its lure, and in spite of an undoubted
gift for it, Sickert abandoned the stage for painting, and
to recall instead the brief but multitudinous hours of a long
life, absorbed as they were by the powers and processes of
pictorial creation. . . . It may be that he altered his personal
style thus, so often, from sheer love of variety, because he
began to like a square beard more than a pointed, in the
same way that he altered his signature, suddenly convinced

that Richard was a much more pleasing name than Walter, that there was thus reason in being Richard, and none in being Walter; it may have been due to the opinion he held, and upon which I have heard him insist, "that an artist should be allowed every kind of fun, including the fun of growing old," or it may be — a point to which I will recur later, and will then elucidate — that these quick changes served an altogether more serious purpose and helped, perhaps in two respects, to promote his painting.

In a fine passage in one of his essays,[5] Sickert describes the sense of urgency which overwhelms an artist who feels suddenly the absolute necessity of drawing a particular person at a particular moment.

The man [he writes] . . . whom I have left standing with a cheroot in one hand, looking out towards the light with his head slightly raised, half in pleasure at the sunshine, and half in a certain inspiration he gets from the memory of a quite trivial incident he is recalling, with an emphasis that makes it important to him, has *got* to be drawn, not only before the sun sets behind the houses of Stanhope Street and puts a cold extinguisher of lead on the whole scene, but long before that. He has got to be drawn before the fizziness in his momentary mood becomes still and flat. . . .

. . . Something of this same sense of urgency compels me to undertake my initial portrait of the man who wrote these words. . . . So often it is the first impression that remains as chief likeness in one's mind, but in his case the image that now assembles itself for me dates from a later period — two or three years, to be precise, after my first meeting with him. And it is singular, perhaps, that I should see this painter, who is so peculiarly the painter of *indoor* sunshine; who could, with a skill unsurpassed by any of his contemporaries, French or English, render the way in which the sunlight,

[5] "A Stone Ginger," *The New Age*, March 19, 1914. Republished in *A Free House!*

coming through a window, nets the spaces in a room, catching in its mesh or web the portion of a table leg, the corner of a table, a piece of a shoe or a hand, or part of the iron framework of a bed, building up of these whole towers and edifices of light — that I should see him, then, standing in the open air.

It was an evening at the end of April, 1918. I had just returned to London from finishing some kind of military course near by. During the three weeks that it had lasted I had seen no intelligent person. I was lodged in the house of a suburban family, and I remember that one of the rooms, commodious but suffocatingly full of small objects, contained a desk at which my hostess kindly allowed me to write letters. On it stood a large calendar, in which almost every day of every week had been marked off and annotated, in the most sable of mourning inks, as the anniversary of some family catastrophe. Sometimes a note of censure was implicit in the tone of the entry — in, for instance, "This morning, thirty years ago, Uncle Arthur's long course of unfortunate practices incurred their melancholy but inevitable culmination" — at others, comment was merely simple and moving — as in "To-day, twenty-four years have passed since Mama found her Maker." But this calendar was the sole object to exhale any originality: all else seemed stale. . . . And yet, perhaps it was those very surroundings that had put it into my head to wire to my brother and ask him to invite Sickert to dinner the night I was returning to London: I knew I could make nothing of this house, and Sickert was assuredly the only person who could have extracted out of it a work of art, able as he was to take the heavy Sunday boredom of the suburbs, and by some magic of hand and eye transmute it into beauty, thus recording it, transfigured and yet true, for as long as pictures endure. . . . All this monotony, however, made my return home, a few minutes before dinner, seem more delightful.

Swan Walk, Chelsea, was a quiet and leafy backwater, with all its buildings on the eastern side. Some of the houses, of sooty, yellow brick, had been erected in the eighteenth century, but the house in which my brother and I were living — and the atmosphere of which, Sickert used to insist, was summed up in Gray's famous line:

> Youth on the prow, and Pleasure at the helm —

was a rather tall modern house, which looked over the wall of the Physic Garden, and afforded, beyond it to the south, a view of the river. . . . As I approached, I saw a tall, bearded man standing in the road. He stood in the middle of this silent and empty road, looking through the archway in the wall, with its iron gate, into the large, green area of the Physic Garden, its strips of lawn varied with early flowering magnolias and other shrubs, and with old mulberry trees, as yet hardly in leaf. Out of all these things the sun was weaving a thousand intricate and living designs, and it shone, too, full upon the face of the stranger, showing it in detail against a background of sooty brick. He did not see me; he thought himself alone; his face wore a peculiarly keen look of observation, or of comprehension, as of someone in the act of saying, "Oh, I understand!" and his eyes held a rapt and penetrating expression. His curling — or rather, waving — gray hair showed at the sides of the half tall hat of rough black felt he was wearing — and then I recognized this stranger. It was Sickert! And the diverse effects I have mentioned were merely part of a new disguise he had adopted since I had seen him a month previously. . . . For the rest, it consisted of a dark poacher's coat with large pockets with flaps, and a pair of shepherd's-plaid trousers. Under his arm he carried a square parcel done up in brown paper. The fan-shaped beard spread out over his stiff single collar and bow tie, and it perhaps made the finely cut face, with its concavities, unusual at his age, seem broader than it was. It blurred, too, a little the boldness of the features, but nothing could obscure the cool keenness of the gray-blue eyes, full of light, or the acuteness of the whole head, which constituted part of its invariable handsomeness. . . . Suddenly he saw me approaching, gave a charming, friendly smile and at once began to sing a verse of a comic song that he knew amused me. It was, he had told me, a song that was said to have been popular with ex-soldiers after the Crimean War, when talk of starting a new conflict filled the air, and it certainly expressed my own views about the current dispute.

> If you'll excuse me [it ran]
> We've 'ad some!

There he stood, in the middle of the empty road, in the sunlight of a spring evening, most carefully rendering the words, deliberately, as if it were a matter of importance, and converting his whole appearance into a box, as it were, for the production of this song.

This is the likeness of Sickert that comes back to me at the moment, though in the two or three preceding years since our first meeting I had been given, goodness knows, the opportunity to achieve a dozen true and striking portraits of the different persons contained in the same man. He was protean; I had seen Sickert as he was, the great artist kerneled in the shell of the strikingly good-looking man-of-the-world, armed with a wit that few could emulate and none surpass, conscious of his powers and able to hold his own in any society (doubtless anyone who, when young, had come under Whistler's influence would have learned both the ways of the world and how to treat them, and certainly Sickert possessed the perfect man-of-the-world's way of rendering to Caesar not only the things that are — or were — Caesar's, but something extra, though perhaps the indefinable and evasive mockery of the artist underlay the whole of this attitude, if one looked closer); I had seen Sickert the good host and kind friend to the young; Sickert the *lion comique*, as Max has shown him, bawling out the comic songs of the 'seventies and 'eighties; Sickert the painter, too deeply absorbed to allow his personality to star for the day in any single one of its particular roles; Sickert the elegant, with the imperial; Sickert the Irvingesque actor, producing effortlessly, sonorously, the great speeches from *Lear* or *Hamlet*, or quoting Latin to me, passages probably from Martial; Sickert full of common sense; Sickert full of mockery; and finally — and it was among my favorites — Sickert the chef, in the white clothes appropriate to the day's trade. Yet none of the aspects he offered in this fashion were without a genuine foundation in his character: he could cook, for example, surprisingly well, this being the result of the interest he took in food, an interest often reflected in his writings, by a phrase or reference, and similarly present in his conversation. Thus he was wont to complain despairingly of Roger Fry:

"Roger's motto is 'I don't care *what* I eat — so long as it comes out of a tin!'"

Into this culinary criticism entered, I apprehend, other reflections of large issue and of wider range; such as that a painter must not use "preserved" models, and, if he wants to paint flowers, or even fruit, must get to work on them quickly, their fragrance and freshness being qualities that he must snatch at, and not labor for so long to portray that they wilt or become moldy, and have to be replaced with thick counterfeit shapes cut out of cardboard or oilcloth. Again he was aware that to perceive accurately, and to work at his best, an artist must be properly nourished — this truth he had no doubt learned in France — and in several of his essays he deplores the growing adulteration of English food, and the consequent poisoning and blunting of men's senses. But then, in all things, he evinced a tremendous feeling for material; and I well remember the air of gravity and concentration with which, looking at me one day, he remarked — for I was in uniform — "You ought always to wear a good blue serge suit." And no picture of him would be complete that did not include the fact that all his own clothes were, if you noticed, extremely good of their kind, whatever the nature of the particular role he might favor for the day or the week.

In these varying disguises, he may, I have suggested, have found, in addition to the fact that they were, each of them, representative, and in addition also to the amount of sheer fun he derived from wearing them — and his immense and vehement sense of fun must always be borne in mind — two definite advantages from the painter's point of view. They may have constituted for him an original form of the usual barrier which every conscientious artist, as he grows older, feels obliged to erect between himself and a world intent on interrupting him and preventing him from working: for everywhere, and especially in England, the arts are regarded — not as a game, for here that would be important, but as an occupation akin to crochet or knitting. Sickert's costumes, and the patter he evolved to fit them, may well have been designed, then, in order to disconcert the studio loafer and the studio limpet. These sudden changes of role disconcerted them, and made them angry. This should have been an *artist*, they would object, and not a tramp, a squire, a gamekeeper, a cook, a tragedian, or a music-hall *artiste:* it was not treating them seriously — and this must prove that Sickert himself was not serious, was not — their favorite word — *sincere. . . .* And beyond, serving this most profitable purpose another can be discerned; an artist is often his own model — after all, you can always paint yourself, it is cheaper and you are easier to find — and, with the aid of these adjuncts, beards, coats, hats and the rest, it was possible at the same time to vary the person before him in the mirror. This method of supplying himself with a model whenever he wanted one he had inherited and adapted from his friend Charles Keene, for whose work to the end of his life he entertained — as did Whistler and Degas — so great an admiration; for it was Keene's custom to keep hanging on pegs in his studio the various disguises he wore when posing for the characters in his own drawings.

Under these disguises of Sickert's certain attributes, withal, remained unalterable: his good looks, his distinction, his wit; but if we looked over his shoulder, what sort of artist was he whom we saw reflected in the looking glass? . . . Certainly, this tall, handsome man with the fine, rather thin but capable hands, had nothing of the inspired dormouse about him — his was another kind of race. In every trait, in every bone, he was *aware*, alert, challenging, not self-conscious, but conscious of himself. He wore, often, the smile of the lion, and no doubt that extra imperceptible drop of adrenalin, secreted by the glands and injected into the bloodstream, which gives the lion his leap, gave Sickert too his approach to pictures, and to subjects of conversation. He sprang. And he guarded the English tradition, which he had rescued from the hands of the mediocre, with something of the growling adroitness with which a lion guards a bone. He was naturally elegant. He drew apparently with the ease, the spontaneous turn of phrase, that distinguished the French eighteenth-century draftsmen. He possessed a most accurate verbal memory, and his talk, full of surprise, was enchanting. Not only was he witty, he was often arrestingly funny. I still remember the impact of certain sentences of his; such as one that I heard almost the first time that I came downstairs into his studio, and which began, "I was standing under the statue of my first father-in-law, in Camden Town." (The first Mrs. Sickert had been the daughter of Richard Cobden.)

In the years in which I saw most of him, though perhaps he was a little neglected at that time by the professional mobs engaged in adapting for the English market the latest Paris modes, Sickert's studio was apt to be thronged, for the young writers of my generation, and many of the painters, revered him; and after us, similarly, the next generation, more especially of painters, such as those composing the Euston Road Group. The later heirs of the English School regarded him as the man who had safeguarded their inheritance, and who, by the virtuosity of his brush, no less than by the choice for it of his subjects, which he never failed to discover in the life round him, had enabled the native tradition to continue. The veins of ore he revealed were indeed rich. He had, from the first, adopted a rigid policy of following the truth, in whatever direction it might lead him. Alone of his contemporaries in this country, he had recognized, first that it was essential for the artist to unearth and expose the current and active beauty of the contemporary world, to find it in the soiled faces, in the shabby clothes, in the infinite variety of the drab and ordinary, and not merely to decorate life, as his first master, Whistler, had been content to do; secondly, to *paint it*, as well as to record it. Where portraits were concerned, he preferred to paint the people of the dust bin rather than the pearl-fettered lay figures and images, embalmed and enameled, of the drawing room. His subjects might have been found by Hogarth: to them he brought the contemporary richness of French art, grafting it onto the rougher stock, without in the least impairing the ingenuousness or other special qualities of the English School. As themes for his pictures, he took the very flesh and bone of humanity, and subjects trite, often, rather than picturesque. He despised no appeal to sentiment in the titles he chose for them, and it was plain that his eye and hand caught fire from his heart. Yet, on occasion, he would voice, in the course of the search for truth that he had set himself esthetically, an antisocial view of the life he loved to transcribe. He did not want the poor, for example, to array themselves in the garb of the rich; he did not desire systems that abolished the difference of dress or rank. . . . Thus, once, in 1917, I related to him how I had been talking to an old man and woman who kept a stall at the Caledonian Market, and how, when I asked if they had acquired any objects since last I had been there, the old man had burst out angrily — for wages were high at the time — with "They *won't* sell! The poor have never been so rich as they are today!" In answer, Sickert, who always liked to take the least popular view — in order, perhaps, that from the ensuing seesaw he could the more easily arrive at the truth — had commented, "All that the artist can hope is that the rich grow richer, and the poor, poorer!" Nevertheless, in his essays, he continually animadverts on a system that taxes charwomen and laborers to provide drawing lessons for those wealthier than themselves. In reality, in practice, nobody was more sympathetic to the distressed, or more kind and courteous to all.

The mastery of paint I have described, by which he was able to show a new beauty in the unbeautiful, he attained — and was only able to attain — because it was based on sound drawing. He continually recalled Degas's example and admonishment in this respect. Nor did he ever tire of emphasizing that the word for *artist* in Greek meant *joiner* in the first place, and nothing more. And his citation of this, in its turn, throws a certain light on his love of squaring-up his drawings. To transfer a drawing to canvas, the custom of an artist is to rule the drawing into squares of equal size, next to cover the canvas with precisely the same number of squares as the drawing, but smaller or larger, as the case may be, and then to copy into each square on the canvas the portion of the drawing contained in the corresponding square. This practice is particularly useful to the painter, because it gives him the precise angle and intersection of a line, where it enters and crosses a square. Where the painting was larger than the drawing, Sickert used, further, often to cut out the little square from the drawing, so as to be able to place it in the larger square of the painting, and thus to be able to measure more accurately still. In time, he came to prefer the look of a drawing that had been squared up, and I have heard him maintain that the process greatly improved the look of any good drawing. In the paintings founded on the drawings, however, all the squares are completely resolved, as in the best carpentry. . . . And, indeed, Sickert was right: the true, the original significance of the Greek word *artist* should be remembered where any art is concerned. To take the writing of prose alone, the joining of paragraph to paragraph, and of meaning to meaning, the transition from one to another, the elision of the unnecessary and elimination of the redundant, and finally, a proper respect for material and purpose, and an absolute control, I take to be its very essence.

As for the principles of painting, he disliked any softness of line and displayed an especial hatred for the nebulous and vague, for muzziness and blur. . . . Some of the opinions in this respect, and in others, which he expressed curiously resembled those of William Blake, an artist for whom he felt no particular love, and of whose writings on this matter I believe him to have been ignorant. Thus Blake, in *A Descriptive Catalogue*, writes: "The great and golden rule of art, as well as of life, is this: that the more distinct, sharp and wirey the bounding line, the more perfect the work of art, and the less keen and sharp, the greater is the evidence of weak imitation, plagiarism and bungling." They agreed, too, about copying from nature, for in his *Public Address* Blake says: "No Man of Sense ever supposes that copying from Nature is the Art of Painting. If Art is no more than this, it is no better than any other Manual Labour: anybody may do it, and the fool will often do it best as it is a work of no Mind." And Sickert often expressed the same view, both in talk and in his essays. After Sickert's own heart, too, had he read it, would have been another passage in Blake's *Public Address*: "We may be Clever as Pugilists, but as Artists we are and have long been the Contempt of the Continent. Gravelot once said to my master, Basire, 'De English may be very clever in deir own opinions, but dey do not draw de draw.' "

We must return, however, to Sickert's studio. It was full, I was saying, and not only with writers and painters. There were connoisseurs and dealers and men and women of the world, and French and Italians; for everyone interested in the arts knew that the cellars of the great Parisian dealers had for years been stacked with his pictures, waiting for death to release into their hands the manipulation of a new old master. . . . But Sickert was not putting up with that; he preferred to give away his pictures, or sell them by the dozen at a hundredth of their value (a matter of which I shall have more to say); he preferred to be a living master, and would by no whit help them. He did not seem to want money; at any rate, he was far from acquisitive. What he did want, no doubt, was sufficient to enable him to paint in comfort (but then, a painter's comfort is how different from the comfort of anyone else!). And though both his genius and his presence compelled the respect of everyone — and most of all of the young who had made a pilgrimage to see him — he was not putting up with that either! (Perhaps he knew there would be enough of it later on.) . . . No, in his own lifetime, he insisted on being alive, a human being and not a monument. So out — or on — with the comic song! Monuments do not sing comic songs, he remembered, and he would roar away suddenly, to shatter a silence in which respect, and even fright, were too conspicuous. He would render the words with all an actor's ability, so that his face, finely cut and intelligent as it was, would momentarily assume the look of one of the obtuse masks of the music hall of thirty years before. . . . But the task that he set himself socially was hopeless. The young respected him all the more for the idiosyncrasies of his character: these alone would have sufficed to make him a center of attraction. But they loved and respected him as the only painter in England whose work had developed as it should — with no evidence, as in many English painters, of arrested mental development — and for his conversation, with its references to giants by now almost legendary, to Renoir and Pissarro, to Whistler and Degas. . . . As a painter and draftsman, he had been a pupil of Degas, as a writer and talker, a disciple of Whistler; what better origin could any living master show?

Moreover, for a young man to have been a friend of Whistler's required bravery; it was no easy task to undertake, and proved — as, indeed, did many other facts — that Sickert was a man of courage. . . . There were barriers to overcome. . . . Let me give an instance. When Conder had been a young artist, just past the student stage, though already of a certain celebrity, he perceived one morning, approaching him along the Chelsea embankment, the figure of Whistler, dressed with his usual dandiacal grace, in his customary frock coat and rather tall silk hat, the white lock just showing under, carrying his short cane,[6] and with the ribbon of his eyeglass fluttering in the wind that followed the river down. Unable to restrain his joy at meeting thus casually in his path so adored an idol, Conder had, with the foolish enthusiasm of his years, darted up to the great man and announced himself with the words, "Mr. Whistler! I'm Conder!" In answer to this information, Whistler had made no remark, had offered no greeting, but had adjusted his eyeglass. After a protracted scrutiny of the young man's appearance, he had finally given judgment on what he saw. With his strong southern drawl, and an air of finality, he had pronounced, "Well, then, good morning, Mr. Conder!" . . . But Sickert had been accepted, had passed these tremendous tests, and had even been privileged to spend an afternoon with Whistler in tearing up canvases. And Mrs. Sickert told me how once, when she had bought a pruning knife, with a curved tip, for use in the garden, her husband remarked suddenly:

[6] Now in the Gardner Museum at Boston.

"That's just the knife that Whistler used for ripping up the pictures he did not want to keep. In Paris one day he sent me out to fetch two of them."

The slashing contest, therefore, must have occurred either just before Whistler was moving to a new studio or, more probably, after Mrs. Whistler had fallen ill, and she and her husband had returned to London. . . . The idea of that afternoon raises so many questions: what was the number of pictures thus slashed, and what they looked like, these ephemeral visions of a divine and dusky nebulosity strewn with stars, these dreams, monochromatic or flecked with color, of persons delicate and ambiguous, who had wilted, perhaps, even when the Master had believed that he had with his habitual deftness and certainty of touch netted them securely, and had tried to pin them out upon the canvas. . . . One wonders how often Sickert too applied the same process to his own similar accumulations; pictures, unwanted by the painter, that in time silt up the long shelf that runs round the top of a studio. To this high repository, safely out of reach, the eyes of studio rover and amateur turn very frequently, longingly surmising what treasures may not lie hidden among those works despised by their authors, notoriously the worst judges of them. Often, indeed, these pictures are those equivocal things that remain only partially created and resist full integration, but that yet many painters cannot bring themselves to destroy. Sickert was more ruthless, though, and once, when Mrs. Sickert inquired of him what had become of his celebrated life-size canvases of music-hall artistes painted in his early days, he told her he had destroyed them because they took up too much room. He added that he had offered one of them, a portrait of herself, to Katie Lawrence, and she had refused it with a classic phrase of contempt:

"What! That thing! . . . Not even to keep the draft out from under the scullery door!"

On the other hand, I well remember Sickert selling for forty pounds to an enterprising young dealer the whole of the litter of pictures stacked on his studio shelf — but these were finished pictures, which, for one reason or another, he had chosen hitherto to retain, and among which may well have been some masterpieces. . . . When I ventured to expostulate with him, asking why he had sold them at so ridiculous a price, he had replied:

"*Supply and Demand*. . . . The inexorable laws of Supply and Demand. There you have it! . . . The young man wanted *my* pictures, and I wanted *his* money."

"But he may sell them cheap and let down your prices," I objected.

Nonchalantly he answered, "On the contrary, it's the dealers' job to keep up the prices. That is why a painter goes to a dealer."

Nevertheless, though he, as we have seen, so rigorously suppressed canvases he had not finished, or with which he was not satisfied, some must have escaped from him into the outer world; for I recollect with what apparent delight he related to me how his eye had been attracted to a certain picture in the window of a shop in the neighborhood of Holborn. He was on the other side of the road, but the vaguely familiar aspect of the canvas caused him to cross and examine it. It was like something he knew, and yet different. . . . Then he saw, stuck above the picture, to the glass of the window, a piece of paper. Printed on it in large letters was the name SICKERT. . . . And, in fact, when he came nearer, he recognized the canvas as one abandoned, when only half completed, some years before. Since he had last seen it, it had been beautifully finished, and had acquired, with every appearance of verisimilitude, his signature.

"I couldn't have improved on the picture myself," he said. 'Now I need never finish them any more — and often it gives me quite a lot of trouble. . . . And I needn't begin them either — Rowlandson and Gilbert and 'Phiz' can do that for me! . . . I only wish I knew the name of the really admirable artist who finishes and signs my things."

On another occasion, when some pictures alleged to be by his hand were coming up for auction, and either a partner in the firm concerned, or an expert who had begun to doubt their authenticity, had telegraphed to him:

DID YOU PAINT THE LOTS SIGNED WITH YOUR NAME AT PRESENT ON EXHIBITION IN THESE AUCTION ROOMS?

Sickert had gone to inspect the pictures and had then wired back:

NO, BUT NONE THE WORSE FOR THAT. SICKERT.

In this same connection, my friend Professor John Wheatley, A.R.A., has told me of how he once visited, in company with Sickert, the mansion of a Glasgow millionaire reputed to have a magnificent collection of modern masters. Wheatley was amazed, on entering, to see opposite him an immense portrait of the Chelsea model he was at that moment painting, but labeled *Renoir* — though Renoir, dead many years, could never have seen her; while even Sickert had been displeased when, on retiring to wash his hands, he found a large faked picture clearly signed with his own signature, and bearing a gold placard with his name on it, hanging on a wall. Subsequently Sickert wrote to the millionaire saying, "I have no objection to your hanging my pictures in your lavatory, but please see that they are genuine."

These episodes had occurred early in the 'twenties, by which time I had got to know him well. At first I had been a little too much in awe of him, for several reasons; such as his great personal accomplishment, his powers, and the fact that he was the same age as my father — at that moment no particular recommendation to me. But these feelings soon vanished, owing to his invariably kind and sympathetic attitude to the young, even to those of unproved talent.

Some years had elapsed between the time I first heard of
Sickert, in the manner I have related, from my sister, who
had not long left the schoolroom, and 1916, when I first met
him. I had returned to London from the Front in the spring
of that year, and was stationed again at Chelsea Barracks:
but it had not been until the autumn that the opportunity had
occurred for Edith to take me to tea with him in Fitzroy
Street. The studio which he then occupied had once been
Whistler's, and arriving there constituted, for the novice, a
rather intimidating ordeal, as well as a memorable experience.
Two factors joined, I believe, to render it alarming; the first
was the narrow, angular corridors and staircases that led to
it — or rather into it — and were unlike anything with which
I was acquainted. These long passages composed of glass and
dingy painted tin, clamped to the sides of the house, suggested, I can see now, a faint prophetic vision of *The Cabinet
of Dr. Caligari* and other forgotten Ufa masterpieces, as well
as something of an Amusement Park, as it is called, of switch-
backs and zigzags and scenic railways, for the staircases
mounted and descended unexpectedly, and the final flight
seemed to leap forward into the studio itself. The second of
the factors that inspired fright was the size of the crowd into
which those last steep steps threw — or tripped — you: for
Sickert was most hospitable, and always invited to his weekly
tea parties a great number of people, especially young artists
and students from the schools at which he taught. The studio,
however, was friendly as well as large and impressive. Indeed,
large and impressive studios were part of the code he recommended, for their own prosperity, to all artists.

"My advice to a young painter who wants to get on is
'Take a large studio! If you can't afford to take one, take
two!'"

Mrs. Christine Sickert must have been away the first time
I went to the studio. . . . Certainly I remember, when, a
week or two subsequently, Sickert came to dine with my

brother and me, that he related to us how he had arranged with her, not long before, that she should join him in London, and that they should stay at an old-fashioned, semicommercial hotel in Covent Garden. It possessed a Dickensian air which delighted him, and for many years he had frequented it for luncheon and dinner, and in consequence the waiters and the porters were old friends of his. It so happened, however, that he had never previously taken rooms there, and now, to his dismay, he had been informed that no female was permitted to spend a night within its precincts. Since it was too late to communicate with Mrs. Sickert, who had already started on her journey, the only thing that remained was for him to try to obtain in this instance a variation of this monastic law. Through his friend the porter, he therefore made a special appeal to the manager, explaining that he had arranged to meet his wife here for a holiday, and the rest of the circumstances. The porter returned from the interview triumphant, and reiterating, "The Governor says all right, for once. . . . But it must be your *wife*, and it must be a *holiday!*"

After my sister first took me to Sickert's studio, I used to go there regularly, and he and Mrs. Christine Sickert often came to luncheon or dinner with my brother and me. From time to time, too, there would arrive a telegram from him in the afternoon, inviting me to breakfast the following morning at 8 or 8:30. . . . In the last years of the 1914–1918 conflict, no district could have appeared to be further away from Chelsea than the Fitzroy area in the early morning. Divided, not joint, they seemed, by the great barriers of the parks, by the empty, canal-like lengths of Oxford Street and Piccadilly; cats arched themselves elegantly on roof tops, there were no taxicabs to be obtained, and only the occasional melancholy clanking of a milk boy with his cart, varied by a desultory whistling (the air attempted would usually be "If You Were the Only Girl in the World," from *The Bing Boys Are*

Here, then running at the Alhambra), would give life to the scene. . . . Always, without exception, I would, the night before, order a taxi to fetch me in the morning — and always, as invariably, it would fail to appear. . . . And here I must divagate, in order to paint the atmosphere of those early mornings; I must take the reader once more into my confidence, to tell him that in those days my temper, inherited from all sides of my family, was still very violent, and explain how it was these breakfast parties that led me in the end to think of a cure. It made me so angry, then, to come down in the morning and discover that no cab had arrived, that for a whole day afterwards I would feel ill, poisoned with my own rage. In order to avoid this consequence, I arranged with Mrs. Powell, my housekeeper, to lay in a store of cheap plates — in those days they cost a halfpenny each — that I could smash on coming downstairs and seeing the street empty. There, on the corner of the dining-room table, just by the hall, I would find a neatly stacked pile of twenty-four plates; which I had proved, by experience, to be the right number to disperse a bad bout. First looking out of the window, to assure myself that the cab really was not there, I would crash them down, one by one, on the parquet floor, or, better, more satisfying still, on the tiled pavement just inside the front door. Thus would my equanimity be restored, and I would go on my way rejoicing. Further, the adoption of this specific provides an infallible cure for chronic — or, rather, spasmodic — bad temper, and I can confidently recommend it to any reader who may suffer from a similar fire in his blood — the only drawback being that it would now come to more than the shilling it cost me to drive away each attack. . . . I told Sickert about the plates, and I remember his saying he would come round one morning in a taxi, pay it off, and help me to break them.

Somehow or other, I would contrive to reach Fitzroy Street, lying newly washed in the morning sunshine. An unshaven foreign waiter or two would be walking hurriedly along on his way to a job, and the dustman, whose dress with its large hat and top boots remained the only pitiful reminder of the former cavalier glory, would be beginning, by his presence no less than by his efforts, to add a note of picturesqueness to the scene; sun, trees and people would appear through a Seurat-like stippled haze. Moreover, every now and then, a charwoman would aid the obtaining of this effect by opening a front door, very suddenly and with a clanking of chains, and shaking out of it, with a flick, a defiant duster. . . . Approaching the door of No. 8, with its iron railings at the side, and the broad, worn paving stones in front, I would ring the bell, which had Sickert's name attached to it, and, after a moment or two, he himself would appear to let his guest in.

Often, as usual, my fear of being late would in fact lead to my being the first guest to arrive. My host would seem very spry. He would probably have been enjoying a swim, or perhaps he would have been working from an early hour. . . . My memory is that he would say he had been working; but Mrs. Sickert told me that while, when engaged on outdoor subjects at Bath or Dieppe, he would make his drawings and color studies before breakfast, and therefore wait to bathe until before luncheon, in London his routine was to swim before going to the studio for breakfast. She added that he often said he had been "working for hours" if he had been thinking of his work, though not actually occupied in painting. Usually he did not work for very long stretches at a period. It was his way to work for a little, then read, probably something that held his attention easily while his mind was really engaged in thinking out the next step. It often surprised her how comparatively short a time he spent in putting paint on canvas. He seemed, she said, to read for the greater part of the day — and yet, somehow, the painting would be done.

[207   ]

Certainly when one went to breakfast with him, he had often been swimming. In this matter he continually experimented. Once, for example, having heard that there was a good bath there, he went to the Y.M.C.A. in Tottenham Court Road. On arriving, he inquired whether, in order to enter, it was necessary to belong to any particular denomination, and received the reply, "No. But there is an age limit." . . . He was a strong swimmer and, since bathing was among his favorite recreations, I may perhaps be allowed to relate two incidents connected with it. . . . Sickert often spent his holidays in the company of his friend and contemporary, the well-known artist Walter Taylor. Contemporary, I write, though to me Taylor, with his red face and white imperial, his prominent nose, slow movements, leisurely gait, and with a little air of a seaside dandy, seemed always to be elderly. Everything about him was leisurely, not least so his voice, with something of an inescapable boredom in its slow, single-toned, unemphatic flow. On the occasion to which I refer, Sickert and Taylor were staying together in Dieppe, and one morning went out to bathe. Taylor was not an accomplished swimmer, and kept fairly close to the shore; Sickert, on the other hand, struck out. When about half a mile from the shore, he turned his head, and to his consternation observed that Walter Taylor was in serious difficulties. Worse still, in a moment he saw him sink. . . . Too far away to be of any use, Sickert thought disconsolately, during his swim back, of the long and woeful search for his friend's body that must ensue. His surprise and relief, therefore, can be imagined when, as he neared the shore, he saw Walter Taylor placidly sitting there in the sun.

"Good God, man!" he called out. "I saw you sinking!"

"Yes," Taylor drawled back with more than his usual mournful deliberation, ". . . I . . . did . . . sink . . . but . . . when . . . I . . . reached . . . the . . . bottom . . . I . . . said . . . to . . . myself . . . 'If . . . I . . . walk . . . uphill . . . I . . . shall . . . get to . . . the . . . shore.' And

. . . so . . . I . . . walked . . . uphill . . . and . . . here . . . I . . . am!"

"Why does anybody ever drown!" was all that Sickert could find to say in reply. . . . And after that he would always maintain that drowning showed a lack of common sense.

The other incident also took place, in later years, near Dieppe. . . . When some distance out to sea, Sickert suddenly recognized in another swimmer, who had not seen him, a dealer. This young man, of nervous temperament, had proposed a year or two before to purchase some of Sickert's pictures, but had in the end failed to do so. He appeared to be by no means at home in the water, and Sickert suddenly burst out of a wave at him with the words:

"*Now* will you buy my pictures?"

While I have been telling you this, Sickert and I have had time to climb up and down the stairs, where the smell of coffee — French coffee, one would say — would greet one. The air of the studio was impregnated with it. Sunlight lay in pools on the floor, and Sickert would move about, talking, now going to take in the bread — just arrived from the shop round the corner, incidentally one of the best bakers in London — now to receive the morning papers, or to keep an eye on whatever it might be that was cooking on the large stove. Great painters are proverbially able to divine the most tremendous patterns in accidental stains, and Sickert carried it further, and could distinguish marvels of composition in a second-rate picture. Perhaps he had bought this the day before in some shop behind Fitzroy Street, and now, between the newspapers and the toast, he would sit down and gaze at it for a moment, silent with wonder. With his very conscious intelligence, he must have himself recognized the existence of this characteristic, for in one of his essays he wrote:

To the really creative painter . . . the work of other men is mainly nourishment, to assist him in his own creation. . . . That is one reason why the laity is wise to approach the criticism of art by an artist with the profoundest mistrust. . . .

So it was, then, that he would contemplate, with a kind of calculating rapture, some flower piece, a small panel of roses, it may have been, painted by a French artist of the 1850's. After a time he would explain its merits, its *real* merits; for, since he put them there, they were real enough, though perhaps absent in this particular piece. Manet, he would remark, though not the greatest of painters, as English people now tried to make out, *had* known how to paint *roses*: that he had known, at least — but this obscure and forgotten artist knew it better! You could see that they had been brushed in rapidly, during the half hour or so in which the blooms were fresh, and before they had changed to something else. They had not been painted to death, nor stumbled and fumbled over for days, until the painter had been obliged to replace them with more permanent models he had made out of old sardine tins. Sardine tins were all right in their way, but a sardine tin wasn't the same as a rose petal. But some people couldn't see that, and they all wanted to paint roses. Roger could scoff as much as he liked, but good painting had always been good painting and would go on being good painting. . . . At other times it would be a cartoon that had caught his fancy. He had cut it out of a newspaper and pinned it up on the wall, and now extolled it. There, if you *liked* drawing, was *drawing* for you; real drawing by a man who, since he had been compelled to turn out something expressively comic every day — every single day, mind you — for many years, had by this time been obliged to find out a little about his job. Or it might be a Rowlandson color print he had discovered. Or, on one occasion, even, the chosen cynosure had proved to be four particularly atrocious Indian color prints — so I call them, though it is impossible to imagine what evil technical process can have been responsible for these seven-armed goddesses, with inflated multiple limbs and naked except for the miters they were wearing on their heads, who pirouetted ungracefully on lotuses, while they displayed their Cambridge-blue charms and handed objects of an equivocal nature to elephants smaller than themselves and colored like blush roses. . . . For a day or two Sickert was fascinated by these, but then, tiring of them, he caused them to be framed, and brought them round to Swan Walk. Indeed, they had composed that brown paper parcel which we saw under his arm as he stood in the sunlight of that spring evening, and he had given them to my brother and myself, with the words, "These may help you to keep straight in your ideals of female beauty."

Other guests would begin now to arrive, and, tearing himself away from the Haselden drawing out of the *Daily Mirror*, or from whatever might constitute the particular favorite of the moment, he would go to greet them. Often I would meet at these breakfast parties Nina Hamnett, Alvaro Guevara, W. H. Davies and Aldous Huxley. . . . Our host would make us sit down at the table, and would hurry round with breakfast, a plate with an egg on it for each of us. Owing to the amount of cooking, serving and pouring out that he was forced to do, he had not always at this hour so much leisure for conversation as his guests would have liked. His talk resembled most good talk in that it contained in its web certain invariable strands, certain immutable monuments that could be invoked for purposes of reference, allusion, comparison and simile, and that also supplied him with an established standard. The Tichborne Case and the mystery of Jack the Ripper constituted two such monuments.

The first, which had come into the headlines when Sickert had been a boy of eleven, had always maintained its interest for him; a special interest, due to the fact that he believed the rejected claimant, who had come back out of the sea, to have been the rightful heir. . . . As for the second, apart from the intrinsic and abiding horror of that extraordinary series of crimes, it interested him because he thought he knew the identity of the murderer. He told me — and, no doubt, many others — how this was. . . . Some years after the murders, he had taken a room in a London suburb. An old couple looked after the house, and when he had been there some months, the woman, with whom he used often to talk, asked him one day as she was dusting the room if he knew who had occupied it before him. When he said "No" she had waited a moment, and then replied, "Jack the Ripper!" . . . Her story was that his predecessor had been a veterinary student. After he had been a month or two in London, this delicate-looking young man — he was consumptive — took to staying out occasionally all night. His landlord and landlady would hear him come in at about six in the morning, and then walk about in his room for an hour or two until the first edition of the morning paper was on sale, when he would creep lightly downstairs and run to the corner to buy one. Quietly he would return and go to bed; but an hour later, when the old man called him, he would notice, by the traces in the fireplace, that his lodger had burned the suit he had been wearing the previous evening. For the rest of the day, the millions of people in London would be discussing the terrible new murder, plainly belonging to the same series, that had been committed in the small hours. Only the student seemed never to mention it: but then, he knew no one and talked to no one, though he did not seem lonely. . . . The old couple did not know what to make of the matter: week by week his health grew worse, and it seemed improbable that this gentle, ailing, silent youth should be responsible for such crimes. They could hardly credit their own senses — and then, before they could make up their minds whether to warn the police or not, the lodger's health had suddenly failed alarmingly, and his mother — a widow who was devoted to him — had come to fetch him back to Bournemouth, where she lived. . . . From that moment the murders had stopped. . . . He died three months later.

Before leaving the subject, I may add that, while I was engaged in writing this account of Sickert, my brother reminded me that the painter had told us that when his landlady had confided in him that morning, in the course of her dusting, the name of Jack the Ripper, he had scribbled it down in pencil on the margin of a French edition of Casanova's *Memoirs* which he happened to be reading at the time, and that subsequently he had given the book away — we thought he had said to Sir William Rothenstein. Sickert had added, "And there it will be now, if you want to know the name." Accordingly, I wrote to Lady Rothenstein: but neither she nor Sir William remembered the book. On my consulting Mrs. Sickert, she maintained that her husband had told her that he had given the volume to Sir William's brother, Mr. Albert Rutherston. And this proved to have been the case. My friend Mr. Rutherston informed me that he lost the book only during the bombing of London, and that there had been several pencil notes entered in the margin, in Sickert's handwriting, always so difficult to decipher.

Sickert would talk more often, however, of beings of another, though scarcely of a less exceptional kind; of Whistler, Degas, Charles Keene, of Toulouse-Lautrec and the curious manifestations of the inferiority complex produced by his dwarfish stature, of Beardsley and Wilde. . . . Wilde he appeared not to have liked greatly, or considered particularly witty, though he admitted that he provided an unusually warm and generous audience for others. Sickert would speak, too, of Frank Harris and his portentous absurdity. Thus I recollect his telling us of a supper party at the Savoy in the 'nineties at which he had been present. It had been arranged, he became aware as soon as he sat down, so that Harris should be able to impress a Scottish millionaire from whom he wanted to borrow money. But his intended victim was singularly hard-headed, tight-fisted and tongue-tied. The silences were long. In one of them Harris boomed out — and he possessed a voice which could easily reach to the further corners of the restaurant — "But what would *Goethe* say?" Whereat, roused by a name so familiar, the people at most of the tables had stood

on their chairs, in order to look dotingly at Miss Gertie
Millar, who was sitting with some friends not so far away, for
they were naturally under the illusion that Harris must be referring to her. . . . Or he would tell us of George Moore —
whom he did not care to see very often in later days — and
of his abiding ingenuousness. Thus, once Moore had sent
for him in the small hours, insisting that the matter was of
importance. When Sickert arrived, wondering what it could
be, Moore had stood up and announced, with that particular
rhythm of voice unforgettable to those who knew him, "I
have just been reading *a* book on Michelangelo, and it *a*-ppears
that he carved the David out of *a* piece of marble that had
been improperly quarried. Now *I* could no more have carved
the David out of *a* piece of marble that had been improperly
quarried than *I* could have flown." . . . And on another occasion, after receiving a similarly urgent nocturnal summons,
he found that Moore had been reduced almost to the verge
of tears by the bewildering difficulty of the problem, recurrent through that day — and, indeed, through the whole of
his preceding lifetime: how to keep his pants in place. . . .
Sickert had been obliged to explain it to him at great length.
. . . "If, Moore, you look at the top of your pants, you'll find
two loops of tape on each side, and if you thread the two tabs
of your braces through them, your troubles will be at an
end." . . . Delighted, dumbfounded, too, by the ingenuity of
the solution, he had replied, "But you are an *a*-mazing man,
my dear Sickert, to discover such *a* thing."

The repetition of such anecdotes fails, I am aware, to convey an impression of the wide range of Sickert's talk, which
rendered him so interesting as well as entertaining a companion. His wisdom derived from life, even more than from
books, though he was a reader both indefatigable and dis-
cerning. He had known so many people of different kinds.
prize fighters, jockeys, painters, music-hall comedians, states-
men, washerwomen and fishwives. He would tell one of Sir

William Eden and his rages (he should have been content to remain a baronet *pur*, I remember he said, and not have tried to become an artist). He told me, also, I recollect, of how the great Lord Salisbury, accompanied by his wife and family, had stayed a summer in Dieppe — I think in the early 'eighties — and of his kindly purchase of a picture. Lord Salisbury was, as all those who have read his life will recall, more interested in science, and in such then recent inventions as electric light, than in art in general; and of modern art he in no way professed to be an amateur. One day, however, he allowed himself to be taken to see the work of a quasi-Impressionist painter, who lived at Dieppe in circumstances of great poverty. Lord Salisbury had felt sorry for the artist, and had determined to help him. And so, on being shown a picture of the river at Dieppe, he had generously said:

"I will buy that river scene for five hundred pounds if you will paint in a boat containing my family and myself."

Enchanted at the idea of a sum that was at least ten times as large as any he had ever asked, and even though, perhaps, a little startled by the stipulation that his new patron had imposed, the painter had eagerly agreed, and had interjected upon the nebulous waters a fishing vessel containing the members of this distinguished English family. . . . This story, in its turn, produced a pleasant sequel, for, remembering it, I repeated it to Lady Cranborne [7] some years later, and asked her if the picture still hung at Hatfield. . . . Its existence had been forgotten, but her mother-in-law, Lady Salisbury, looked for it, and sure enough, it was found, as described, put away in the attics there. [8]

Another small incident of which Sickert told me, and that had occurred at a luncheon party at Dieppe about the same time, I have always remembered, for I regard the reply it

[7] Now Marchioness of Salisbury.
[8] I had forgotten — if Sickert told me — the name of the artist. But Lady Salisbury informed me that the picture was signed *A. Vallon.*

enshrines as a classic instance of French wit. Among the several guests had been Cham,[9] the celebrated French caricaturist of the epoch. He had sat opposite a young French nobleman, who bragged unceasingly, and to the general annoyance, of the grandeurs of his father's château. At a moment in the middle of luncheon, when he was describing the stupendous loftiness of the ancestral dining room, Cham, unable any longer to endure in silence such boasting, interrupted, saying smoothly:

"*Chez-nous, c'est tout à fait différent. Le plafond de la salle à manger est tellement bas qu'on sert seulement des soles frites!*"

Sometimes, again, Sickert would talk of the London of his youth, telling me of my grandfather Londesborough's horses, of his coaches and carriages, which had been especially fine, for — in this resembling so many English artists before him — Sickert possessed a keen eye for horseflesh and a smart turn-out. And usually, in all that he said, there was an element of the unexpected, both in phrasing and in opinion. . . . Let me try to give an instance of, at any rate, the last.

In the spring of 1919, it had been planned to hold an exhibition in London of etchings by Félicien Rops. The Customs House officials, however, having opened a parcel containing them, had pronounced them obscene, and had ordered them to be destroyed.[10] This caused an uproar among art lovers.

---

[9] Cham, or, to give him his real name and style, Amédée Charles Henri, Vicomte de Noé, came himself of a noble French family. He was the second son of Jude-Amédée, Comte de Noé, a peer of France, who had married an Englishwoman. Cham was born on the 20th of January, 1819, on the island of Noé, near Miranda — the same place from which his family had taken their name some thousand years previously. He was educated for the army, but abandoned this career for that of caricaturist. In spite of the wit of his onslaughts, they were so scrupulously fair that, when he died in 1879, a friend suggested that upon his tombstone should be cut the words, "*Quarante ans d'esprit, et pas un de méchanceté.*" Sickert, who entertained a great admiration for the work of this spirited and prolific draftsman, frequently referred to him in his writings and conversation.

[10] An account of this typically Anglo-Saxon incident follows as Ap-

Everyone, in studios and galleries and museums, rose up in arms about it — a great artist like Rops to be treated in such a way! Questions were to be asked in Parliament, and there was talk of a deputation to the Prime Minister. . . . One morning, when I went to breakfast with Sickert, and arrived there a moment or two later than usual, I found him already discussing the matter with some of his guests. He appeared to be genuinely pleased at the action of the officials, and enthusiastic in his praise of them.

"They ought to make the Customs House into the Ministry of Fine Arts," he was saying. "Here Rops has deceived all the critics for years into thinking him a great artist. But you can't monkey about with the Customs House! You can't take *them* in! They saw through it in a minute, and said, 'That's not *Art:* that's PORNOGRAPHY!' — and they're quite right. . . . But nobody before them had had the wits or the courage to say it! . . . I wish one of them could be given Konody's job on the *Observer*. . . . I daresay the postman — there he is, by the way! — would do just as well. *Common sense*, that's the thing. . . . You can't better common sense, whether it's politics or business or art!"

He always seemed to be in good spirits in the morning, but breakfast was passing quickly, the big bowls of coffee were empty, and the guests began to leave. Sickert got up to escort Davies to the front door, fearing that the wooden stump that served the poet as a leg might give him trouble in mounting or descending the steep stairs. He watched him dipping slowly away down the long street, a large bundle of etchings his generous host had just given him held under his arm. . . . Sickert seemed to have enjoyed himself, but no doubt he was glad to settle down to work, to shut his own door and know that he need not — and would not — open it.

If it were usually in the morning or at teatime that my

---

pendix A, page 341. It is an excerpt from Arnold Bennett's *Things That Have Interested Me.*

brother and I saw Sickert at his studio, it was in the evenings, generally, that he came to our house. . . . Just as Margot Lady Oxford, if she wished to talk herself, used to rap on the table and say sharply, "*Let* us have *general* conversation," so at dinner at Swan Walk and Carlyle Square, Sickert, in similar circumstances, used to call out, "Poets and Poetesses! Don't all speak at once!" (My sister, accustomed to regard herself, and to be regarded by others, as a poet, not as a "poetess," nevertheless in this instance did not in the least object to this mode of address from Sickert, and when I asked her the reason, replied that it was as if he had said "Tigers and Tigresses!") . . . Many evenings there come back to me: who were the others present? . . . Well, from time to time, among others, van Dieren, Arnold Bennett, C. R. W. Nevinson, Aldous Huxley, Nina Hamnett, Guevara, William Walton, Roger Fry, Madame Vandervelde, Clive Bell. There were evenings when, after dinner, charades would be acted in the drawing room. Sickert would not take part in them, but would remain in a corner of the room, declaiming *Hamlet* for his own edification, and totally absorbed by his performance. . . . Or it might be that we would walk to a party in the vicinity — though, on occasion, we had to traverse comparatively long distances. Indeed, my mind returning to those days, it seems to me that every little street in Chelsea, every yellow brick and stucco wilderness in South Kensington, has echoed at some time or other to a solitary voice chanting the dying chorus of a comic song of the 'seventies and 'eighties.

I recall later evenings, too, and one night at dinner in my present house in Chelsea, after we had left Swan Walk, comes back to me particularly. (It has already been mentioned in print by Frank Swinnerton.[11]) Those present were Sickert, Arnold Bennett, Frank Swinnerton, Massingham, the editor of the *Nation*, Percy Wyndham Lewis, William Walton, my brother and myself. . . . Sickert was in a peculiarly brilliant

[11] In *The Georgian Literary Scene.*

mood, led the evening and was audacious as a matador. I do not think that Lewis enjoyed this scintillation. (It did not seem to him to come from the right quarter.) Even Arnold, an old friend of Sickert's, seemed a trifle dazed. Towards the end of dinner a controversy arose, and Sickert just danced round the rest of us. Arnold's stutter became even more pronounced than usual, and after a prolonged effort to speak, while his mouth was open, and he was just going at last to say something, Sickert remarked, as one might of some very brilliant young dealer in paradox. "*Now*, what's he going to say, I wonder!!!" Sickert then lit a cigar and, nipping round the corner of the table, pressed one upon Lewis, with the words, "I give you this cigar because I so greatly admire your writings." Lewis switched upon him as dazzling a smile as he had had time to prepare, but before it was really quite ready, and he had succeeded in substituting this genial grin for his more usual expression, Sickert planted the goad by adding, "If I liked your paintings, I'd give you a bigger one!" [12] . . . Lewis, at this, became very angry, though, typically, not with Sickert, but with the rest of the company. As a punishment, he refused to accompany us to a party at Lady Ottoline Morrell's to which we were going on, and instead returned home. But not before he had accepted an invitation to luncheon with Sickert two days later. No doubt the prospective guest intended to have it out over the meal, but when he arrived he was disconcerted to find his host dressed as a chef in white jacket and high white linen cap standing on the doorstep in Fitzroy Street ready to welcome him. Moreover, Sickert would only talk French that day, of how he had cooked the luncheon, and of food in general. And Lewis, who, quite apart from the bone he had brought with him to pick, had come here, at the

[12] In *The Hunters and the Hunted* my brother records the following note from his diary, dated January 1919. "Sickert compared Wyndham Lewis's drawing to the hippogriff which disdains entry for the Derby because of its race. He compared Lewis, also, to Balzac's Prince de Bohême and to Byron."

worst, to talk of himself, grew furious at being thus prevented from getting round the beefsteak, as it were, to this other, and to him more important, topic.

That, then, is the story of a battle which had its origin in a cigar — a *Manila* cigar, for Sickert always carried on him about six or seven large Manilas in a case, and used invariably to smoke them the wrong way round. In an essay, my friend Clive Bell [13] has suggested as a reason for it Sickert's desire to show "how unlike he was to other men." But a more likely explanation is one that I can produce from my own experience, that to smoke Manilas the wrong way round is the best way, and actually the right way, to smoke them, for, compared with more expensive cigars, they are apt to draw badly if you light the wide end. Sickert once explained this to me, and I have proved it to be true. And, since he always bought and smoked Manilas in his own house, this may have led him, if elsewhere he were offered a Havana, to smoke it from habit in the same manner. . . . But there were also other reasons for his smoking them, and for his lighting the narrow end. The late Professor Sir Walter Raleigh, who had as a young man spent two years in the East, had originally recommended him to smoke Manilas, because no guano was put on the fields in which the leaves for these particular cheroots were grown, and they were therefore much healthier than any other cigars. He had told Sickert at the same time that the natives, even the young girls, always smoked them, and in this same fashion, with the wide end in their mouths. . . . These points are not, of course, important in themselves, but they fit into a more important subject: for it would seem to me that if Sickert, for the sake of the fun to be derived from it, ever posed, it was in a precisely opposite direction: in order to prove that the artist was exactly the same as other men.

Other occasions come back to me: I recall Sickert dining with me one night in '22 or '23 at the Marlborough, to meet

[13] In the *Cornhill* for May 1944.

Professor Tancred Borenius and Bernard d'Hendecourt, the French connoisseur and collector. After dinner, Sickert recited to us limericks by D. G. Rossetti. Subsequently he wrote them down for me in pencil, because he said that, except for himself, there were few people living who knew them. One, about Sandys, began:

> There is an old painter called Sandys
> The victim of his own glandys . . .

It is perhaps better to break off here.

Another, concerning Prinsep, runs:

> There is a Creator named God
> Whose creations are sometimes quite odd.
> I maintain — and I shall —
> The creation of Val
> Reflects little credit on God.

Finally, there is one devoted to Whistler, and written **when** first he came to England.

> There's a combative artist named Whistler
> Who is, like his own hog hair a bristler,
> A tube of white lead
> And a punch on the head
> Offer varied attractions to Whistler.

I recollect, too, Sickert attending one of the annual banquets of the Magnasco Society in a private room at the Savoy. My brother and I, together with Professor Borenius, who was also a friend of Sickert's, had been among the founders of this body, formed to foster an interest in the Italian Virtuoso Painting of the seventeenth and eighteenth centuries that Ruskin has taught English taste to condemn. For one evening the walls of the room in which we were to dine would be hung with fine examples of the art of that epoch lent by members of the Society, while during the meal a small orchestra played music appropriate to the feeling of the pictures, though, it is true, of a later date; such music as that of Donizetti, Verdi and Rossini. After dinner there were speeches, and on this occasion Sickert delivered a long speech upon painting. Alas, no one was present who could take down a report of it. . . . At about the same time each year that these banquets took place, the Society held its Annual Exhibition, usually at the Galleries of Messrs. Thomas Agnew in Bond Street. The exhibits consisted of works lent, again, by members, or borrowed from the various great collections of such pictures that still exist — or existed — in country houses. Among them, however, we sometimes included examples by English masters of the same period. . . . Sickert always visited these shows, which delighted him. And he was especially fascinated by the pictures and drawings of that English master, still a little neglected, Marcellus Laroon. I refer to this partiality of his for a reason, which will become evident in a moment.

In October 1918, during one of my periods of twenty-four hours' duty as Captain of the King's Guard, Sickert came to dine with me at St. James's Palace. It was the first time he had been there; he enjoyed it, and was in enchanting mood. Several rather conventionally minded young officers were also on duty, and present at dinner, but Sickert got on beautifully with them: indeed it was perhaps the kind of company he liked best. I remember my relief that night when he foretold, with an appearance of certainty, basing his statements on deductions from former experience, that the war would be over very shortly, and that as soon as it stopped, war hysteria would vanish suddenly, and the public would refuse to read any book or look at any picture concerned with that long-enduring and tedious subject — and he was right; for a full ten years we were free of it, until the return of the portentous war novels, of enormous length, by German pacifist authors, announced, like the opening theme of a Wagnerian opera, that a new war was on its way.

Sickert examined the dining room most carefully. He noticed everything and commented on it — on the character of the long, red-papered dining room, with its supreme air of English tradition and of being situated in London, even of *being* London or one of its important constituents. He looked most carefully at the prints in black and gold frames that hung on the walls — prints of officers of the King's Guard in other days, when they were dressed in long scarlet coats, the tails looped back, and wore white wigs on their heads, and cocked hats — and inquired the history of such things as the hoof of Napoleon's charger Marengo. Just as Peele has said that

His helmet now shall make a hive for bees,

so the relic of a charger famous as Bucephalus now lay, with no sound of martial clatter, upon the white tablecloth, finding a base use as a receptacle for snuff. . . . And Paul, too, the celebrated waiter of the King's Guard, interested Sickert, with his quick eye for the individual, and he said that he would like to draw him, and proceeded to make arrangements to that effect, though I am not aware whether he put this project into execution.

Paul was a very old Frenchman, so lightly made as to appear almost transparent. He possessed small, rather aquiline features, his white hair curled round his head, and white mutton-chop whiskers added a needful air of substantiality to a figure which could have belonged to no profession except that he followed, and to no nation except that which gave him birth. When he spoke English, moreover, his tongue betrayed a most endearing French accent, so French as to make him seem almost a stage Frenchman, while the deft, polite quietness of his manner made him seem, too, a stage waiter. All his life he had been an ardent Bonapartist, and as a young man had served in the Imperial Army at the time of the Franco-Prussian War. Even that catastrophe, which he had watched developing at close quarters, and its results, had failed to disillusion him. His devotion to the dynasty, and in especial to the Empress Eugénie, was of an unfailing and most touching quality, and he always carried on him a brown and by now scratched photograph of her as she had looked nearly fifty years before in her full beauty. This photograph, signed by the Empress, was that which had been issued to the troops when the war had opened. Since 1870 Paul had lived in England, and had been, for most of the intervening years, a waiter on King's Guard: nor during the whole of his lifetime had he once returned to his own country, though so near, for he had vowed never to go back to it until France had defeated Germany in war. Meanwhile, he had attended the officers of the Household Brigade with assiduity and tact, had almost helped to shape the education of them, advising them, for example, on the proper choice of wines, but without ever allowing even the youngest or most sensitive to feel that his man-of-the-world status was in any way impugned. He was, indeed, a model of discretion. Only when at last the hour came for which he had so long been ardently hoping, and England declared war on Germany, he had been unable to conceal his joy. Not even his beloved Empress, in her retirement at Farnborough, could have been more furiously glad. . . . Tonight old scores were wiped out, and a settlement that would last for a generation was near. He and Sickert talked together in French, and Paul pulled out of the inner pocket of his coat the signed photograph, now faded to a tone of sepia or light tobacco, and showed it to the painter.

It was, indeed, a delightful evening: Sickert, who could if he wished be provocative, was all the same very adaptable, and, as we have seen before, would take a great deal of trouble to get on with every sort of person. He and some of the others present may not have shared many traits or interests in common. . . . But there came only one moment of tension, when Sickert remarked at dinner, apropos of the reactions of English people, in a voice loud enough for the whole table to hear:

"And no one could be more English than I am — born in Munich in 1860, of pure Danish descent!"

Then, indeed, came a moment's hush. . . . I record the incident here because I believe that what he said then contains an important truth. He was sometimes prone to emphasize his foreign descent. (I remember, for example, that he told me of the friendly cobbler who lived in the same street in London as the Sickert family, and who, thinking, in the English way, that it was necessary to shout and explain things to all foreigners, however well they spoke English, would always, when Sickert and his father passed his shop, point at the porpoise-hide bootlaces that were his pride, and roar at the top of his voice, "Papooze's 'ide!'") Yet nobody *was* more English than Sickert, either as man or as painter. And it may well be that his northern foreign blood afforded him just the requisite impetus to understand especially well this country and its ways. It endowed him, perhaps, with a sharpened eye to note the peculiarities of our idiosyncratic island, and a pencil tilted at the precise angle to record them. And if this be so, it may have prompted Sickert to see, consciously or subconsciously, a resemblance between his own origin and career and that of Marcellus Laroon,[14] and so have been responsible

[14] Marcellus Laroon was the second son of Laroon the Elder, who had painted draperies for Sir Godfrey Kneller. Laroon the Elder, though born in The Hague, was the son of a French painter who had settled there. The real name was Lauron; but as everyone called him Laroon, Marcellus, in his statement quoted in *Nollekens and His Times*, tells us that himself always wrote it that way. Marcellus was a real Cockney, having been born at his father's house in Bow Street on April 2, 1679.

In his youth Laroon the Younger was a proficient musician. As a boy he became page on various diplomatic missions. He then went on the stage for two years, but threw up this profession — he had appeared at Drury Lane — and joined the Foot Guards. During his career he fought in Spain, as well as Flanders, and was for twenty months a prisoner on parole at Najera. After having served with distinction, he retired with the rank of captain in 1732. His third and most notable career was that of a painter, in which he spent the last forty years of his life. Born some eighteen years before his friend Hogarth, he outlived him by eight years, dying at York on June 2, 1772, at the age of ninety-three.

Laroon appears to have been of a rollicking disposition, and J. T. Smith

for the interest in him that I have noted. Like Sickert, Laroon the Younger had been brought up in England, though of foreign blood. Like Sickert's father, Laroon's father was an artist and had settled in England. Similarly, the first profession which Marcellus Laroon had adopted for himself had been that of an actor, and afterwards he had helped to found the English tradition in painting that Sickert had, a century and a half later, seized on and, by his example, enabled to continue. It is true that Laroon, though a most delightful and characteristic painter and draftsman, was not comparable to Sickert in the greatness of his art; but in his time he had been the foremost portrayer of the contemporary English, and especially London, scene, and in the most English way. He, also, had found inspiration in the life round him, painting scenes on the stage, village weddings, and the levées of the nobles of the time, attended by their loafing bodyguards and tradesmen. The identical quality of being able to see the typical English environment from both inside and outside, that had inspired him, was perhaps responsible, on the night in question, for the pleasure Sickert so plainly took in his surroundings.

I continued to see a good deal of Sickert until I suppose the late 'twenties or middle 'thirties, when his retirement to Broadstairs, and my long voyages to such distant parts of the world as China and Central America, prevented us from meet-

---

in his *Nollekens and His Times* relates that Mr. Welch, father-in-law to Nollekens, said that whenever Laroon was mentioned in Henry Fielding's presence, the novelist — who had also been a magistrate — would remark, "I consider him and his friend Captain Montague and their constant companion Little Cazey, the Link-boy, as the three most troublesome and difficult to manage of all my Bow Street visitors." J. T. Smith goes on to say that the portraits of the trio had been introduced into Boitard's rare print "The Covent Garden Morning Frolic"; in it Captain Laroon is depicted as brandishing an artichoke, Captain Montague is seated in drunken state at the top of Bet Careless's Sedan, which is preceded by Little Cazey on foot. Cazey, he goes on to add, was eventually transported for stealing a gentleman's gold watch.

ing. Also, I thought I felt in him what, alas, I have now come to feel in myself, the sense that no longer is one a multi-millionaire in minutes, and that life, with its accidents and illnesses, is not long enough even for work. And, as a young man, Sickert, with his attraction, his wit, his social aplomb — all of which made many hundreds of friends for him — must, though obviously always a fanatic for work, have loved also to squander his time as well as use it; because the young artist, in the same way as every other young man, feels all eternity before him — we are all born immortal, and only lose that property as we grow older — all eternity in which to experience life, to talk, to observe, and learn, and feast, and enjoy.

From Broadstairs, from time to time, would come a story of the painter, typical of him and of his wit, based on exaggeration. I heard, for example, that he had confessed to a friend that he had found all the pupils in the School of Art he had started there so gifted and so promising that he now discovered that he had awarded each of them a life scholarship, and was in consequence bound to teach the whole school every day for nothing. Or sometimes, again, one would meet him in a picture gallery or at a theater. Thus my brother saw Sickert in 1934 or '35 at a gallery, where he was examining with minute care a picture by Charles Robinson, and professing for it the greatest admiration. Sacheverell observed, "It's extraordinary: he's the brother of Heath Robinson!"

"Yes," said Sickert, "and you're Osbert's brother — or he's your brother! Which is it?"

It was clear, then, that as an individual, though he was growing old, he had changed by no particle; but it was obvious also that as an artist he was still evolving, his genius expanding. The technical innovations and developments of his later style, however, puzzled many of the public. As Canaletto and Guardi had made use of the camera lucida, so Sickert seized on photography for the purposes of his art. . . . He maintained that the traditional method of portraiture, by which the subject of the portrait sat to the painter day after day, for hour after hour, had become obsolete, and used to declare that for the artist "to demand more than one sitting was sheer sadism": photographs from many angles and by different lights could now afford him all the help that was needed to obtain the perfect likeness. This system, though, made life so easy for the sitter that even he could not believe in the new freedom with which science, coming to his rescue, had presented him. For a proper resemblance, he remained sure, it was necessary to suffer. . . . Many of the artist's later portraits are splendid: but his attitude misled many people who were resolutely looking in the wrong direction.

Thus, at last, the long hours spent in staring at prints and engravings, and at old copies of newspapers, were beginning to bear fruit. In 1927, he began to paint his grand series of "Echos," as they were called. The first of them was taken from a scene on the lid of a mid-nineteenth-century china pomade box, and they were all of this kind, adaptations, transposed to a larger scale, of works by other older artists. But, because of this, and because also Sickert had reverted to the ancient studio practice for large pictures, of having assistants helping to prepare the ground, and because, still more, of his ineradicable sense of humor, the virtues and importance of these works have been minimized and in some quarters dismissed. Nor was it entirely the fault of the critical that this was so, for Sickert could never restrain his wit. . . . One day, for instance, in the 'thirties, my brother met him at the Leicester Galleries, where an exhibition of his later work of this kind was in progress. Sickert turned round, after looking at a picture, and remarked to my brother:

"It's such a good arrangement; Cruikshank and Gilbert do all the work, and I get all the money!"

He enjoyed saying it, and said it, fortunately, to my brother; but he would not have hesitated to make the remark

to anyone, and the dull might have taken it for the truth;
they would have thought that, in fact, he was plagiarizing.
Whereas, in reality, among the "Echos," derivative though
they are at first sight and admittedly, there are yet certain
paintings more magnificent than any that the artist had hitherto achieved. Always, up till now, he had been a painter of
tones; that is to say, the tones and colors had been separate
entities in his mind, he had thought of a canvas first in terms
of tone. But now that he adumbrated from a preconceived
germ these huge compositions, filled for him, too, with an
intense character of the period and locality in which they had
originally been designed – qualities that he loved in pictures
for their own sake, and for which he had always searched –
for the first time he was set free, because all these matters had
been already thought out for him. Thus released, he was able
at last to see the whole work in terms of abstract color, as it
were. In consequence, now, in his old age, his personality
united with a lifetime of technical achievement unrivaled in
English painting to discover a fresh territory, the very existence of which had remained up till now unsuspected, even
by his admirers. But it takes many years before the public will
forgive anyone, and especially a veteran, for discovering a new
land. The old country is good enough for them, they aver,
even though, as in this instance, the artist is able to develop the
new, and imbue it with a sumptuousness to which they have
not been used. So, in these "Echos," Sickert proved himself to
be a splendid and audacious innovator in color, and the canvases of his last years blaze with a richness that indicates the
ultimate fulfillment and fructification of a painter's genius,
owing to decades of perseverance in practice and experiment.

CHAPTER VIII

W. H. Davies

WILLIAM DAVIES — W. H. Davies! I had long known the name as that of a distinguished and individual poet: but I first came to think of him as a person, to know about him, as it were, in three dimensions, instead of seeing him only flat on the page of a book, from the conversation of Nina Hamnett, with whose work — and with whose delightful autobiography [1] — my readers will undoubtedly be familiar. Always she manifests a particularly fine flair for people. Generosity, moreover, is so marked a feature in her character that she longs to introduce her friends one to another, to make presents of them in the same manner in which in those days she gave away drawings by Modigliani and Gaudier-Brzeska as though they were twopenny prints, albeit she was never in very comfortable circumstances, and with the passing of a year or two these drawings were to become extremely valuable. Thus, on the afternoon in the spring of 1917 of which I am talking, when I went to have tea with her in her studio in Fitzroy Street, though she showed me drawings she had done of many other friends, of, let us say, Sickert and Roger Fry and Michael Arlen and my sister, of Icelandic poets and South American painters, and of herself, both clothed and naked, as well as several of W. H. Davies, it was solely of him, her latest discovery, that she would talk. She was almost alone of our generation in that her bump of reverence was fully developed — and lacking such a sense no true artist can live; its absence impoverishes the soil so that it yields but a stony and withered

[1] *Laughing Torso*, by Nina Hamnett. (Constable.)

crop. In those years, however, as today, it was not a fashionable virtue; it is easier to be funny about poets than to give them, alternatively or in addition, their due. But I have always remembered Nina Hamnett telling me how, when she first came to London from Wales, she would wait for hours in the street outside a famous painter's house in order just to catch a glimpse of him if he should chance to go out, and so too, now, as she took the last drawing of Davies and propped it up on a table for me to look at — and a splendid drawing it was, with its air of certainty and the fine modeling of the head — reverence as well as affection entered into the enthusiastic tone with which she said, "You *must* meet him."

Accordingly it was not long before she took my brother Sacheverell and me to tea with him, or before we had become as fervent in our praise of him as she was. Indeed, in the space of the next few weeks we seem to have become old friends, and certainly from that time until he left London in 1925 we saw a great deal of the poet. But though he called me "Osbert" very shortly after we met, some years went by before I was privileged to call him "William," for Davies manifested his own individual ways in everything, and one instance of this was to be seen in the strict principles which he had worked out for himself to apply to the mutual use of Christian names and surnames. If he liked a man, Davies would soon call him by his Christian name, but that man would be expected to continue to call him "Davies" in return until several years had passed, when, if still approved, he might be allowed to address him as "William." On the other hand, albeit he called a woman by her first name, she must always call him "Mr. Davies." Moreover, even these universal laws found an exception where married women were concerned; there his strong sense of propriety, coupled with an innate fear, I think, of husbands enraged at another man's familiarity with their wives, never permitted him to call them by their Christian names.

Most certainly he was a man with whom everybody must have wished to be on mutual Christian-name terms, for there can never have been anyone to whom friends became more, or more quickly, devoted. His whole nature seemed to have been designed to call out their affection, and in its simplicity, combined with a certain shrewdness, offered the appeal of pathos as well as of originality and genius. Further, his approach to his fellows was unusual. From his point of view, all men were alike, and he judged them with the same benevolent but appraising glance — his head held, like that of a bird, a little on one side, whatever their standing might be in the eyes of the rest of the world.

To illustrate this trait, so that its citing can be seen to be part of a true analysis of character, and not, as it may sound at first, a merely obituary commonplace, let me give an example of it. . . . Lord and Lady Oxford and Asquith had always been very kind to Davies, and he cherished towards them feelings of especial gratitude and affection, because Lord Oxford had been Prime Minister at the time that Davies, on the recommendation of the late Robert Ross, had been awarded his pension. Thus, during the First World War when Lady Oxford — Mrs. Asquith as she then was — organized on behalf of one of the charities in which she was interested a reading by celebrated poets of their own poetry, Davies gladly consented to appear among this band. The room was filled that evening with the perishable flower of Mayfair and the *immortelle* of Bloomsbury. At the end of the proceedings, when Davies went up to say good-by to his hostess, and to congratulate her on the result attained, he took a final glance at the audience, now dispersing, and added:

"It's been very successful: and you've had quite a nice lot of the neighbors in, too."

His birth and career had, in fact, rendered him independent of class feeling and nearly blind to the indications of it that existed in that bad old world before a universal Maison-Lyons culture had blanketed the ancient follies of the European tradition. . . . Davies came of Cornish descent: but he was brought up in Newport, Monmouthshire, by his paternal grandfather and grandmother, his father being dead when he first remembered, and his mother — whom he seldom mentioned — having married again. In addition to his grandparents and himself, his home consisted, he says, of "an imbecile brother, a sister . . . a maidservant, a dog, a cat, a parrot, a dove and a canary bird." He does not tell us to what profession his father belonged, but his grandfather and uncle, I know, each owned his boat. In his poems, and still more in his superb autobiography,[2] we often find portraits, or reflections, of them. In the second of these he tells us that his first recollection was of sailing as a small boy from Newport (in which town, in the Church House Tavern, he had been born) to Bristol on the *Welsh Prince*, a schooner that plied then regularly between the two ports. He was taken on this trip frequently, since his grandfather was a friend of the captain's, and would stand beside him on the bridge all the time, except when he went below to visit the saloon cabin for refreshment. He records that returning from a rough voyage at midnight, the old man was wont to pause in the empty street and to address the sleepers behind the flat and slumbering façades with the angry demand:

"Do you know who I am? *Captain Davies*, master of his own ship!"

In the daytime, too, he liked, now that he was always at home, to parade the street in which he lived and inform the women — for almost every woman in it had a son or husband or brother at sea — if the tides and winds were favorable.

This upbringing, and the consciousness of his ancestry, made Davies retain all through his life a great feeling for the sea and for ships. I remember, for example, how, when, on

[2] *The Autobiography of a Super-Tramp*, by W. H. Davies, with a preface by Bernard Shaw. (A. C. Fifield, London, 1908.)

one occasion of many, I took him to tea with Violet Gordon Woodhouse, to hear her play the harpsichord and clavichord, she showed him — for she felt instinctively that he would like it — a bottle containing a little full-rigged ship, and that he regarded it gravely with a connoisseur's interest, and then inquired of her, "Do you come of seafaring folk too?"

Davies's grandmother, a Baptist by denomination, was of a more austere and religious turn of mind than her husband. She was inclined to resent the fidgeting of the retired mariner, for he was always opening the door to look out at the stars, or to see if the wind had changed, and then going down to the kitchen to make sure that his family were comfortable, as though "he had just made his way from the hurricane deck to inquire after the welfare of the passengers." This conduct would cause the old lady to say every now and then:

"Francis, do *sit down* for a minute or two," to which he would reply, as if giving orders to a ship:

"Avast there, Lydia!"

Davies once told me that he remembered his grandmother smacking him severely after some manifestation of childish sin, and saying between blows:

"If-you-go-on-like-this,-you'll-be-no-better-than-that-young-Brodribb-cousin-of-yours-who's-brought-disgrace-upon-the-family!"

"That-young-Brodribb-cousin" was, in fact, known to the theater-going audiences all over the English-speaking world as Henry Irving: but the old woman always referred to the stage as "the Devil's Playground," and that her relative was the idol of the whole country, acclaimed everywhere, to her signified nothing; indeed worse than nothing. The wages of sin were death, and not even a knighthood — the first ever conferred upon a member of his profession — could modify that well-known decree, or moderate the sentence of doom that it pronounced.

Directly one knew of their relationship, it was plain that, distant though it might be, William Davies bore a likeness to Irving. The face of the poet manifested precisely the same bone structure as the mask of the great actor (and the similarity was especially noticeable in the fine and tragic cast of Irving's head taken after his death). And here, if the reader is to get to know him properly, it is extremely important that I should describe Davies's personal appearance; because the outward aspect is a matter to which today people pay too small attention. Our neglect of nature's so obvious hints is the measure of how far we wander from the truth, as though bees were suddenly to become so self-important as to refuse to take a flower's scent for true guide to its nectar. There is much that I would like to say along these lines, but I must confine myself to reminding younger writers of how essential it is for an author to be able to render the superficial as well as the deeper aspect of anyone of whom he is writing. In a novel, as in work of a descriptive order, the visual sense is all-important — each character must be seen; and in this connection Somerset Maugham once remarked to me that no writer who could by his words summon up for a reader the personal appearance of a character could be considered as without talent; it was the first requisite, and the most severe test of his powers.

Davies's face, then, though it resembled that of his cousin in cut and construction, had in it nothing of the actor, nothing which suggested, as Irving's face did so clearly, that it was a mask designed by the years to display on the boards, with the aid of make-up, various emotions, and that in its present form it was only to be worn off the stage. At first sight, he appeared more Spanish than British in type, and after I had met Manuel de Falla, I noticed from time to time a likeness in the look of the two men. Though their features were different, the head of the Welshman, with its fine, rugged quality, exhibited the beauty of a Gothic stone head, as did the Spaniard's, and there was something in each of them that seemed to belong to a race immeasurably old, perhaps to that ancient Pelasgian people from whom both Iberians and Celts claim to descend. His mold of face was rather long and aquiline, but with broad high cheekbones, and all of it, chin, mouth, long upper lip, nose and high forehead, was finely sculptured and full of character. Features and hair both exhibited a naturally proud, backward slant or tilt, though there was no arrogance in him. His eyes were dark and gleaming, and his skin possessed an almost nautical tinge, the look of having been exposed perpetually to air and wind and sunshine. He was broad-shouldered and vigorous-looking, but of less than middle height. Having lost a leg, he wore — for he could not afford the expense of a modern artificial leg of metal — a heavy wooden stump, which made a wooden sound as he walked, and gave him a particular slow gait, making him raise and dip his shoulders as he moved. It never, though, until the very end of his life, prevented him from going for long walks, or enjoying them. When he spoke, his voice, with its soft Welsh rhythm and intonation — he pronounced "man" as "mun," and "Mr. Asquith" as "Mr. Usquith" — was singularly attractive and beautiful, but in it was to be traced, too, I used to think, a disarming and pathetic diffidence, not easy to account for, since, when I knew him, he was sure both of himself and of his poems.

Davies was proud of his poems. He knew they were good and made no secret of their merit. The last time I saw him — two months before his death — he referred to the fact that my sister had asked permission to reprint some of his poems in an anthology, and added reflectively:

"You know, Osbert, altogether over a hundred lyrics of mine have been published in anthologies — and that is ten times more than any other living poet has — even De la Mare!"

This attitude made him all the easier to get on with, because, for example, I could attack in print other Georgian poets as much as I liked, and it would never occur to him, any more than to myself, that these strictures could apply to him, so certain was he of the worth of his work and of our admiration for it. On the other hand, it inspired him, too, with a certain simple consciousness of his dignity and what was due to it. No one could have called him conceited, but he liked to be given his place and was, even, a disciplinarian on those occasions on which he thought it had not been properly recognized.

For example, in the early days of our friendship, he wrote to my sister. She did not at once reply, and he reprimanded her for this when they met.

"I wrote to you two days ago," he said.

"Yes, I know, Mr. Davies. Thank you very much."

"Yes, Edith, and when I send you a letter, *I expect you to answer it!*"

On another occasion, about the same time, when she went to tea with him, he showed her a drawing of himself by Nina Hamnett. The artist had portrayed him sitting at a square table, on which, at an almost ostentatious distance from him, stood a bottle of port and, pushed away still further, a glass. When my sister, after examining the drawing, said how good she thought it, and how much it resembled him, he appeared to be displeased, though quite gently, and said:

"You know, Nina really ought *not* to have done it. . . . She ought *not*. It doesn't do for a man in my position — and it was Nina who bought the port!" [3]

This anecdote must not be taken, however, to mean that he disapproved of wine, for, as will be deduced from his poems, he was no puritan, and he seemed to have inherited in his disposition more qualities from his sailor grandfather than from his Nonconformist grandmother. In his autobiography, he accounts for his liking for liquor by the fact that he was born in a public house, and that, through this, he "became

[3] Miss Hamnett tells me Sickert supplied the money for it.

acquainted with the taste of drink at a very early age, receiving sups of mulled beer at bedtime in lieu of cocoa or tea. . . ."

Certainly in the years of which I speak he possessed an almost Chinese attitude — I mean by this, the hedonistic, ingenuous attitude in this country attributed to the Chinese poets — towards wine and the other sensual pleasures. Wine made him happy and he loved it, though only to the degree that it made him feel happy. And, of course, it always represented to him luxury, in the same manner that a pineapple personified it for Arnold Bennett (so long as a pineapple sat, crowned with its green tuft, in the center of the dining table, Arnold felt that he was successful, secure, and leading a life full of wealth and romance). Moreover, the drinking of wine made a gathering into something more memorable, more festive, "a party." And Davies looked forward immensely to parties, though he considered himself ever at a disadvantage in society, for he maintained that he lacked all conversational powers, and attributed this imaginary deficiency to the fact that, since he had heard so much slang throughout his early life, his thoughts naturally first decked themselves out in it, and that, this being so, "the shame and confusion in good company" made him "take so long to undress and clothe them better . . . that other people grow tired of waiting and take upon themselves the honour of entertainers." [4]

Herein he shows himself, of course, too humble; it was merely an exaggeration of the ordinary man's occasional fear of indulging involuntarily in overstrong language before company unsuited or unused to it. Though not, perhaps, quick in talk, he was not unduly slow. His fascinating voice alone would have ensured him a hearing, while what he said was always worth waiting for; he hardly ever spoke a sentence that was not tinctured through and through with his delightful and rare personality. . . . Perhaps he rather dreaded, as well

[4] See *The Autobiography of a Super-Tramp.*

as looked forward to, entertainments, but he would be un-usually excited before them, being essentially sociable. This trait showed itself in the way his whole appearance altered when he saw a friend. A charming, long-lingering smile would light up his rather somber face — which, as a rule, wore an expression of seeing life very clearly and daring to confront it — and it would assume a glow of pleasure.

Particularly, I think, he looked forward to entertainments at a late hour, because they presented him with the oppor-tunity of wearing evening clothes — more of a symbol, even, than wine — and thus of testifying, to himself as well as to others, how far he had traveled, to what an altitude above his tramp status his poems had brought him. No doubt, too, he liked the dress for itself. Indeed he and Arnold Bennett were the chief protagonists in London of unusual evening shirts. Arnold's, frilled and ruffed and ruched and pranked out, were a conscious, even intellectual presentation of the *joie de vivre* of a flamboyant personality, all mixed up with a lifelong ad-miration of Balzac and his works, whereas Davies's were the subconscious expression of himself and his dreams. They were less diverse in form than Arnold's — indeed, they were always the same — but they were none the less rich, and of the finest napery or damask, as opposed to Arnold's linen. Their pat-tern, further, was invariable, the front being composed of a number of shiny squares, each of which displayed in the mid-dle of it a shiny lily of the valley. . . . But all these character-istics, all these modes of self-expression, all these curious veins in a nature complex despite its apparent and beautiful sim-plicity, were fused to make his exquisite poems; poems that appear as natural and sweet as a blackbird's song — and, in-deed, with his dark and sparkling eyes, and in the way he would occasionally hold his head, he did, at times, seem a little to resemble a very wise old blackbird.

Davies was the author of many volumes of poetry and prose, and it is less easy with him than with the average writer to disentangle his personality from his work. In consequence, I must quote from his books more extensively than from those of various other characters that help to compose this volume. His most famous and beautiful poems possess a world-wide celebrity and are now better known perhaps than his prose works. Of these, *The Autobiography of a Super-Tramp* is a beautiful, touching and illuminating record, with the quality of suddenly throwing light upon dark places, so that things which have not been understood before become clear. . . . Once, for example, only a year or two ago, I watched a tramp walking through Hyde Park. It was midday. He was plainly full of energy and loved life, a tall, burly man, with a bushy black beard, and an air of crazy bonhomie; a most unusual type that suggested power, and combined certain physical qualities that are to be seen in the portraits of Henry VIII and of the late Mr. William Whiteley, though his eyes were wild and roving. He did not look particularly dirty, but his clothes were torn to shreds, his trousers and boots being a perfect cat's-cradle of string, and albeit he wore a not intolerably battered bowler hat at a jaunty angle, his jet-black hair and beard were long and unkempt. He was carrying, I noticed, a great many large, crumpled, brown paper parcels. I watched him. . . . Just beside the stone bridge that crosses the Serpentine is a bench, set a little way back from the path. Here he sat down, placing his belongings beside him. The next thing he did was to undo the largest parcel. I thought he must have in it something to eat — but no! After removing fold after fold of paper, he produced a very small bit of broken looking glass and a comb, and proceeded to an elaborate toilet, holding the mirror up, so that he could part his hair and comb his beard, and smiling in it with a rather fixed and sinister grin, so that he could see how his teeth were looking. . . . I was amazed at all this care of the person on the part of so cranky a tatterdemalion, and often used to wonder what it meant. A year later, however, I came on the following passage:

W. H. Davies

It has become a common expression to say "dirty tramp," or "as dirty as a tramp"; but this is not always true, except occasionally in the large cities; although such a term may be applied morally to them all. There is one species of tramp who wanders from workhouse to workhouse; and this man, having every night to conform strictly to the laws of cleanliness, is no less clean, and often cleaner, than a number of people whose houses contain bath rooms which they seldom use. Another species of tramp is proud of being a good beggar, who scorns the workhouse, but who knows well that a clean appearance is essential to his success. For this reason, anyone that enters a common lodging house can at once see what efforts are being made to this end. It seems a strange thing to say, but the dirtiest-looking tramp is often the most honest and respectable, for he has not the courage to beg either food or clothes, nor will he enter the doors of a workhouse. I have seen this so often the case that I would much prefer to believe a dirty ragged tramp who might tell me that he had a good home six months previous, than to believe his cleaner namesake, who seems so eager to impart this information unsolicited. It is certainly the man who has had a good home, and has been waited on by other hands, who soon succumbs to a filthy condition, when it becomes necessary to wait on himself by washing and patching his own clothes; and the higher his former position has been the lower he sinks in the social strata.

After reading these words, one more problem had been solved, or at any rate a corner of a curtain had been lifted. Another mystery even Davies can never explain: how, subject to the life he describes, he was able to *become* a poet. His education must have been fitful, to say the most of it, but he wrote in a beautiful, small, clear, educated hand. . . . The books which his grandmother read, and strongly recommended to young William, were *Paradise Lost*, *Pilgrim's Progress* and Young's *Night Thoughts*. Against all others she warned him, but he contrived as a youth to read Shelley, Marlowe and Shakespeare. At fourteen or fifteen, he was apprenticed to the picture-frame trade, but, being consumed

[241]

with a passion for reading, could not apply himself sufficiently
to this craft ever to have a hope of becoming a master of it.
(During this period he went so far as to compose and cause to
be printed a poem describing a storm at night.) After his
apprenticeship was finished, he tried to persuade his grandmother — his grandfather being by now dead — to finance him,
so that he might go to the New World, but she refused. He
then took work for six months in Bristol, whence he was recalled home by the old lady's death. Here he found that her
estate was in the hands of a trustee, and that she had left the
profits of it to be divided equally, every week, among her
three grandchildren. Accordingly he obtained for himself, on
account, an advance of fifteen pounds, which seemed to him a
boundless fortune, and embarked for America, where he
quickly adapted himself to the life of a tramp. . . . Thus an
access of fortune had been directly responsible for his re-
nunciation of an ordinary working life.

Through spring and summer and autumn as a rule he
begged his way — though sometimes he was engaged to pick
fruit, strawberries being the first crop. During this period of
five years he made some eight trips to England with cattle.
Usually he and his fellow tramps, by a convenient arrangement with a conniving sheriff, spent the winter in prison, so
as to be sure of at least a modicum of food and warmth during
the winter months. The sheriff of the town would see that
they were sentenced to a month's detention, and when that
sentence had expired, they would — though not before they
had given the friendly dignitary their promise to return the
following year — remove themselves to the next place, and
there again seek the sheriff's aid, being rewarded with a further
month of the state's hospitality. After five years of this life,
Davies returned to England, meaning to settle there for good.
His first act on arrival was to go and see his mother. It was
evening when he knocked at the door, but she immediately
called him by name, and when he said, "That's me!" she re-

plied, "Yes, I thought it was your knock," as though he had left but the day before. . . . Soon he became dissatisfied once more, and this time decided to seek his fortune in the Klondike. He reached Canada, but in the act of train-jumping there he met with an accident, through the stupidity and negligence of a fellow tramp, and in consequence his leg had to be amputated. As soon as he was well enough, he left Canada for London.

Here he lived in doss houses on the money inherited from his grandmother. . . . Shaw, to whose kindness and discernment Davies owed his first fame, says on this point: "The exact amount of his independent income was ten shillings a week. Finding this too much for his needs, he devoted twenty per cent of it to pensioning necessitous friends in his native place; saved a further percentage to print verses with; and lived modestly on the remainder." He had now, at the age of thirty-four, begun to write poems, and a publisher informed him that he would accept them if Davies would pay twenty-five pounds towards the cost of issuing the book. To raise this money, he decided to have four short poems printed, and himself to sell them from door to door. Alas, even this printing was estimated to cost thirty-five shillings, and he had only contrived to put aside thirty-one shillings, so he was obliged nearly to starve himself in order to save the missing four shillings, at the rate of a further two shillings a week off his eight-shillings-a-week income. And when the poems were at last printed, he did not sell a single copy, though he made a house-to-house visitation in the suburbs. Most of the people he called upon were poor, and badly educated. They looked at the poet in amazement when he offered them a printed sheet for three-pence. One richer woman, with a servant, gave him a penny, but refused altogether to accept the poems which he proposed to give her in return. When he reached his doss house again that evening, he burned every single copy. Now, with the same object of a book in view, he started to peddle boot-

laces and needles and pins, which seemed less humiliating;
but he was not used to this trade and allowed his wares in
a few days to get rusty from damp. Begging seemed simpler
again, so once more he reverted to it, and threw in a little hymn-
singing as well. To this he took with all the fervor of his
race, who love to sing, until his more experienced companion had to warn him that he was using his voice too vigor-
ously, after the fashion of a healthy man, and had better
"cut the difficult high notes short," as though he had "spasms
in the side." . . . Finally, he was able to put by enough
money, and the poems were published. He sent a copy of
them to Shaw, addressed from "The Farm House, Kenning-
ton." Shaw tells us that the address surprised him, and that
he did not suspect at first that the name of the Farm House,
like those of various Paradise Rows and Nightingale Lanes,
was ironical and disguised the identity of a doss house.

The summary which I have given above of this poet's
amazing career is derived entirely from *The Autobiography
of a Super-Tramp*, for he seldom, when I knew him, referred to his adventures in America. Perhaps he felt that he
had written all that he had to say about them, or perhaps
the memory of those times oppressed him. Once, however,
he described to me an appalling razor-slashing contest he
had seen in the New York slums. Two rival gangs of Negroes,
holding the shafts of the instruments in their hands, with the
back of the blade bent back against their knuckles, so that
the edge itself was immovable, had attacked one another
with wild cries. Soon blood was spurting everywhere. But
this did not stop them. The fighting became wilder. Again
and again the battling bands hurled themselves on the foe,
nor did they desist until the police, in great force and with
considerable difficulty, divided them and arrested the living.
This demoniac scene had left upon him, as will come out
later, an abiding impression. . . . And, on another occasion,
when sitting next my sister at dinner, their talk turned on

starvation, and he told her how once he had come very near to it, being lost in the Arizona Desert. He remarked that all the stones in it had looked to him like loaves of bread.

"I wonder you survived," my sister said. Drawing up his body and inflating his chest, he preened himself and replied: "Well, you see, I'm a well-set-up mun."

Of his days as a tramp in England, equally, he said little, though I recall one curious incident and its sequel, which he described to me. It is possible that he may have printed an account of it himself elsewhere, but it is of too much interest for the reader to run the risk of losing it, so I record it here as he told it to me. He did not say exactly when its first part occurred, but presumably it must have been very early in his career; perhaps during one of the intervals when he returned to England by cattle boat from the States. . . . One evening he was sitting near the stove in a tramps' doss house in Lambeth. It was cold and wet outside. The room was lit only by the glow of a large brazier, which emitted suffocating fumes, but Davies sat near it on a broken wooden box and tried to read by the glow of the cinders. The general noise and rowdiness made such an attempt at concentration most difficult, for it was Saturday night, and as many of the occupants as could afford it had got drunk. I do not know if Davies had read Robert Greene; if so, he will have realized that Greene's world still survived within these damp and scabrous walls. The very names of the tramps, peddlers, loafers and pickpockets with whom he consorted were but modern varieties of the Elizabethan mumpers and coney catchers: Brummy Tom, Fishy Fat, Never Sweat, Cinders, The Snob, The Masher, All Legs and Wings, Red Nosed Scotty and the rest of the band. The singing, shouting, roaring, swearing, dancing seemed insupportable, exaggerated and magnified as they were by the bareness of walls and floor. In the whole room he was the only quiet man, except for a mysterious stranger who sat opposite and talked to no one. He too was trying to read, and something in the look of him made Davies wonder who he was and regard him attentively. Indeed he would have liked to enter into conversation with him, but the man seemed absorbed in his book, or else in melancholy thoughts, and a sort of shyness and restraint came over Davies and prevented him from making any attempt at it. . . . Many years later, however, he happened to meet Francis Thompson, and recognized in the features of the famous poet those of the stranger in the Lambeth doss house.

Davies's career, as detailed above, affords the perfect grounds for arraigning both Capitalism and Socialism. That for so many years such a man should have been obliged to lead this life is plainly sufficient to condemn the system in which it was allowed to happen. On the other hand, in a Socialist state he would have been deprived, being a *rentier*, of the ten shillings a week he had inherited. Worse still, he would have been obliged to work instead of being allowed to idle, and thus he would have forfeited the leisure in which to practice his poetry, and the singular experiences that had both nourished his imagination and shaped his character. . . . The perfect poet of the proletariat — in a sense in which our middle-class-conscious schoolmaster poets, with their dry and doctrinaire catalogued points of the law, decorated with tags of classic learning, cannot ever hope to be — he never wrote of great public enterprises, dams and factories. Though he lived in the cities, he walked for choice down country lanes, and it was the life of tramping the roads in America and England, of beggars' lodginghouses and of going to prison, that gave birth to such lyrics as this:

THE BIRD OF PARADISE

Here comes Kate Summers who, for gold,
   Takes any man to bed:
"You knew my friend, Nell Barnes," said she;
   "You knew Nell Barnes — she's dead.

"Nell Barnes was bad on all you men,
  Unclean, a thief as well;
Yet all my life I have not found
  A better friend than Nell.

"So I sat at her side at last,
  For hours, till she was dead;
And yet she had no sense at all
  Of any word I said.

"For all her cry but came to this —
  'Not for the world! Take care:
Don't touch that bird of paradise;
  Perched on the bedpost there!'

"I asked her would she like some grapes,
  Some damsons ripe and sweet;
A custard made with new-laid eggs,
  Or tender fowl to eat.

"I promised I would follow her,
  To see her in her grave;
And buy a wreath with borrowed pence,
  If nothing I could save.

"Yet still her cry but came to this —
  'Not for the world! Take care:
Don't touch that bird of paradise,
  Perched on the bedpost there!' "

During the years that I saw most of him, from 1917 until
he married and left London to live in the country, he appeared to be very happy. His civil-list pension of seventy-five
pounds a year had been doubled by "Mr. Usquith," and,
with the values acquired in his earlier life still governing his
existence, such a sum represented to him a Croesus-like opu-
lence. I recall that once I went to see him just after he had
been to look at the collection of ancient and modern paint-

ings belonging to a well-known connoisseur, who, though by no means rich, had, through his knowledge and discernment, contrived to amass a gallery of pictures that would have done credit to an ample fortune. Davies had been impressed by many of the objects, especially by a newly acquired Gainsborough. I was astounded when he described this to me, for I knew what huge sums the works of this artist fetch. I remarked:

"How clever of Richard! How did he manage to get it?" To which Davies answered solemnly:

"Well, you see, it's the immense wealth of the mun."

He lived during most of the period of which I am writing at 14 Great Russell Street, not far from the British Museum, though on the Tottenham Court Road side of Bloomsbury Street. I still can never pass through this neighborhood without thinking of him. Notwithstanding the hideousness of the enormous stone Y.M.C.A. palace which occupied the half of the street nearly opposite, his part of it was pretty. There the houses are set back, so that, more than a street, it becomes a *place*, being much broader than is usual in London and lined with small eighteenth-century houses of three stories. Davies inhabited a room on the first floor. It had pleasant, low proportions, and two windows, old and well-made, but, in spite of them, the place was rather dark because of its wallpaper. In the middle stood a table — no doubt that on which Nina Hamnett had depicted the bottle of port previously mentioned — covered with his writing apparatus, and one wall supported a large case full of the signed volumes of poetry presented to him by his own contemporaries, or by the young who so greatly admired him. In spite of the sociability of his disposition, he liked very much to be his own master, to go and come, or read or work quietly, as he felt inclined, or sometimes just to stay at home and puzzle over various new accomplishments which he still found troublesome. Alas! Money brought, as well as pleasures, its own

responsibilities, and, for instance, the drawing of checks itself proved a ritual not always easy to acquire. Indeed this,
and with his dislike of cats and Negroes, the difficulty of
telephoning (a means of communication increasingly forced
upon him by the growing number of his friends), and the
conduct of a neighbor, constituted — apart, of course, from
the horrible and pointless war in progress, which continued
to darken life and all its background — the only things that
endangered his peace of mind, his innocent bliss.

To take the check-drawing trouble first, one afternoon
Sacheverell and I went to visit him unexpectedly, and found
him seated before his table. His face wore a look of mingled
gloom and bewilderment. In front of him was a checkbook.
Obviously some connection must exist between his aspect
and this latter object, and we inquired what was the matter and if we could be of help. . . . For a long time he would
not confide in us, for he was very nervous of being chaffed
in such respects, but finally, after extracting a promise of
secrecy, he explained. He had been asked for a subscription,
and the secretary had remarked airily, "Don't make the check
out to me, draw it to yourself." Davies had felt that to show
ignorance on this point, or to ask for an elucidation, would
impair his status as a man-of-the-world, so he had returned
home to pass a miserable hour or two in pondering what the
mystic phrase could signify. . . . He had not the slightest
notion of how to set about his task. Yet, if it got out, the
situation would seem so ridiculous, he felt; people would be
as surprised and amused at such an unexpected lack of
savoir-faire as if D'Orsay or Brummel had been found incapable of tying a cravat.

For the same reasons, he also carefully concealed other
difficulties. One afternoon, however, my brother and I went
to see him to arrange about his coming to dine with us the
following evening. There existed some doubt as to whether
it would be possible for him, and eventually Sacheverell said:

"Well, don't bother about it: leave it till the morning, and let us know by telephone."

A look of the utmost suspicion — into which entered as well a kind of wiliness — came over Davies's face. He watched my brother intently for a moment or two, and then said:

"Now, Susshie, don't get me on to thut."

He thought we had discovered one of the cunningly guarded secrets of his existence: the telephone was an instrument he never could master, and he well might speak down the earpiece and hold the mouthpiece to his ear.

As for cats and Negroes, he was inclined to believe that both species knew instinctively of his pronounced antipathy for them, and, withal, were to that precise degree the more attracted to his vicinity. The fact mentioned earlier in these pages, that in New York he had seen Negroes fighting with razors, had added to the sentiments of disgust and aversion he had always entertained for them, a feeling of almost superstitious horror. Yet he noticed that numbers of black men were apt to pass by his door — if, indeed, they did not stop, specially, to loaf outside it and to shout. . . . The true explanation, of course, was that Bloomsbury has ever been particularly cosmopolitan, people of all colors dwell in its lodginghouses, while, further, these men had probably just that very moment left the austere but hospitable precincts of the Y.M.C.A. building opposite. . . . Nevertheless, Davies could never be persuaded to view the matter in this light. His attitude towards it resembled that of Blake in some of his inspired aversions: he seemed to perceive in the passing of these shadows made flesh and blood, or in their waiting outside his door, something that was beyond our sight, the manifestation of a deep struggle which he imagined must be visible to every one else as well as to himself.

He told me of the worst instance of this haunting of him by Negroes that had occurred. One evening, some of them had gathered at about midnight outside his door and had actually begun to fight, shrieking and yelling. While the struggle was still in progress, Davies had gone downstairs, slipped out of the door unobserved by the black men, and, in spite of the fear inspired in him by the police — a terror to which I shall allude later — had fetched a constable to the scene. . . . Of course, by the time the policeman arrived, the gang had disbanded and all was quiet. Davies, however, was angry and on his mettle. He expostulated, and told the policeman that it was his duty to prevent the Negroes fighting outside a door. For his part, the constable declared stolidly that there were no Negroes here, and never had been any, and, alternatively, that if there had been, he had not seen them. This drove Davies to fury, and he produced the name, hitherto carefully saved up, of his most powerful protector, the man who liked his poetry and had doubled his pension, the Prime Minister himself.

"If you don't stop them another time, I shall tell Mr. Usquith about it; Mr. Usquith is a friend of mine, and will insist that you put an end to it."

He had, indeed, unlimited faith in Mr. Usquith, but the policeman made it plain that he simply did not believe a word of this boasting, was not for a moment to be taken in by this rather shabbily dressed little man in front of him, with his strong Welsh accent, who pretended to be a friend of the head of the Government. *Was it likely?* Indeed he looked at the poet with such an air of mistrust and, even, hostility, that Davies, fearing that worse might come, retreated hastily into the friendly shadow of his house. . . . But the episode had left him feeling humiliated.

Cats were worse than Negroes. Black men at least were human, shadows to our light, but cats were messengers from the Devil. They plagued him and sang unceasingly to him from the moonlit angles of roof tops. The name of the animals itself proved a source of vexation to him, for he grew

to suspect — and not without reason — my brother and myself
of trying to induce him to talk of them because of the beautiful way in which he pronounced the word "cat," turning it
into a slow, soft "cut." While formerly I used to ascribe the
horror he felt for them to a reasonable cause, that they were
the enemy of all birds — creatures to which he was devoted
— with the passage of time I came to realize that in origin
it, too, was superstitious. . . . Thus, one afternoon when I
went to see him, he told me, with a look almost of awe, as
well as of distress at the recollection, of how, when he had
gone to bed the previous night at about eleven, he had at
once fallen asleep and been vouchsafed a vision of a large
tabby cat, which had sat on his chest and tried to suffocate
him (an ordinary enough nightmare, but he clearly did not
accept this idea when I advanced it). Fortunately, he said,
he had been woken up, before the dream cat had been given
time to finish his evil work, by the man who lived above him,
who, thinking, since it was not yet midnight, that Davies
would still be sitting up, had called in on his way upstairs
to see him. But what had particularly impressed and dis-
quieted Davies was that this man had told him that he had
found outside the room a huge tabby cat pressing itself
against the door, as if determined to get in, and that it had
taken him some moments to drive the creature away and
enter himself. . . . Perhaps the real explanation of this story
is that Davies's dislike of cats was founded (as it is said to be
in general) on their smell — which in some persons allergic
to it produces a kind of asthma, though the victims may be
unaware that they suffer from it — and that this smell, reaching him, had communicated the thought and fear of cats to his
subconscious mind.

Davies himself always maintained that he was not in the
least superstitious and, indeed, in his *Autobiography of a
Super-Tramp*, gives us what he claims to be the only instance
of a terror of this kind assailing him, and I remember him,

too, telling me of it. The occurrence had taken place one September, when he was starting to tramp back to London from Somerset. Towards the end of the day in question, he found himself skirting a park, in which he did not like to rest, because he felt sure there would be many keepers there to protect the game. After proceeding about two miles, he saw a suitable field a little way off and — for night was coming on fast — turned away towards it. When he reached it, he listened to see if anyone was about, but all was silent. Accordingly he picked up one of the wheat sheaves, which were standing as usual, clumped together in threes, and was about to lay it flat for part of his bed when he heard a wild laugh, harsh and mocking. At once he dropped the sheaf and bent down, sure that someone was watching him — but nothing more happened, and he thought that whoever the spy might be must have passed on. He therefore proceeded to make his bed with the stacks and stood up — only again to be greeted with several shouts of derisive laughter. Even now, the fear that he felt was not superstitious, for, as he says, a homeless man goes in terror of the living and not of the dead. He stood still; the laughter stopped, but every time he moved it began again, until he picked up a stick and prepared, as he thought, to meet the maniac who must be watching him. This action caused such savage paroxysms of laughter that they determined him to abandon all thoughts of rest and to quit the place at once. As he moved towards the gate, the laughter began again, this time continuing until he had run a long way down the road. For this once, superstitious terror entirely possessed him. . . . Afterwards, when he had reached a village — and he did not stop running and looking back until that moment — the only solution of which he could think was that the voice belonged to an escaped pet bird. But he never himself really believed in this explanation.

Whether or no Davies was superstitious, the chief trouble that he suffered in Great Russell Street — worse than any I have yet outlined — was material enough. . . . A Belgian refugee streetwalker lived in the next house, in a room adjoining his own, and, entertaining at all hours of the night, would be noisy and disturb him. At first, then, it was just a clash of hours, but, odd as it may seem, when the prostitute found out that her neighbor was a poet and poor, this made her venomous, and she used deliberately to rouse herself at three in the morning in order to disturb his rest and disorganize him for his day's work by thumping out tunes on the piano with hands that in their heavy clumsiness resembled clubfeet. He often used to complain to us about it, and once, with a sort of puzzled and grieved expression on his face, he added:

"And I am always so sorry for those girls, and have done them many a kindness."

In the protracted warfare which had ensued between Davies and this neighbor, in the end he won, but not, as it will emerge, without the aid of auxiliaries, or without being obliged to mechanize the forces at his disposal. . . . The details of this victory had vanished from my memory, until my friend Richard Church, who knew Davies very well, lately reminded me of them. One night when the woman was being more than usually obstreperous, Davies had got out of bed and knocked on the wall. To this protest she replied by bawling her national anthem.

"So I waited until dinnertime next day," Davies related, "when I knew she'd be asleep, and then *I* knocked on the wall, and sang *my* national anthem, 'Men of Harlech.' "

Even this had failed to quell her, but Richard Church had gone to see Davies one day and found him quietly triumphant, with a particularly secretive air. He confessed, at last, that two friends of his had obtained for him a mysterious infernal machine, which Davies could set going before he went out, and which yet, even in his absence, continued to madden his neighbor. Later, he confided to Richard Church that it

[254]

was "the Sitwell brothers" who had provided it, and that "Osbert had brought round the instrument, unknown to the police!" . . . Richard Church entered into the conspiracy as dramatically as he could, his curiosity having been aroused by these references to the machine. . . . At last, after much pressing, and after having obtained a strict promise from his friend not to disclose any information he received to the authorities, Davies slipped his way into the back room — into which no one but he had ever penetrated — and returned after a moment bearing in his hand — a metronome! (This my brother and I had brought from Renishaw, where, when my sister was a small girl, it had helped to regulate her playing of the piano.)

Such private horrors and difficulties as I have described in no way, however, interfered with his enjoyment of life, which was very strong. And one of the reasons, I hold, for his happiness during these years was because his range of acquaintance continued to extend. The characters of the new friends he made interested him tremendously, and he could ruminate upon them when alone. All the same, the people he saw regularly were few: the contemporary to whom he was the most devoted — and whose work as a poet he chiefly admired — was Mr. Ralph Hodgson; and Hodgson's celebrated bulldog could also be numbered among his favorites.

Concerning his opinion of his peers, the only person towards whom in talking Davies betrayed some feeling of jealousy was Walter De la Mare, though he is so delightful, so generous and unself-seeking a man and so exquisite a poet. Not that Davies did not admire his work, but he considered himself as a rarer poet, and yet one possessed of more humanity. The two men were of the same generation, and, in the words of Blake:

> The poison of the honey-bee
> Is the artist's jealousy.

And the emotion that Davies manifested could be regarded in itself as a compliment, a tribute to a rival. . . . The only person for whom, on the other hand, he actually cherished an *animosity* was the late Sir Henry Newbolt. Him he suspected — most unjustly — of lauding de la Mare because he had been Newbolt's discovery, and of continually comparing the two poets in literary papers, always to Davies's detriment. Still worse, he believed — though it was difficult to find out on what authority — that when Newbolt had been asked to be a signatory for him at the time that the pension was to be awarded to Davies, Newbolt had refused to enter his name "on behalf of a person who had once robbed a poorbox" (an incident alluded to in the *Autobiography*). If not in the best of humors, Davies used to dwell a good deal on these presumed attitudes of Newbolt's, and one day, when I came to see him, he remarked:

"I have been thinking of Newbolt again, Osbert. . . . People always compare his face to an eagle's; but to my mind it much more resembles a vulture's! There's something cruel and predatory about it."

As a rule, however, he was unusually generous in his judgments of people, especially of the young, for whom he loved to trace out great careers. He would tell them in some detail and to their faces what he saw they would be in the future, saying such things as, "I can see Robert as Poet Laureate," or whatever it might be, but in a voice which carried no trace of mockery, but only a soothing sense of conviction, so that I reproduce his remarks concerning Newbolt solely because, in the same way that a knot gives character to a tree, so this manifestation of his nature, albeit some may regard it as a blemish, nevertheless may enable others to see the entire graining of the man and seize upon his whole unique quality. Everything pertaining to him was steeped in the peculiar essence of his personality, and his few enmities, slight in themselves and in their cause, yet sometimes seemed to hold

for him the same sort of symbolic importance with which
Blake, again, invested his dislikes. Blake's diatribes against the
talented, cultivated and good Sir Joshua Reynolds, or against
Lafayette, seem to us in themselves to be singularly pointless, yet even today they maintain at least the interest of
their *intensity* and, further, help us to comprehend the nature of his genius. So, too, with W. H. Davies, these deep personal feelings illustrated both the mingling simplicity and the
intricacy, like that to be observed in Gothic architecture, of
his nature.

Now he seemed only to make new friends, never new
enemies. Harold Monro, the poet, and then editor of *Poetry
and Drama,* was an old and valued friend of his — as, indeed,
of so many contemporary poets. Under Monro's auspices
Davies had met Epstein at the Poetry Bookshop, and the
sculptor had modeled the poet's head. The sittings had taken
place at Epstein's studio at 23 Guilford Street in 1916, and
in the course of these sessions a friendship had sprung up
between the two men. The bronze that resulted is perhaps
the best portrait extant of the poet, the only one that gives an
idea of the modeling of his face, the subtle planes round
temple and cheekbone and eye, and of his somber expression.[5]
Nina Hamnett introduced him to many people she thought
he would like, and I helped, too, to widen his circle. Siegfried
Sassoon he knew already (*he* was permitted to call Davies
"Bill"). But through my brother and myself he made the
acquaintance of Aldous Huxley, and also of Robert Nichols,
who at that period lived in a fine romantic frenzy of poetry
(I remember some years later, after Nichols returned from
Japan, going to see Davies, and his saying to me, "Robert
Nichols wants me to give him lessons in writing *sonnets.* . . .
But, you know, you can't *teach* a mun to write sonnets.")

It was through us, too, that Davies met his rival in shirt

[5] One of these bronze heads was presented to the Fine Art Gallery of
Newport, Wales, by the late Viscount Tredegar.

fronts, Arnold Bennett, who immediately appreciated his extraordinary character. I can still see Arnold laughing with delight at the things he said, and smacking his thigh as he tried to master his stammer and answer him. Then, too, there was Sickert, who, when I brought Davies to see him, was equally enchanted with him, and angry at not having met him before; he reproached me bitterly for it, and at once gave him a complete set of twenty or more etchings. When subsequently I said to the painter, knowing that at the time he was in financial straits, "How generous of you to give all those beautiful etchings to Davies!" he said, "What else could I do! . . . I never find anyone who understands a single thing I'm aiming at, and then you bring along an old tramp with a wooden leg, and he at once understands everything I've ever attempted!"

Davies hung these etchings on his wall, above the Epstein head, for he was very proud of them, as well he might be. Henceforth I used to meet him often at Sickert's studio, sometimes at that artist's breakfast parties which I have pictured with some elaboration in the last chapter. I recall that one day, when Sickert and I were walking down Fitzroy Street away from his studio, we met Davies and Aldous Huxley walking towards us, for they were coming to see the painter. Aldous looked very tall and young at the side of his elder companion. When we had advanced within greeting distance, Sickert remarked to me, but in a loud voice specially designed to reach them:

"Look! Here we have the comparative stature of Prose and Poetry!"

I do not think either of them — and Huxley regarded himself at that time mainly as a poet — much cared for this summing up.

It will be seen, notwithstanding, that if the entering upon so many fresh acquaintanceships at an age approaching fifty constituted in itself an excitement, it carried with it also its own cares. Davies now viewed himself more than ever in the light of a man-of-the-world, and I remember his confiding in me his plans for going away to stay with some new friends.

"I've got to buy a suitcase — but I know where to find a secondhand one, with lots of labels on it . . . *they expect that.*"

Though he used often to come to stay with my brother and me at Swan Walk, alas, he never treated us even to a glimpse of the labels, so that I still do not know whether they were English, European or world-wide in their scope.

Sometimes we would ask him to dine and sleep for a single night, but as a rule we would invite him from Friday to Monday, especially so that he could obtain at least some respite from his piano-playing Belgian neighbor, whom the end of every week seemed to drive to musical frenzy during the small hours. . . . Nina Hamnett was usually present at the dinner parties for Davies, and another friend of Davies's and our own, a young Icelandic playwright, Haraldur Hamar, known as "Iceland," in opposition to the name of a more celebrated friend of ours, the South American painter Alvaro Guevara, who was called "Chile." Hamar — a friend of Augustus John's, and an inmate of the Café Royal — was for many years a figure in the English Bohemian world. He was small and dark-haired, and his highly colored face carried with it a suggestion of the ventriloquist's dummy, though his wild and flaming green eyes gave the lie to such a conception of him. His plays were never produced, and he lived on a very meager allowance, often spending on drink the money he should have reserved for food. When cash came his way he was extremely lavish. On one occasion when somehow or other he was enjoying a windfall, I remember that he decided to buy a really smart suit. He asked my brother for the name of his tailor, and there chose the stuff. Next, he begged Sacheverell to help him by being present at the ensuing fitting. My brother accordingly accompanied him to Conduit Street; but the head cutter seemed to be very surprised when, on taking off his old clothes in order to try on the others, Iceland's vest and pants were found to consist entirely of newspapers pinned together. Alas, whenever he came to dine, the Norse tendency to strong liquor soon asserted itself, and as the correct ancient Norse procedure consisted in breaking a glass in order to bring good fortune, and because he was very kind and wished us good fortune, he would leave behind him a trail of broken glasses in the dining room — much to the dismay of Davies, who always minded an untoward occurrence more than his hosts. It was after dinner, too, that Iceland's mind inevitably occupied itself with a metaphysical problem: was it not possible to fix your likeness forever in a looking glass by applying, as you gazed at your own reflection in it, some substance to its surface? This preoccupation of his formed the germ of the very beautiful and moving poem by Sacheverell Sitwell which I reproduce at the end of this volume.[6]

By nature, Hamar was extremely generous. He never tried to borrow money from his friends, and much resented his inability to return their hospitality. Nevertheless, on one occasion he gave me a beautiful drawing by Nina Hamnett which he had bought from the artist; and on another he succeeded, indeed, in extending to me the most unusual and original invitation I have ever received. . . . During the First Great War, I was in bed, fast asleep, at three o'clock on a winter's morning — having gone to bed about eleven after a quiet evening — in my bedroom on the second floor of our house in Swan Walk. Dimly, through my deep slumber, I was perhaps conscious of some disturbance, of a hammering at the front door, far below. . . . Presently, however, my light was switched on, and my servant woke me up with the following announcement.

[6] See Appendix B, p. 343.

"Mr. Iceland's compliments, sir, and he's sent word round to say that he and Mr. Augustus John have broken into a cellar, and will you join them at once!" [7]

It will be seen from the above that Iceland was a good friend, and possessed character, but I think it was his plight —rather similar to that which formerly had been his own— his never knowing where the money for his next food or lodging was to come from, that aroused Davies's interest and pity. Though often angry with him, he continued to see him, and it distressed him, even, if one of Iceland's friends were to tell the young man plainly that his plays would never be produced.

When he came to stay with us, Davies always traveled the whole distance from Bloomsbury to Chelsea on foot, carrying a small bag — unlabeled. Sometimes Iceland, who cherished a tremendous admiration for the poet and had constituted himself at this time a sort of self-appointed bodyguard, accompanied Davies, but generally he arrived alone. He particularly loved to walk by the river from the Houses of Parliament as far as the Physic Garden, over which our house looked. No doubt, if his only real leg became tired, he took a short rest and refreshment at one of his favorite public houses on the way. The attraction to him of the Embankment, however, consisted in the contrast it offered between the warehouses and huge black factories opposite Pimlico, and the idyllic beauty of the neighboring Battersea Park which lay at dusk like a sleepy wood across the water. I suppose, though he loved London, that he always missed the country. . . . At any rate, I recall in this connection a small but a singularly impressive incident which occurred after dinner one hot summer evening in June or July. It was growing dark, and the dining-room windows were wide open. I noticed a sudden look of intentness on Davies's face, and he

[7] Mr. Augustus John tells me he was not present. But that is the message which reached me.

lifted a hand, and said, "Hush! . . . There's an owl!" Our
ears could not reach so far, but he had heard it right across
the river, from Battersea Park. He had then been a long time
in London without leaving, and in his expression was all the
lighted rapture of his countryman's soul — *countryman* is too
insufficient a word, and *tramp* too derogatory — with its memories of a long and intimate experience of fields and woods, of
sighing dawns and long, cool evenings trailing into black
night. . . .

But, though Davies loved these things, he loved, too, more
urban entertainments. In consequence, during these short
visits to us, besides organizing dinner parties of people whom
we knew he liked or thought he might be glad to meet, we
used often to take him to a music hall. Sometimes there would
be ten or twelve of us, sometimes only Davies and ourselves.
Usually we chose the Chelsea Palace, because it was the nearest to us of the theaters, the turns were not too sophisticated,
and the best seats cost only three and six, or half a crown.
Davies was as fond of this sort of performance as we were;
indeed his pleasure in it was so great that it was a source of
delight to his friends to watch his rapt and glowing face. Nor
could he bear to miss a single item of the program. Thus, on
one occasion, being annoyed at having been taken out before
he had enjoyed his full money's worth of turns, he subsequently confided to a friend his distress at my brother's and
my conduct, in the words:

"I'm worried about those two boys. You know, it isn't
the thing — they're so *extravagant*. They take seats for themselves and for me, and then they come in after the beginning
and leave before the end!"

I think, too, that his beautiful manners and almost exaggerated fear of hurting people's feelings may have entered
into this complaint; he feared that our going away early
would be noticed by the artistes, and might cause them distress.

One of the performances I remember extremely vividly; because the chief turn consisted of four performing elephants, and after the whole entertainment, when Davies and my brother and I were walking back to Swan Walk down Oakley Street, the elephants passed us. They were — for it was a dark night — marching in single file, and, by the simple expedient of each holding on with his trunk to the tail of the beast in front, they never lost touch. The stately procession merged into the murky obscurity, which itself, by the lowered lamps of the last war, seemed to be fashioned of elephant hide. It was a cold night, but perhaps the heat of the stage, or the natural nervousness of an artiste, had made them thirsty, for when we reached the Embankment the object of their pilgrimage became plain. The fountain near the opening to Church Street has four compartments filled with water, and each elephant set himself to drain one of these quarters, leaving no single drop behind. Davies was enchanted with the cleverness of the animals, and we became so interested in them that we followed them as far as their stables, which stood opposite Old Chelsea Church, and finally saw them put to bed.

After October 1918, in which year Diaghilev's Russian Ballet reappeared in London, we used often to take Davies to the Coliseum and, later, to the Alhambra. But though he immensely appreciated the art of this company, and especially delighted in such ballets as *The Good-Humoured Ladies*, nevertheless, at the Coliseum, where their performance occupied about a fourth of the whole program, he still showed himself very loath to miss any of the subsequent turns, however banal they might be.

Davies would also often go to visit my sister and Helen Rootham, who for many years shared a flat in Moscow Road, Bayswater. . . . Edith had met him for the first time when I took her to tea with him in Great Russell Street during the rationing days of the 1914 war. On that occasion he had given her an unusual greeting, saying, directly she entered his room:

"How d'you do? . . . You can have *one* cup of tea, but no more. . . ." After a pause, and in confirmation . . . "I shall be *glad* to give you one cup of tea."

In spite of the initial misunderstanding about the letter — which I have mentioned earlier — they had quickly become friends, and I remember his looking at her one night, when they were both dining with us, and saying — I repeat it because of the simple splendor of the phrase:

"Edith is always as fine as a queen."

And, much later, when she wrote to him to ask for permission to include a poem of his in an anthology, he replied, saying that he would leave it to her to choose which she liked; "You are always right about my poems," he added.

He used also to walk the whole way from Great Russell Street to Bayswater when he went to see Edith and Helen. Often he would not tell them he was coming, but, on arrival, in order to give them a pleasant surprise, he would hide behind the door and jump out at whichever of them happened to open it. He never doubted for an instant that his unexpected presence would gratify his friends, and — unlike the majority of men and women similarly sanguine — he was perfectly correct in his assumption.

It was impossible, as I have said, to know him at all and not at once to feel for him a special respect and affection. Further, it seemed natural to talk in front of him as though he were a lifelong friend of the family. For his part, he was extremely interested in the details of his friends' lives, and would often recur, when next he saw you, to what you had said the last time, however petty the matter might be, always beginning in a surprised, puzzled voice, with the words:

"I've been thinking of what you told me."

Thus, it may be that, in discussing before him small family troubles, we had indicated that my father was a man of unusual and determined character and far from tractable — even at times, in his own favorite phrase, *très difficile*. At any rate, Davies once said to my sister:

"I've been thinking of what you told me. . . . I wish I knew your father, Edith. I believe I should be able to talk him round."

Davies used frequently to attend my sister's tea parties, which took place every Saturday, in the two small sitting rooms of the flat. Here she and Helen fed their friends on strong black tea and glazed, delicious halfpenny buns that seemed for once to have retained the taste and luscious quality of the buns one ate as a child. Owing to the extraordinary mixture of the people she gathered together — relatives, old friends of my mother's, scared but tittering, who had never hitherto heard even the name of a poet, famous poets, schoolteachers, the most advanced musicians and painters, hunting men, doctors, philosophers, zoologists, economists, and one or two persons who seemed to exist for no other reason than that my sister was sorry for them — these afternoons became renowned for the incidents that they produced.

For example, Davies arrived rather late one afternoon, when the rooms were already full, and apologized, as he entered, in the somewhat unexpected words:

"I'm sorry to be late, Edith, but there were a lot of police about."

The relatives, the old friends of the family and the hunting men winced and cast an eager but timid eye beyond the door, at the collection of hats and umbrellas; it was what they had expected, the culmination whereunto this sort of company inexorably led.

Edith, however, herself not quite grasping his point, looked at him inquiringly, and he proceeded to elaborate it.

"You see, Oxford Street was full of them, so I had to come here by side streets."

His horror of the police was, no doubt, in essence the peculiar fear universally felt for them by the inmates of the doss house, by tramp and beggar and street singer. In Russia, it would be the aristocrat who would have to bolt down dark alleys: but here this fear of the police — which often, on the other hand, takes the form of snapping fingers and saying, "*I'm* not frightened of them!" — was still the dividing line between master and employer, bourgeois and proletariat. In Davies's case, moreover, an influence from his childhood served as the especial foundation for a terror that had been later intensified by the experience of many years as tramp and hawker. In his autobiography he relates how, as a schoolboy of fourteen in Newport, he formed a gang of youthful desperadoes, who made a practice of entering big shops and stealing things — cakes, confectionery of all sorts, books and even bottles of scent. One day, however, a member of the gang, in a large store, dropped a bottle of scent he had just stolen, and, losing his head, instead of pretending that he had knocked it over, made a dash for the door. At this the whole gang fled, pursued by a crowd shouting "Stop thief!" Davies says that this "terrible cry, taken up by one and another, took all the strength out of our legs, and our sheer terror brought us to a halt. In five minutes we were captured and crying over our ill luck in a prison cell." Subsequently Davies and his chief lieutenant were sentenced to twelve strokes each with the birch rod. . . . Thus did the policeman's shadows, as in the harlequinade, first impinge upon his life.

After Davies married[8] in 1925 he left London. The chief reason for this, he told us, incidentally, was the amount of unnecessary correspondence in which, if he were in London, he found himself involved: yet even towards this nuisance, which has been the bane of the lives of so many writers be-

[8] Mrs. Helen Payne, on December 29, 1925. . . . He had given up his rooms in Great Russell Street, and had lived latterly at 13 Avery Row, Brook Street, W. 1, in rooms which he rented from Olaf Baker, the Quaker poet. He first lived in the country at "Torleven," Cantelupe Road, East Grinstead.

fore and after him, he showed the intensely individual nature of his reactions. "I can't manage it, Edith," he said to my sister — "the postage comes to eight shillings a week." Accordingly, he settled first at East Grinstead, and later at Nailsworth in Gloucestershire. Here he was not far from Mrs. Gordon Woodhouse at Nether Lypiatt. When she heard he had come to reside in the neighborhood, she wrote, inviting him and his wife to luncheon. In reply, she received a letter [9] which opened with a simple, trumpetlike tone of self-assurance, "Only fancy two celebrities of our note living so close to each other and not knowing it!" . . . We saw little, alas, of Davies after he left London, except when we went to stay with Mrs. Gordon Woodhouse. On these occasions, however, she would always arrange for the Davieses to come to dinner, sending her motor over for them, or sometimes going to fetch them herself. And it was during one of these drives — the last time, I believe, on which he came to Lypiatt — that, in referring to the poem he had written to her, on first hearing her play now many years earlier — which I quote in the next chapter — he said (and I reproduce the remark only as an instance of his simple but justifiable pride, so different from self-glory or conceit):

"Well, I did do you well with that poem, didn't I?"

These dinner parties were usually composed of the same people, Violet and Gordon Woodhouse and Lord Barrington, and my sister and myself. And Davies was on his special Christian-name terms with all of us, except Violet, whose status was immutable.

Sometimes, in these later years, twelve months or more would have elapsed before I saw him again at Violet's, yet the skin strangeness that usually interposes itself between friends who have not met for a long time, the trying mutual adjustment of two atmospheres, which as a rule takes a day or two to accomplish, simply did not exist. He would talk as if we

[9] Headed Shenstone, Nailsworth, Glos., and dated August 31, 1931.

had met every day, asking after old friends, telling us of Jim, his pet toad whom he fed regularly with saucers of milk — and whom, according to Mrs. Davies, he "encouraged" — of what he had been writing, and of the trials to which he had been subjected as the result of the cruel overcharging by unworthy members of the medical profession in the neighborhood.

"Of course, I can pay," I remember him saying, apropos of this, "but it will spoil my Christmas."

Naturally I did not now hear so much of him, either, as when he was in London, but a friend told me that not long before, at Christmas, he had been invited to a party given by a rather bad artist who lived in the vicinity. One of his host's two sons, observing the expression on his face, came up to him and said:

"Are you bored?"

Davies, with his simplicity, replied, in a tone of agony, "*Oh, yes*, I am, I am! . . . But I'll stick it!"

The last time I saw him was at his own house, about a month after the collapse of France in 1940. He was too ill to come over to dine, so my dear hostess motored me over to his new home, "Glendower," to which he had moved not so long before. It was a lovely drive, through precipitously hilly country covered with hanging woods. I had not been in the English countryside since I had returned, about six weeks before, from Italy and the South of France, and it seemed to me that it had decked itself out in that particular glory with which it seems to oppose public or private misfortune. Never had leaves been more green or prosperous, woods more cool, or streams clearer. A narrow road, with a wonderful view over the long stone town, straggling along the river, wound up the steep side of the hill on which the house was situated. . . . We had been nervous that we might not be able to see Davies, for there had been no way of letting him or Mrs. Davies know that we were coming. However, we were fortu-

nate in finding them at home, and in the fact that he was out
of pain at the moment, and able to receive and talk to us.

I thought William looked very ill, but his head, so typical
of him in its rustic or nautical boldness, with the black hair
now graying a little, but stiff as ever, surrounding the high,
bony forehead, seemed to have acquired an even more fine
and sculptural quality. He was full that day of plans for his
garden — a small terraced garden that ran along the slopes
above the house and caught all the sunshine. Whilst he was
on the lawn, just outside the window, talking to Violet Gordon Woodhouse, and explaining what alterations they had
made, and what others they intended, I was able to ask Mrs.
Davies the nature of his illness. She told me that his heart was
ailing and showed alarming symptoms of weakness, and that
the doctors attributed its condition to the perpetual dragging
weight of his wooden leg which for so long he had been
obliged to carry; but he did not know how sick a man he was,
and imagined himself to be suffering from indigestion, as to
his face the doctors pretended his complaint to be. Moreover,
Mrs. Davies, with her solicitude for him, never allowed him to
realize the seriousness of his illness, for the consciousness of it
would only have afflicted him still further. In his gentle way,
he was already nervous about himself. When Mrs. Davies
took Violet Gordon Woodhouse up the hill to show her the
improvements, he talked to me of himself. And I can still
hear the puzzled tones of his voice, full of pathos, as he
said:

"I've never been ill before, really, except when I had that
accident and lost my leg. . . . And, d'you know, I grow so
irritable when I've got that pain, I can't bear the sound of
people's voices." And then, after an instant's pause, he added,
"Sometimes I feel I should like to turn over on my side and
die!"

I am sure, all the same, that he did not know he was going
to die. The rest of his talk was most cheerful and reassuring.

. . . I remember that he spoke of the growing expense of life, and added, rather grandiloquently:

"After the war, I may be forced to part with my collection."

By this he signified the Epstein bronze head and the set of etchings by Sickert, but he said it in a fashion which inevitably called to mind such other patrons as the Lords Hertford or Mr. Gulbenkian.

I asked to see Jim, the toad, but it was dead. . . . Then we went out to meet Violet Gordon Woodhouse and Mrs. Davies, who were coming back down the hill, and one of the party said what a pity it was that a house in front and a little below blocked part of the view, and Davies, I recall, told us how, some fifty years before he had come to live here, it had been built especially for that obstructive purpose by a spiteful neighbor, who, when he had finished his wicked work, dropped dead. As he related in considerable detail the story of this old feud, of which the four stout walls in front of us were still the solid materialization, bearing witness to it today, he contrived, because of his own simplicity and concern at the evil of the action, to invest the narrative with a palpitating Homeric interest that made every minute point in it as important as a similar incident in the *Odyssey*. Of this quality, he was, in conversation, the only living master, able to impart it to anything of which he spoke.

Alas, this was the final talk we were ever to enjoy with this extraordinary and memorable being, who, for all his humility, bore about him something of the primitive splendor and directness of the Elizabethan age; in which, as his appearance testified, he would have been equally at home. No one who knew him will, or ever could, forget him, even had he never written so many lovely poems, fresh and exquisite as flowers, to keep his memory alive; nor will anyone who knew him ever be able to recall him without a smile of pleasure and regret, without tenderness, and without gratitude for a character that was no less remarkable in itself than in the genius it

supported and nourished, and of which even the little blem-
ishes and flaws were singularly endearing. I had one more
letter from him. But he died on September 26, 1940, when I
was at Renishaw. Gordon Woodhouse and Lord Barrington
went over from Lypiatt to attend his funeral. Owing to the
difficulties of the time, they were the only two persons present,
besides the widow and members of the family, at the obsequies
of this man of genius.

CHAPTER IX

Violet Gordon Woodhouse

MRS GORDON WOODHOUSE! . . . Violet Gordon Woodhouse. . . . The reader of this history of my life is already familiar with the name, which has sounded out, like a theme, throughout its pages. In the course of my days I have consorted more with original artists than with executants, but of the latter Violet was both the most exceptional and the one I knew best. It is true that by the range of understanding she exhibited in her art, she ranked also as a creator, and that she herself had at times composed, but these works, remarkable though several of them were, have vanished, and only one little song, written in 1894, is still in existence. So that it is as a performer that she must be considered, and because the echoes of even the greatest music die, at any rate to our ears, it is all the more necessary that some testimony to her and her powers should be compiled, and accordingly I record my evidence. Her personality and the taste through which she expressed it, and of which I shall have more to say later, were so strong that I believe I could anywhere immediately recognize an object she had chosen: just as, now that she is dead, every time I pass through the hall here at Renishaw, where I write, and see, lying on an oak chest, a scarf she gave me, the very first glimpse of it, so typical in its colors and weftage of her individual choice, strong and evocative as a perfume, at once administers to me the shock both of her magic and of the fact that she has gone, and kindles in my heart an immense personal regret, not in any way lessened by the fact that I have

[272]

known only two women of genius, and that she was one of them.

Part of her genius consisted no doubt in the assurance wherewith she had found her medium and made it her own, taking to it as a swan to water. Indeed her instruments suited so well her personal style that it seemed by the very look of her seated before one of them as if she had been created to play them. Obversely, in other hands they might have been obsolete, and they, perhaps, needed her too, great virtuoso that she was, to shape once again the vehicle of pure music. . . . There was no special reason, I think, in her background to account for her great gift. She came of the well-known Sussex family of Gwynne of Folkington, which has produced inventors and great engineers, and both men and women of character and distinction. Her father had no musical interest, and her mother sang sweetly, but in the convention of Victorian after-dinner singers. Violet, however, had been taught music from her earliest years, and during the two or three months every year that the Gwynnes spent in London, she was taken regularly to concerts and to the opera. From 1888 to 1900, her music teachers were first, Oscar Berrenger and then Schönberger and in 1890, Arnold Dolmetsch, the most celebrated maker of both harpsichord and clavichord, and the most notable advocate of them as against their supplanter, induced her to adopt the harpsichord [1] instead of the piano. (In her musical life she was most deeply influenced by him, by Ethel Smyth, and by Rubio, to whom we will recur later.) In the decade between 1920 and 1930, she in her turn exercised a profound influence on Dolmetsch, by persuading him to create the small clavichord that is now the only type made. Subsequently, my friend Thomas Goff began to design his unrivaled instruments, and it belonged to the magic that sur-

[1] The harpsichord on which Violet Gordon Woodhouse learned is now in the possession of Lady Headlam, of Holywell, Durham, and is in full working order.

rounded her character and playing, that an age, so poor in this kind of music, should have matched in quality with their great exponent, the maker of these at one time almost extinct instruments. Almost extinct, I write, yet, though the mention of ancient instruments might to some minds carry the suggestion of a certain preciosity, she completely rid them of this peril: her fire burned their rind away, and revealed the flaming core of all music. In her art, as in all else, she was surprising, because, rooted in the past, it flowered in the future, and knew no present tense. Her playing of Bach upon the harpsichord pointed a way beyond the contemporary schools of cold, competent pianists let loose, like so many correct and inharmonious blacksmiths, in a boiler foundry.

Though, in a sense, as we shall see, for a great executant she led a very private life, sheltered by devoted friends, yet her span had been full of people as well as music, and she had met in it — ever since that evening in 1879 when, as a child, she had first encountered a genius, and had sat on Sarah Bernhardt's knee after a charity performance in the St. James's Hall — many persons of most unusual gifts. . . . I will therefore prelude my more detailed portrait with a sketch of her sitting side by side with another genius, but of a very different order, will try to give some impression of an afternoon when she played the clavichord to Bernard Shaw, for he seems to offer to her, even physically and in the texture of his clothing, a great contrast. Besides, though the meeting took place in one of the last years of her life, and under the shadow of the Second World War, it was typical of delights that could only be tasted in her house — or rather, flat, for in this instance the scene is pitched on a wide upper floor in Mount Street, on an afternoon of late autumn; to be precise, at about 3:45 on November 20, 1943. . . . Both my hostess and I shared a tremendous admiration for Shaw, and for the courage of his attitude towards the war, but, as it happened, she did not at first invite me on the day in question, for she thought I was still away in the country, working at the first volume of my autobiography. The occasion had been brought about by her saying to my brother that she would play for him, and then, on being told by her friend Miss Emery Walker that Shaw wanted to hear her once more, by her writing to him suggesting that he should come to Mount Street at a quarter to four on the day that Sacheverell was going to be there, and offering to play the clavichord for him for an hour until tea, so that he could return home before it was dark. The answer came on a postcard:

Sachie and the clavichord will do me nicely. G. B. S.

Subsequently, Violet had learned that I was in London and had asked me to join them. . . . I made my appearance at the flat punctually at 3:45, to find Miss Emery Walker at the window, watching for Shaw in the direction of Berkeley Square — for, at the age of eighty-seven, he had announced his intention of arriving on foot from his flat in Whitehall Court, situated some two miles away on the Thames Embankment, and she wanted to be ready to meet him at the door. . . . A moment or two later, tall and straight as a tower, he could be seen striding buoyantly along the empty street below. . . . In a few moments he had entered the flat, and at once his full, Irish voice, speaking with its multitude of inflections mirroring the emotions of conversation, poured into the room its resonance, bringing with it a tremendous sense of personal energy. Except when being played to, he talked the whole time. Almost as soon as he arrived, I remember that someone — perhaps I myself — mentioned to him the raids, for bombing was reaching its climax, and Shaw remarked:

"I hate all this destruction. Every time a bomb falls on Berlin or London it kills a number of young Europeans: a fact which, as an old European, I deplore."

But he scarcely looked an *old* European, and I recall that — for I had not seen him since the death, a year previously, of

Mrs. Shaw, whose long illness I knew him to have felt deeply
— when I said how glad I was to see him plainly in such good
health, he replied:

"At my age you are either well or dead. I have passed
through my second childhood and got a sort of second wind
as a widower. I never felt my wife's long illness as a weight
to be carried; but when it suddenly lifted, there may have
been some unconscious relief; for I used to say that every
death is a relief to the survivors. But I have never grieved
since I was a small child, and then for half an hour only. And
as to loneliness I have my mother's love of solitude."

After this, he began to talk to his hostess of music, and then
— perhaps recalling that my father had died, too, a few months
earlier, and that he had not seen me since that event — broke
off in what he was saying, turned to me and inquired, in a manner that suggested it was a question he had long intended to
ask me:

"*Was Sir George Sitwell a nice father?*"

The question took my by surprise; and I shot out a thunder-
ing NO which was a pure reflex. When I recovered I softened
it with the hackneyed phrase, *Yes and No;* but it was too late:
I had given myself and my father away irrecoverably. Readers of my autobiography will understand.

When Violet Gordon Woodhouse was about to begin,
Shaw would not sit in the armchair that she, with her usual
grace and quickness of movement, had pulled for him near
her and the clavichord. . . . Instead, he chose a chair with a
long, stiff back, and sat very upright in it, and almost touching
the instrument, while she played Bach and Scarlatti to him. I
was placed next to him, and took the opportunity, while he
was intently listening, to examine him very closely. I noticed
in particular the fineness of his hands, which, albeit they
afforded an impression of being powerful, had long fingers and
delicately shaped oval nails. His eyes watched the keyboard,
and his long bearded face had assumed an expression of both

solemnity and of mockery, if this be not a contradiction in terms, as well as of that benevolence which the giant classical masters never fail to summon up in the hearts of all lovers of music. . . . I did not think that this great man, about whose genius I have elsewhere in the course of my autobiography declared my unequivocal opinion, appeared to be any older: he might still have passed for a man of sixty, though his hair and beard had grown a little whiter and he was certainly thinner. But this last change in some respect made him actually look younger: in the manner, for example, in which the joints of his knees and elbows showed more than formerly. And undoubtedly with every passing year he became more, rather than less, Irish, until now his whole appearance proclaimed him to be what he was by descent: an Irish gentleman — or, as he prefers to call it, an Irish downstart.

When Mrs. Gordon Woodhouse stopped playing, we had tea and Shaw began once more to talk. Now he would not speak of the war, but confined himself to telling us of Sir Edward Elgar, and of how the famous English composer had liked to play, over and over again, the gramophone records made by Cicely Courtneidge and Jack Hulbert, alleging that in them he found the secret of the perfect use of rhythm. . . . He asked me, too, I remember, what I knew of the Comma of Pythagoras, and when I admitted my ignorance in the matter, added that he himself had not the slightest idea of its nature, but that he had found it was easy to obtain in musical circles a high reputation for learning by, from time to time, sprinkling the talk with this phrase: he offered me this information as a handy tip, and advised me to make use of it.

At 5:30, after eating two pieces of toast and butter, he set off again on foot for home. It was dusk now, but though there was an almost complete blackout, and he had brought no torch, he insisted on returning alone, as he had come, and we could only watch him walking away into the darkness.

While Violet Gordon Woodhouse was playing to us, I had

[277   ]

been able to observe her as well as Shaw. As usual, I had
admired the elegance of her carriage, as she sat there, and
marveled at the strength and nimble swiftness of her small
hands. The roughness and pale tones of Shaw's clothes —
though, contrary to public opinion, they are always of fine
quality — contrasted with the dark sepias and blacks of the
velvets she was wearing. Her small size and lightness of frame
made him seem even larger and more robust, for all his thin-
ness. He in his presence seemed a summary of droll and
startling common sense, a robust epitome of the ludicrous
unreason of reason, yet like the great comic dramatists of
earlier ages like Aristophanes, for example, he belonged to the
air and earth: whereas, if the basis and substance of each
body were an element, hers was fire, all fire. This was the
very essence of her aspect, of her moods. She was a phoenix;
and a phoenix is in private life no very easy subject for a portrait. To a writer, the difficulty and, at the same time, the great
attraction of attempting to pin down such an appearance, and
of trying to focus for the reader the character that animated
it, is precisely the same problem that fascinated certain painters, among whom were El Greco and Tintoretto, when they
occupied themselves with the rendering on canvas of flames.
Her fragile mold, young, as I must continually emphasize, with
some kind of magic, even when she should have looked old —
the same kind of magic, indeed, that emanated from her whole
personality — provided the appropriate vessel for this fire, and
resembled its smoke. Light, elegant and supple in the way
she moved, she walked very rapidly, talking at the same time
eagerly and spontaneously as a child, for her mind kept pace
with her step. An unusual gaiety that quelled and overran
the opposite strain of melancholy in her nature animated her
conversation and actions, except when, on rare occasions, the
smoke veiled the fire and some somber mood laden with mortality would descend upon her, causing her dark eyes to
smolder sullenly; for illness and death were two things of

which, with her unquenchable flame, she could not bear to
be reminded. Her vital fire appeared, indeed, to have halted
old age itself, and during the thirty years of our friendship she
never changed, but remained a young woman until the last
years of her life. The only alteration visible in her was that
her hair had turned white, and she had in consequence become
a young woman with white, instead of black hair. Her laugh
remained happy and casual, and her voice was strong and
beautiful as that of a bird, able effortlessly to raise itself above
the level of the talk if she wished to make herself heard, yet
without any increase apparent in its volume, so that no one
would ever have heard her shout. Fire was in her speech too.
In fine, in everything she looked or did or said, this element
burned. Yet her voice also a little resembled that of a child,
and her character, though far from simple, held something in
it of a child's simplicity and power to be swept by primitive
emotions; loving, hating, stubborn, beautiful, impulsive, generous and sometimes perverse, she followed her own way, uninfluenced by opinion, and clung to her own ideas with all a
child's obstinacy: because she formed and formulated them
with her heart and not with her head. Her heart, however,
was truly Christian, and compassionate in its original meaning;
she felt the sorrows and misfortunes of her friends, or of those,
even, whom she had met casually and liked, with real passion.

It was, in fact, through my sense of this quality in her, and
through my being able to respond to it, that we became
friends after our very first meeting. This had taken place at her
house, in late July, 1917, at the southwest corner of Ovington
Square. Here, in a large, finely proportioned room which
had once been Bartolozzi's studio, she played, when in London, every Sunday during the 1914–1918 war to a crowd of
friends and musicians. . . . I shall never forget the impact of
the atmosphere, so unlike any other I had known — warm, and
full of gaiety, beauty and, at times, a faint, luminous sadness:
still less is there likely to pass from my memory the shock of

the whole new world that her playing revealed. Never, for example, until that instant, had I realized the greatness of the harpsichord as a vehicle, neither the immensity nor the grandeur its sound possessed. Her surroundings, too, the furnishings of the room with their dark surfaces licked by flames, impressed me by their strangeness. On the Sunday in question, though, I was no less overwhelmed by the splendor of her playing than conscious also of the fact, underneath the surface, that she was suffering, and I realized a little later how almost unbearably distressed she was at the news that had come to her in the past few days that the War Office had announced Denis Tollemache — a great friend of hers, and a kinsman of mine, though I had never hitherto met him — as missing. I determined to try to be of some help in the matter, and fortunately through the good offices of Lord Carisbrooke, and the kindness of his brother-in-law, King Alfonso, I was able to obtain for her very soon the news that Denis Tollemache was alive, and a prisoner of war at Freiburg. Thereafter she always reserved for me a specially cordial welcome, being grateful to me for what I had done — since the thought of anyone dear to her being in bodily or mental pain was intolerable to her, and could induce in her anger as easily as sorrow. Her moods were swift, ardent and unpredictable. And there were moments, I suspect, when she could have set fire to the world with her rage, just as, at other times, I have seen her make it glow with gaiety and affection, or make it blaze with great comfortable fires to warm those near her.

We must return now in more detail to the matter of her appearance and address, because they were so pre-eminently the sheath of her spirit. She was as different from others in person as in the character of her talent. She might have belonged to a nation of her own, which in a sense she did: to that legendary nation of human genius, of all epochs, who, in their whole sum, form so noble and rare a race. . . . If, then, you were a friend of hers, her face would lighten directly you entered the room — for she was adept at welcome — and she would rise from her chair and would seize your hand and race you off into another room, to show you some treasure she had been recently given by one of the many persons who loved and admired her: some object that had lately — perhaps for a whole week — captured her imagination, a book, a carving, a lacquer box, an ancient toy, a china figure, a fish of supple silver scales from Mesopotamia, or a bracelet, jeweled and enameled, that represented a snake, from India; always something with its own peculiar and elusive beauty, which she had, as a rule, first perceived and which she alone could have brought out for others. If she gave a friend a present — and this must have happened every day, for she was generous beyond the dreary bounds of common sense — it would be completely individual, so true to her being as to seem part of herself. Everything about her was homogeneous: her looks, her possessions, the way in which she dressed, for example, in smoky garments, mottled, dark but never funereal, satins and silks with many points of light, flecks of scarlet — flashes of the flame. All these attributes were natural to her, and could have found their expression through no other personality. In flowers her taste would perhaps have been summed up in the fritillary, with its dapplings and checkered snakeskin pattern, except that this plant lacks the gleam of fire. Her fastidious personal elegance, exemplified in this range of color, was intensely feminine, like that of some velvety dark moth, queen of the summer night, sailing, with its sable richness, its subtle markings of ivory and dove gray and fawn, and its almost hidden gleams of orange and scarlet, into a room, there to perfume the whole air: but, unlike that winged creature, she was intensely warm-blooded, created fire, had been born to arouse affection and love.

Her houses, too, resembled her dress and adornments in their style and coloring (even the food she offered you in them was deliciously unlike that you ate elsewhere — a fact

[281]

due chiefly, no doubt, to the hospitable and epicurean care of
Gordon Woodhouse). Though during the time I knew her
she several times changed her place of residence in London —
first from Ovington to Brompton Square, then to Porchester
Terrace, and finally to the flat in Mount Street — yet these
houses, albeit they varied in size and situation, remained in
their essence the same. Always they were hers recognizably,
even apart from the sight of the several harpsichords or clavi-
chords, impressive or elegant objects in themselves, though
usually clad against the cold in thick rugs — all except the
most beautiful in tone of her instruments, a small clavichord
by Thomas Goff that always stood, covered with an Indian or
a Paisley shawl, in the corner of the drawing room. These
rooms were full of her pervasive but intangible influence, the
same colors and glints and gleams of fire, the same feeling
for the texture of objects and materials, the same books in
fine old editions — which she so greatly loved, continually
reading aloud with an infectious enthusiasm her favorite passages in them, or calling to one to look at the illustrations —
the same kind of feathery flowers in the same great Dutch
bouquets, standing formally in vases, each blossom glowing,
because of the way it was arranged, with its own peculiar
value, the same unquenchable hospitality, the same unique but
familiar pattern of gaiety, of new finds in the art of life, and of
treats for others, the same warmth and the same incomparable,
almost indefinable, charm and fascination. And whether she
was in London or in the country, you would always notice in
her rooms one or two of the beautiful carvings in wood of her
friend and neighbor William Simmonds, whose work she so
greatly admired.

She had owned, since she married, several country houses:
first, from 1900 to 1908 she lived at Southover Grange, near
Lewes; then, until 1923, at Armscote House, near Stratford-
on-Avon. These I never saw; but in 1923 she, Gordon and
Lord Barrington, their lifelong friend, moved to Nether

Lypiatt Manor, a tall William-and-Mary house, built of stone, the color of a guinea fowl's plumage, and standing on the top of a steep hill near Stroud, and above the valley of the Severn. This old palace in miniature — for such, with its complex architectural organization of iron grille and of gardens and outhouses as formal as a fugue by Bach, it seemed — constituted a perfect setting for her. Beyond the world of music stood the farm, conducted by Lord Barrington, and the orchards and kitchen gardens, presided over by Gordon Woodhouse. These factors helped to tinge the general atmosphere with a sense of the unvarying English traditional background; orchard and farm and potting shed overflowed, as it were, into the lower story of the house, into the more masculine rooms, comfortable studies and smoking rooms, where, among the pieces of solid 1790 or 1800 mahogany and well-worn carpets and chairs, had strayed baskets of apples and pears, shallow wicker trays of walnuts, even, occasionally, vegetables — a turnip or a carrot — roots of flowers, a piece of bass, so that by the contents of the room, even coming out of a trance in a vacuum, you could judge of the season outside by these traces of the earth's fruits dropped from the cornucopia of some English Goddess of Plenty. The rooms above, superbly paneled and richly colored, seemed always to be filled with sun — though I thought, sometimes, with the vanished sun of another age, which glowed also upon the garden. With its high yew hedges and stone walls, with its exquisite dark-toned flowers — for example, bergamot, *moisia* roses, columbines in various shades of night and flowing water, and among the shrubs a honey-scented *ceanothus*, the spicy blossom of which was the color of Violet's hair, and another that was hung with shapes like small red lanterns — it provided endless pleasures for hostess and guests. Here, before going upstairs to the drawing room to practice, she would walk, straight and supple, swift as a wind, round the confines, so as to breathe the sharp hilly air; or she might take you to see the tomb of the horse of Judge Coxe (who had caused the house to be built); an animal whose specter is said to haunt the place, so that the clatter of his hoofs is heard on Christmas Eve, or obversely he is seen galloping soundlessly through the wood, where, at the top of the hill, rises the gray stone obelisk under which he lies buried, and on the base whereof, to relieve you from being worried by the phantom, you are supposed to deposit a copper or two; or to see her feed the Italian green lizards that would flash with emerald fire as they flickered at her out of the interstices of the loose gray walls in which they lived, beneath the green grass terraces. Or, again, she might run you at great speed to feed with sugar Cupid, a young and most handsome Herefordshire bull that might have been drawn by William Blake. (So impulsive in her generosity was she to all living things that once when, on a dark and cheerless day of winter, a guest asked "Where is Violet?", a witty friend Norah Lindsay, who was also staying in the house, replied, "Oh, she's out buttering the lawns for the birds!") There would, when you stayed with her, be picnics too, or motor drives to places she had discovered for some particular charm: to Bath, so that she could buy presents for her friends; to Lydiard Tregoze, to see the tombs of members of the St. John family in the church, or to that singular Oriental vision, Sezincote, which first provided the theme on which King George IV and his band of landscapists and architects had founded the variations that became the Royal Pavilion at Brighton. . . . Often, however, Violet would stay for days within the bounds of her house and garden, or would only go beyond them to take walks, long but wind-swift, over the steepest hills, for the beauty of Nether Lypiatt ever delighted her; and I recall how, as she lay ill in London, almost within the casting of Death's shadow, she told me, with a special and lovely rapture in her voice, of the sort of enchantment its aspect bore during what proved to be her last stay there, three months before, in the peachlike glow of a fine September.

Her musical life, however, naturally centered in London, which she greatly loved. It was there that she liked to receive her friends and to play to them: for, since she realized to the full the nature of her medium and the capacities of her instruments, and that they had been intended, when they were the musical expression of their day, to be heard in rooms — in palace rooms and chambers, it may be, but not in concert halls, for which they had never been designed — she preferred to play in her home rather than to give concerts; more particularly because clavichord and harpsichord are both so sensitive to change of atmosphere and temperature. (Indeed, if she gave a concert or traveled, Mr. Henry Tull always went with her, to tune her instruments.) The fact, however, that she disliked playing in large public halls may have persuaded the unmusical, and those who borrow their ears from others, to underrate her tremendous gift, because their stereotyped minds insisted on hearing only what they had come to hear, the quaint music of vanished ages, faded and related to folk art. But though Violet Gordon Woodhouse so well understood humble things and simple people, her technique was essentially aristocratic. Even the English folk tunes, to which, by her unrivaled sense of rhythm, she gave a new and living force, never built round one cottage walls, but instead revealed landscapes by the great English masters. I apprehend, too, that the apparatus of beauty and private luxury by which she was surrounded rendered those who regard art as an iron ration, unpleasing in itself, and only to be taken in times of national emergency, dismayed and a little angry; as, too, did the fact that she was so well guarded against the world's buffetings, not only by a circle of devoted friends, almost by a court, but by those who lived in the house with her, or were always in it or near it: Gordon Woodhouse, Lord Barrington, Denis Tollemache, and in former years Max Labouchère.[2] Yet it proved

[2] He was wounded and taken prisoner in March 1918, and died the following month.

impossible to blunt that extra sensitiveness of the artist, which in so high a degree she manifested, even though the hard corners were softened by the loving affection of those about her. . . . Nevertheless, the company of these friends, and the work of her several devoted servants, all went to build up this atmosphere that I have tried to describe, and which she, of course, dominated by her presence.

Here in London, people were brought in flocks to hear her play, and the members of her domestic circle were often hard put to it to dissuade her from expending her every ounce of energy: but she and Gordon continued to be endlessly hospitable. . . . Though on occasion, when her audience, basing anticipation on previous experience, confidently expected her to perform for an hour, she would, on the contrary, and very probably because she happened to have taken a dislike to someone who had been brought into the room, sit down, give one short piece, and then jump up from her chair and shut the instrument, clavichord or harpsichord, very deliberately and with an air of utter finality (indeed, at these times her face would wear a look of such irremediable obstinacy that it would take a hardy person, or one who did not know her, to ask her to continue); yet I have known her equally to play for an entire afternoon and evening, pouring out her treasures because she enjoyed it, even though people unworthy of her art were present. Her taste was eclectic in music as in persons. In the same way that her rendering of early English music showed the utmost love and understanding, so in the great preludes and fugues of Bach she evoked their portentous grandeur in a manner to be obtained by no other executant on no other instrument. Again, in her rendering on the clavichord of Scarlatti's compositions — many of which, now that, alas, she is dead, may never be heard again — it was possible to detect the thousand contemporary and living sounds of the streets of such southern cities as Lisbon, Seville and Naples: castanets, bells and bird songs; sounds which, as Sacheverell

Sitwell first pointed out in his *Scarlatti and His Times*, contributed so largely to that composer's music. Of Mozart she
was a perfect exponent, and she loved, in comparatively
modern music, the work of Wagner and Debussy, and of Delius. (He, like Vaughan Williams, Percy Grainger and Ethel
Smyth, wrote or arranged a piece for her.) I have heard her,
when the mood took her, play on the clavichord fragments of
Mendelssohn, and dances by Béla Bartók, and on the harpsichord two dances by Gounod, and even waltzes by Kreisler;
compositions most unsuitable to this medium, a purist would
have pronounced, which she yet made to warm the heart and
to glitter in a fashion unparalleled.

As for her manner and execution, no one who played on
these instruments approached her in technical skill or comprehension of their purpose, nor in her spirited and precise
seizing of rhythm. After her death, a friend aptly wrote of
"the gypsy rhythm in her wrists": and this, I think, she derived in part from her own being, in part from the example
of the great Spanish instrumentalists; especially from the advice of Rubio,[3] who was perpetually praising her, and urging
to fresh efforts, or criticizing unsparingly the way in which
she had formulated some phrase. (No one asked him for this
advice, but without stint he gave it.) . . . She had known
many Spaniards, to whom by temperament she showed a
natural affinity — indeed, her mother's grandmother was said
to have hailed from Spain — and her playing seemed to hold
for them, on their part, a special attraction. She had met Sarasate, being taken to meet him in Arbos's rooms in Savile Row
in 1893 or 1894 by his only English pupil, Nettie Carpenter.
Arbos and Casals were frequent visitors to her house before
the 1914 war, as later was Segovia. Other Spaniards were continually being brought by Rubio to hear her play. (I remember
well in 1917 and 1918, for example, a Spanish Basque monk,
Brother Elizondo,[4] who used to attend nearly every time she

[3] See *Left Hand, Right Hand!* pp. 234, 235.
[4] He was later killed in a motor accident near San Sebastian.

[287]

played and greatly influenced her. And the presence of the Spanish contingent, together with old Rubio's vociferous but sibilant ejaculations (for though he had lived in this country thirty years, his confident English lapsed with every other word into guttural Spanish sounds which could not be interpreted, and he still retained in it the lisp of the Emperor Charles V), tinged the afternoon with that vivid and indestructible quality belonging to all things Iberian, and canceled out the occasional polite ineptitudes of assembled English music lovers.

Though the slightest deviation from the ideal he had conceived of how Violet *should* play prelude or fugue would make Rubio furiously angry, he nevertheless particularly reveled in her playing of Bach. And, in all truth, it was a great musical experience. Under her hands the harpsichord, as I have said, was no small and ancient instrument, but a whole young orchestra in sound. The great and vibrant chords came rolling out with that exactness of rhythm, vivacity and deep musical comprehension that distinguished her above all executants, save such another artist as Paderewski. All this beauty, however, that she dispensed with such lavishness and apparent ease, was, notwithstanding, founded on the discipline won by the hardest work. In the long span of our friendship, albeit Sacheverell and I owe her countless hours of enchantment — sometimes just because we were in her company, at others, because she played for us — yet no single occasion have I enjoyed more than that of which I will now tell. . . . I was staying at Nether Lypiatt, and one morning I happened to be sitting in a corner of the drawing room, when Violet came down. Fortunately, she had not observed me. She opened the harpsichord, raised the top of it, lifting it open, pegged it — all this time I stood motionless — and proceeded to sit down and practice. So intent was she on the job before her, that of phrasing and rephrasing a fugue of Bach's over and over again, that I was able to remain, enthralled, in the room for over an hour while she engaged in an astounding personal combat. I have never been more interested than in this process of wrestling with an angel audible, if invisible; a struggle to which she perpetually reverted, renewing the attack from a different angle, and not ceasing until she had achieved a victory whereby she had mastered every thought and feeling that the greatest of European composers had expressed within the strictest bounds of his art.

Many incidents in connection with Violet and her guests rise in my mind as I write — some of them enchanting, others absurd: for she carried with her a small world, subject to its own laws, and rich in its own kind of occurrence. . . . One incident which always greatly amused her, and which, there-fore, I select to relate, took place when Picasso was brought to hear her play in the late 'twenties. . . . Her own taste in furniture and painting was so individual and unaffected by the mode, either general or particular, that some of her friends who were, in an esthetic sense, fashionably minded were from time to time inclined to try to persuade her to let her decora-tive inclinations run on lines more approved by the *cogno-scenti*. Then as now, they adored Picasso, and for several days before he arrived, one lady who was an old friend of Violet's came to implore her to remove from her walls certain pictures. These hung in a small room through which he would have to pass. She had bought them from an old gentleman, who devoted that part of his time left to him from his study of the Gothic ages to a portrayal, in pure, bright, almost encaustic tones of paint, of sailing ships in full rig against a flat sea, covered, like a head with curls, with conventional foam-tipped waves. But Violet was not to be persuaded, for she had pur-chased these strange creations because she rather liked them, and because she liked also and wanted to help the old antiquary artist who had executed them. Her friend represented to her that they were bound to horrify Picasso, to such an extent that probably he just would not stand for it and would leave the

house directly he saw them. . . . But when the day arrived,
and with it the great painter, on the contrary, the moment he
saw them he had eyes for nothing else. Continually he went
back to look at them once more. Eclectic as he is in his genius,
he doubtless perceived in them some original vein that had not
yet been exploited, some vision he had not yet essayed. Finally
he offered, slap-out, in front of everyone, to buy them!
In the result, Violet's crestfallen friend and the gang who
supported her esthetic opinion had completely to reverse
their views, and to express enthusiastic admiration of these
works.

Picasso was only one among many eminent men and
women: for though, as I have suggested, Violet Gordon
Woodhouse at moments indulged audiences which were not
entirely discriminating, there can yet have been few music-
loving artists and writers, and still fewer musicians, who did
not at some time go to her house. Rodin had, for example,
come over specially from Paris to be present one afternoon
when she played at her then London home, 9 Park Place.
Delius was a friend, and dined with the Woodhouses the night
before he first conducted *Koanga* in England, at the St.
James's Hall. Madame Adelina Patti was an old friend, for Mr.
Gwynne's was the only English house to which the great diva
ever went, and whenever Madame Patti was in London between 1890 and the time of her death, Violet Gordon Woodhouse would always be sent for to play to her in her private
suite at the hotel where she stayed. Ellen Terry, Bruno Walter, Sir Henry Wood, Rachmaninoff, Diaghilev, Stravinsky,
de Falla, Karsavina and Madame Blanche Marchesi were
others — names chosen at random — to whom she played. My
brother and I were continually to be found in the house, and
took many writers to hear her; my sister was also often there,
and on several occasions Violet Gordon Woodhouse brought
round a clavichord to Carlyle Square, or to my sister's club in
London, and played it there to us and our friends. Violet also

used regularly for many years before the 1939 war — and this is an honor of which I am greatly proud — to transport, on December the sixth, my birthday, a clavichord to the house in South Street of Lady Aberconway (who always gave me a luncheon on that day), and afterwards Violet would play to a group of our friends in order formally to celebrate the occasion.

Among those whom my brother and I took at various times to hear this great artist play were T. S. Eliot, Bernard van Dieren, Wilfred Owen, Aldous Huxley, Arthur Waley, Ezra Pound, Robert Graves, Robert Nichols and Siegfried Sassoon. In the last two years of the 1914 war, when W. H. Davies used to come to stay with my brother and me from Saturday to Monday in Swan Walk, as I have described, we always used to conduct him to Ovington Square about four o'clock on Sunday afternoon; one of us, tall and clad in the Brigade of Guards gray greatcoat, with brass buttons, striding along on either side of his smaller, but thick-set, figure, with its dipping gait. Being a genius herself, Violet Gordon Woodhouse of course identified, on her very first meeting with the other extraordinary and fascinating individual, the same quality, the identical power of seeing beyond the mountain ranges and molehills that hedge us in, that he equally recognized at once in her. Because of this, perhaps, they soon became fast friends, and Richard Church has mentioned to me Davies's description of his visits, of how vividly Davies told him, with the Welsh lilt and accentuation of his speech, and with his way of softening all *a* sounds, of the "rupture," as he pronounced it, that he had felt when he heard the harpsichord, and of Mrs. Gordon Woodhouse, who in spite of her ability was good and charming and "not like a really educated lady." One of the results of these visits was that Davies wrote and dedicated to her the beautiful poem with which I end this portrait. He brought it to her with the true words, "A woman like you should live forever!"

ON HEARING MRS. WOODHOUSE PLAY
THE HARPSICHORD

We poets pride ourselves on what
  We feel, and not what we achieve;
The world may call our children fools,
  Enough for us that we conceive.
A little wren that loves the grass
Can be as proud as any lark
  That tumbles in a cloudless sky,
Up near the sun, till he becomes
  The apple of that shining eye.

So, lady, I would never dare
  To hear your music ev'ry day;
With those great bursts that send my nerves
  In waves to pound my heart away;
And those small notes that run like mice
Bewitched by light; else on those keys —
  My tombs of song — you should engrave:
"My music, stronger than his own,
  Has made this poet my dumb slave."

CHAPTER X

Rex Whistler

REX WHISTLER! . . . To those who knew him the name *Rex* could signify only one person: a young man of great and lovable character, and possessed of such various talents in the arts and decoration as in their sum to approach genius; talents that were very high in quality, and innate, no less than cultivated through a sound intelligence and an exquisite sensibility. . . . At the very mention of his name, after this interval of five years, anger at the waste in war of so valuable and irreplaceable a life is the first emotion to be experienced, and then a thousand meetings with him and glimpses of him surge up in the memory: Rex on a sun-spangled spring morning that had somehow strayed into the fold of autumn, when he took the part of a shepherd in a scene after Watteau that was filmed among cows and sheep on the little hills above the water meadows at Wilsford; Rex, up ladders, painting walls at the Tate, at Lympe, at Brompton Oratory (to see him engaged in such work was itself a diversion for onlookers, and an endless source of delight: for one idea would succeed to another with a rush and, without suffering the regrets that a less gifted man might have experienced, he would, out of his wealth, destroy what he had the moment before so beautifully adumbrated, for he was as prolific in execution as in conception); Rex at Kedleston, whither a party of us had gone for the afternoon from my home, suddenly disclosed to view lying prone on a damp gravel path, and totally absorbed in drawing a garden urn; Rex at Renishaw staying up late to finish the design of a book cover that should have been rendered to the

publisher several days previously, or talking with — or, rather,
listening to — my father, who so greatly admired his gifts, or
driving a motor over the hills round Chatsworth with a no
doubt deceptive air of gay inconsequence, or staying at Bal-
moral (where, on arrival, he promptly settled himself down in
Queen Victoria's chair, in which no one had been permitted
to sit since her death, and when I hastily but quietly remon-
strated, saying, "Rex! That's Queen Victoria's chair, and no
one is allowed to occupy it!" answered defiantly, presuming
it to be a joke, "Nonsense, Osbert!"); Rex at hotels and inns,
motoring round Rome, or at the Station Hotel at Inverness,
where after dinner he drew caricatures for an hour, altering
one person into another with a superb ingenuity, or having
luncheon at an inn on the Great North Road, and observing
with fascination and intentness a ferocious row that had
broken out between a butcher, who had dropped in with a female friend for a meal, and the proprietor (the culmination
came when the butcher, who possessed the bulk and powerful
physique of his trade, rose from his chair, till he towered above
the innkeeper, a spindly little man who most elaborately presented himself as a *character*, sportingly rigged out in stock
tie, riding breeches, gaiters, check coat, riding crop and straw-
in-the-mouth, and, glaring down at him like the Chinese God
of War, roared out, "If it weren't for this lady being present,
I'd throw you, you little beggar, through your own plate-
glass window"); or Rex catching a train in a whirl of lost and
last moments. Or I catch a glimpse of him again at Renishaw,
whither we had arrived by motor from Scotland late at night,
beginning, about midnight, to rearrange the furniture in the
Great Drawing Room, and, in spite of the fatigue engendered
by a long journey, staggering about under the immense weight
of a Roman baby in marble which he had moved, and for
which he was now unable to find a place.

In addition to these and innumerable other images of him,
the name *Rex* spelled an infinite charm to which all responded.

So greatly overworked, so often wrongly applied has been this word, that its use is apt now almost to color its subject unpleasantly, yet here it has to be employed, for no other noun suffices. In this instance, the charm was genuine and spontaneous, composed of warring factors, of a defensive carapace of apparent vagueness, which we will later analyze, and of an intense concentration, of knowing really exactly what he wanted to do, of sophistication and innocence, all blended by a peculiarly personal style. It must also be said that his great gifts, his success in many fields, and his popularity when a very young man with all those who knew him, or indeed met him, left him completely without conceit or vanity. It would also be true, I think, to use about him another hackneyed, by now even slightly rancid expression, and to say that he had not an enemy in the world; for even those whom he disliked liked him. But he was, albeit very good-natured, far from being easy or lazy in his judgment of people, and so the phrase holds no offense, indicates no lack of spirit or absence of a critical sense. . . . And as I think of him, I almost expect to find waiting for me on the post table below one of those letters from him which his friends knew so well, addressed in that fine, flowing hand, written in sepia ink, and containing pages headed or illustrated in his own inimitable fashion. Of these, I, together with most of his intimates, must have received scores during the span of friendship: but, alas, many of them my own carelessness and the passage of the years have conspired to mislay.

All the more anxious am I, therefore, that a similar fate shall not overtake the memory I cherish of his appearance, so typical of his character and enchanting. . . . There were about his aspect two obvious but contrasting impressions: one that, by the cast of his features, he might have lived in the middle of the English eighteenth century; the other, that physically he would have been equally at home here a hundred years later; he belonged solely to those two epochs. . . . To be more detailed, he was of moderate height, rather tall than the reverse, not sparely built. His profile was determined, even stubborn; but the really remarkable thing about it was its eloquence. Not that his full face lacked the capacity to convey meaning — far from it — but, whereas with others it is the look of eyes and mouth which reveals the mood of the moment, with Rex a glimpse of his head in outline, even when caught sight of across a room, declared his present state of mind. This significance of profile he obtained unconsciously by the variation of the angle at which he carried his head, usually tilted back a little, like that on a Greek coin, and it helped to give him a very individual bearing. . . . To continue the physical description: his upper eyelids were high domed and well shaped, imparting to the face the look of nobility that nearly always accompanies this particular physical conformation, and his eyes, of greenish hue, were properly recessed; his nose, slightly bridged, had well-cut nostrils, while his upper lip was noticeably long. His complexion was pale — not in the least that he looked delicate in health (indeed, when you considered how hard he worked, or rather in what bouts of hard work he engaged and the irregular hours at which he then ate and slept, it was amazing how seldom he was ill; there was, in fact, a certain unexpected but agreeable toughness about his whole physique and personality), but that color did not come easily to his face. In general, his air was one of distinction and authority. He did not care for long walks, and would walk rather slowly, with a look of meditation, often moving his head from side to side. His speech, in which the words were apt and well chosen to a singular degree, was quick and impetuous, and his laughter, which was frequent, seemed to fall suddenly, without his consent, out of a state of gravity and abstraction. His nervous energy must have been considerable and, as nearly always is the case with artists, he expended it with prodigality. He was, when not drawing, seldom still or in repose, but often drumming with his hands on a wooden surface, till at times I was obliged to protest:

"Rex, remember you're not a woodpecker in the mating season."

He would talk with animation, moving as he spoke. He could talk while he drew, and drew constantly and with facility, and the presence of people in the room, watching him, seemed in no way to deter him.

Professor Henry Tonks, who had taught Rex Whistler at the Slade School, and who was far from easy to please, told me that during the entire course of a lifetime he had met only two or three people who were natural draftsmen, and that Rex was one of them. And he went on to elaborate his use of this phrase, saying that even as a youth Rex had been able to draw anything put down before him, and to give it form and content, whether it were a rose, a hand, a vase, a human being. In fact, he was a draftsman by birth, as well as through study, and just as the Chinese allege that when they first behold any object their immediate reaction is "What will it taste like?" so Rex's first thought, I believe, would have been "How should I draw it?" Drawing was the purpose, the business, the pleasure of his life, his everyday life; but, industrious though he was, he also liked, contrarily, to take his ease, to lie late in bed if he were tired, to talk when he felt he ought to be working, to draw with brilliance what particularly he wanted that day to record, but not always to be obliged to carry out the commission waiting for him at the moment. Often he would put this off to the last minute, but when finally he set to, it would be to proceed with an admirable concentration, and an often startling rapidity. I have seen him suddenly, for example, at Port Lympne, climb up on a chimneypiece, and paint on a Charles II mirror that hung above it a design in silver, so executed that it appeared to be engraved on the glass, of a palm tree, a cupolaed tent with a scalloped edge to its canvas cornice, an opening, by which a warrior, wearing a toga, reclined, and the partial outline of a fat cloud that yet gave the whole of a Mediterranean sky — all in the matter of a few minutes. Nothing could have been more of an entity, or more finished.

It is hard to say where talents so exceptional, and so un-usual in their epoch, began, in what heredity they were rooted, or what influences in formative years worked on his mind. He told me once, in reply to a question, that what had first impelled his eye and hand to assume their so individual angle and direction had been the result of going to see his younger brother, Laurence, at school among the melancholy and stony splendors of Stowe, its temples crumbling now among the ancient trees and reflected in weedy and dying pools. But this answer, though interesting, hardly accounts for the talent which moved the hand more than does any other unrelated fact — such as the knowledge, for example, that he was born at Eltham in Kent on Midsummer Day 1905. . . . As for heredity, at any rate in my opinion, it exercised a greater influence upon him than did living people; though this is not to deny that he was most affectionate and sympathetic, in addition to being most successful, in his re-lationships with them. But there was about him an integrity that at times might be called obstinacy. Thus it interested me to be told by a friend of both his and mine that when she first saw Rex, she knew, or believed she knew, precisely how he had looked, as well as how his character had grown, at every stage in his life. That is to say, that it was possible to picture him, to a greater degree than with anyone else, as a small boy and thereafter consecutively through every development; even through those years to come which in the end, alas, were to be denied to him. This sense of personal and fluid continuity derived, no doubt, from the fact that there were no scattered or dissipative elements, nothing schizophrenic in his nature: which, on the contrary, offered a remarkable at-one-ness that enabled him to remain childlike — though in this term I do not include any faintest suggestion of childishness. And it may have been this same unbroken and simultaneously existing growth of the spirit — though in all truth his kindness and innate gifts, his charm of mind and manner, were sufficient by themselves to account for it — yet it may have been, I suggest, this same curious quality that was in part responsible for attracting to him people of all ages. It used, for example, often to be said of him by his friends in conversation that he was devoted to children: but this axiom is to be questioned. I doubt if he was really especially fond of them. Obversely, the children, I hold, collected him. They certainly wanted to be in his company or near him, long before he proceeded to draw for their amusement.

It will be deduced from what I have written above that attempts to bend his will would not have been easily successful; because his nature, though affectionate, would only receive those influences exactly suitable and necessary to it. He remained with his feet set on the paths he intended to follow. Though his whole approach was traditional, yet in everything he originated and evolved his own methods. Thus a stranger, noting the way in which Rex held pen or pencil, would have concluded that he was determined to make it as difficult for himself as possible. He appeared to grasp it in his right fist. In reality his forefinger was on the top of the pen, but pressed far back, the second joint into less than a right angle, the top joint below the nail into an angle the other way, re-entrant. Across this top joint, the thumb was bent, holding the pen very tightly. The other three fingers were folded down, close together, the tips being pressed against the lower part of the palm, where it joins the ball of the thumb, while the outside of his fist often rested on the table — for the effect of holding the pen in this fashion is to throw the hand over to the right. The pen would thus be slanting at an angle of about 45°, more or less across from right to left, parallel with the front of the body, instead of pointing forward at a lower angle in the ordinary style. . . . Rex himself affected to think it a ridiculous way to hold a pen: but he continued to grasp it in the same manner, for it afforded him great control; and when you came to regard it a second time, your impression would be one of restrained nervous energy and of the crispness he secured by his method. Nevertheless, at first sight, his grip of his instrument would suggest to you the manner in which a child might draw. And in fact he had held it thus from his earliest years, for his mother has related how a nursery governess tried gently, and fortunately without persisting, to teach him to re-arrange the grasp of his fingers. . . . As in this matter, so in others, the methods by which he pursued his natural aptitudes, and the way in which he applied himself to their cultivation, met with little interference. At home, he encountered no opposition, but on the contrary — and of how few artists can this be said! — received every encouragement to prove he could establish himself along the lines and in the direction he desired. And it may be to this circumambient atmosphere of affectionate support in his childhood and youth that he owed, when he grew up, his amazing and uninhibited facility.

To revert to his manner of gripping his pencil, Mr. Laurence Whistler informs me that he has on occasion seen his brother open his fist, in order to make sweeping lines, and grasp his pen in more conventional fashion. Yet you could tell instinctively that any *outside* effort to persuade him to hold his pen differently would have been doomed to failure. Even had the amiable nursery governess persevered, it would have been in vain. He only forsook a method of his own if he himself had decided to abandon it — as, for example, when he discarded, at an early age, the habit he had formed when very young, of drawing the human figure from a most unorthodox approach, beginning with the feet and proceeding upwards! He told a friend the following story of how he had adopted this mode. . . . The first picture he could remember copying was that of a barefooted angel in a reproduction of an Italian picture — a Fra Angelico or a Botticelli — which hung fairly high up. Rex was a small boy. He knew the picture intimately from gazing at it across the room, but to copy it he approached so near to it that his eyes were just on a level with the angel's foot. He therefore decided to draw this member first. And from this beginning the inclination stayed with him for some years to continue to draw in the same manner. . . . But when I mentioned this tale to Mr. Laurence Whistler, he said it was new to him, and that in his opinion the reason that his brother had formerly been in the habit of starting at the feet was that, if he drew first the head, he found it difficult to know at what point on the paper to begin. By the time he reached the feet, he might find that they were either above or below the road on which they were supposed to be walking! And Rex in later years would often roar with laughter when he came across some early drawing, executed on this system, which contained only legs reaching up to the knees, or perhaps a pair of boots striding along, but carrying no body above them.

Though Rex's nature was independent, and somewhat aloof, as I have tried to indicate, mention must yet be made of the possible influence exerted by one family in his life. While at the Slade School, he had become acquainted with Stephen Tennant, then a fellow student, the youngest son of Lady Grey of Fallodon,[1] who, as Lady Glenconner, occurs frequently in the previous volume of this autobiography. Her house became for Rex, as it had been for me some ten years before, a second home, and the particular cultivated and kindly atmosphere he found there probably stimulated him and accustomed him to seeing many kinds of people. . . . There was always a certain inconsequence in the air, and I recollect Stephen Tennant telling me how deeply distressed Lady Grey had been to hear that Rex, so young a man, and gifted visually to such an unusual degree, was threatened — as it was thought — with some malady or defect in the eye. She

[1] Lady Glenconner married Viscount Grey in 1922. See *Laughter in the Next Room*, footnote, p. 109.

said, accordingly, that she was determined he must take the best advice possible, and generously announced that she would see to the matter herself, make an appointment for him, take him to the house, and accompany him during his visit. The day came, and Rex Whistler and Stephen Tennant, and their respective mothers, set off in Lady Grey's electric brougham. On and on drove this machine, until it began to seem to some of those inside the vehicle that the direction it was taking was a strange quarter in which to find a great eye specialist — Harley Street was left far behind. On and on it hummed, through the outer suburbs of London, until at last they arrived at their destination and realized, as they were shown upstairs, that Lady Grey, an eager and convinced spiritualist, had made the appointment, not with a celebrated oculist, as they had thought, but with a clairvoyant or witch doctor of some kind. . . . It must be recorded, too, that it was at Wilsford, Lady Grey's country house, that Rex met first the late Miss Edith Olivier, who throughout his career gave him the greatest encouragement, and that it was through her — for she lived in a house in the park at Wilton — that he first came under the Palladian spell of that great house and domain.

So far we have mentioned, but have not examined, the painter's heredity. The Whistler family came from Hampshire, where, apparently, all bearing the name originated. The ancestors of James McNeill Whistler, for example, can be traced back to the main stock living at Fowlescourt in the sixteenth century, and are thus connected with Daniel Whistler, the friend of Pepys. There was also, Mr. Laurence Whistler tells me, a poetaster on the same side, a friend of Shenstone's, who was the author of several books now forgotten, and of a poem on flowers, the first two words of which used to amuse Rex: "*Th' Auric'la* . . . . ." But the link, if it exists at all, between the families might be more remote than the sixteenth century, so that at best it is tenuous. . . . Of more direct interest is the fact that, through his mother, Rex Whis-

tler was a great-great-grandson of Paul Storr, the most famous
and original of Regency silversmiths.

Whatever, then, may have been the past or present influences at work, Rex Whistler was in his full development a
living and fiery paradox, both typical of his age and anachro-
nistic. His pleasant and ingenious art, which matched a certain
modesty of aim with a great breadth of achievement, could
have existed in no other age save that in which it flowered,
and yet was almost wholly dependent on the past for its inspiration. He never allowed any fear of prettiness — a quality so
difficult to formulate in art — or of humor to curb his exuberance. Uninfluenced by the currents of his time, there
was to be detected in his work no sense of struggle, except the
continual battle to achieve outer beauty, of which he was so
avid. He surveyed the world that existed, and recorded it, or
in its place created another, with equal naturalness, ease and
elegance. Albeit by temperament a Cavalier, through days
when, in the ceaseless war waged between Cavalier and
Roundhead, the Roundhead was on the point of scoring one
of his recurrent victories, delusive as repulsive, yet he seemed
to enter without effort upon a kingdom of his own. He was
competent, and seemed almost to have been chosen by the
Time-Spirit to heighten in England the sense of delight in
living, just before the moment when the word *Austerity* was
to take to itself a new sub-fusc and squalid twist of meaning.
As well as being able easily to entertain and please the multitude, he was well qualified, too, to enrich the mansions of the
prosperous with designs and artifices of every sort, as few
artists had latterly, for a century or more, found it within
their power to do. In his wall paintings and decorations, his
was the old, but at present unusual, aim of wishing to please,
amuse and astonish; the same motives that had inspired the
frescoed halls of the late sixteenth, and of the seventeenth and
eighteenth centuries. The exercise of his art and the successful
consummation of the task he had set himself entirely occupied

him, and as he contemplated the beauties of the visible world, to which he was so abnormally sensitive, he was not moved to anger, neither to denounce his patrons nor to engage in propaganda for their overthrow. In short, he considered art to be the artist's whole business.

His standing as an artist is somewhat difficult to define. Those afraid of prettiness, of delicacy of line and of ingenuity, would, as they looked at his creations, murmur the word *pastiche:* but there was, in all truth, little or nothing of it to be detected in his work. In one branch alone, that of book illustration — notably *Gulliver's Travels* — he proved as original in his summary of a past epoch as Aubrey Beardsley had been in his drawings for *The Rape of the Lock*. It was equally impossible to fathom how either artist, with the little experience of his years, could yet have come to know so much of a past period, and at the same time, having seized it through the imagination, be able thus individually to re-create it. . . . And book illustration, it must also be remembered, was only one of the arts that Rex Whistler practiced. Wall paintings, gala decorations of all kinds, bookplates and jackets, work of every sort in the theater, for plays, ballets and operas, all these came within his range, and with all of them he was continually experimenting, moving on, thinking out new devices and effects. . . . On the other hand, it would do him a disservice to place his drawings side by side with those of Michelangelo or Rembrandt: no, his art, though it extended in so many directions, was yet confined by its own solid red-brick walls. By nature he was essentially English, and the comparison which his brother has drawn in his essays,[2] between the art of Rex Whistler and that of William Kent as a decorator and designer, I consider to be no less just than suggestive. Rex Whistler seemed similarly to excel in any form of decoration, without putting himself to extravagant trouble: but he was

[2] *Rex Whistler, His Life and Drawings*, by Laurence Whistler. (Art and Technics.)

both a better draftsman than Kent and a painter of sounder judgment, of more pleasant color. His rooms are painted with a higher degree of imagination, and are more personal in inspiration: while in addition his architectural drawings, and memorably those notes he made in drawings of Rome and its neighborhood, entered in his sketchbooks, were finer, more characteristic than anything Kent did. (These books have unfortunately vanished, but they will surely one day reappear in the sale room.)

It must be taken into consideration, withal, that Kent found in a flourishing condition all the arts to which he contributed, whereas Rex Whistler had to revive and inspire anew several that had latterly, until his advent, begun to languish, notably the arts of the book jacket, the bookplate, the headed writing paper, and of the *Toile de Jouy*, as well as of the painted room and, eventually, of the theater. In this last medium his energies during the final few years of his life before the 1939–1945 war were largely absorbed, and it seems probable that had he lived his remarkable talents would have found in it their fullest and most abiding expression. He delighted in anything to do with the theater, in the Crazy Gang of the Palladium hardly less than in the Diaghilev Ballet, in Bud Flanagan hardly less than in Chaliapin: he could whistle through his teeth with a music-hall expertness, and, as he drew, would often imitate the manner and repeat the patter of Max Miller, "The Cheeky Chappie," or talk of some recent Shakespearean production with a yet critical enthusiasm. The theater, for its part, quickly comprehends character and distinction; and these qualities doubtless helped him to obtain his own way, in the execution of his general designs as of their details, without resort to threats or loss of temper, while, in addition, those working with him loved him, admired his extreme ingenuity, and therefore liked to do his bidding. And in this respect, it is significant that I have several times been hailed on buses and in trains by stagehands and others connected with the profession, who remembered me as a friend of his, and accordingly wished to give me a word of greeting.

An artist is often said to lose by being worldly, but Rex Whistler was worldly in the best sense, able to enjoy and command situations and to appreciate all the finer points of subtle social intercourse. That he happened to be as delightful in his personality as his art was pleasing indubitably helped him in the realization of his genius — for that most rare essence was what, within certain limits, he possessed — but at the same time might have led the envious and the bad-tempered, who believe in the necessity for the artist to be continually rude and bad-tempered, to disparage it (for to be pleasant in art has long been out of fashion). His company was so agreeable, and so much sought after, that it would have been easy for him to have wasted his time. He was the least snobbish person I have ever met, equally at ease anywhere, whether in a palace or a laborer's cottage, and wherever he went he compelled affection. It was as impossible for a stranger to meet him and not instantaneously to like him as it would have been equally impossible on that first occasion not to have been enchanted and astonished by his versatile and spontaneous gifts. . . . Of these, I recollect, he would speak with a genuine modesty, and in instance of this I recall that he gave Betty Robins, my butler's daughter, who was then, in the summer of 1935, a child of nine, a colored drawing of a bouquet of flowers on a small sheet of writing paper. It was delightful, gay and elegant, and when her father thanked him for it, he added solemnly, "One day it may be worth ten pounds."

Rex answered, laughing, "In that case, for heaven's sake, book me all the orders you can, Robins — I'll be delighted to give you thirty per cent!"

Though direct and integral in the manner I have suggested, he was yet superficially adaptable, and his manners were so distinguished, his manner so natural and attractive, that people thought he liked them as much as they liked him — indeed, he made friends effortlessly. But it was never difficult for someone who knew him well to tell whom, if he were to meet, he would dislike: he was discriminating, and pretentiousness, conceit and affectation enraged him. Moreover, in spite of his pleasantness, he held strong opinions, in politics as much as in the arts and literature. . . . Yet, having written the words above, it is plain to me that I may run the danger of over-simplifying for the reader the traits of a most subtle character. For example, his hatred of the Nazi regime has been stressed by other writers. It is true that he loathed it, because he loathed oppression and barbarism. But always, at the same time, he saw, and would admit, that if he had been a young German the system might have appealed to him, for he understood how impossible it would have been for a German youth not to have been captivated by the spectacle of such a temporarily triumphant nationalistic racket. And then once more he would qualify that opinion, when he recollected how differently Germans of other years and background must feel about it. Thus, in short, though he could see many sides to a question — a trait which in others would often signify an uncertainty of character — he was decisive in judgment, and by no means uncritical, or even uncensorious, of either people or institutions. . . . I remember, for instance, being amused by his impatience with the fashionable intellectual world when it had taken to wrestling with Einstein. The word *Relativity* at that time boomed through the speckled and daubed chambers of Bloomsbury with somewhat the same cultured but bovine iteration that we noticed during the course of the last volume had attached itself some ten years previously to the name "Doë-rain." And Rex one day said to me irritably, "If only Rodolphe and Immermann" — I here produce new names for both painter and critic — "could get away from their boring obsession with Einstein and Relativity! They obviously don't understand it, and had much better get on with their work. What they ought to be doing is looking at the light, or trying to paint it." . . . Again, the scenic art of the theater at times drew forth some of his sharpest comments (though, in general, his attitude to fellow artists was kind and charitable). Thus on one occasion he attended a performance of an opera of Rossini's. The sets had been planned by a man of fashion, now turned theatrical designer, unfortunately without much talent to underwrite his change of profession. In the middle of the Shipwreck Scene, painted somewhat ambiguously and amorphously, Rex suddenly turned to David Horner who was with him, and remarked:

"I've often seen a ship wrecked on a rock, but I've never before seen a rock wrecked by a ship!"

He possessed, too, a temper, the existence of which could be traced through his growing pallor, in the end to culminate in a touch of green, and at several exhibitions of modern paintings to which I have gone in his company, and elsewhere, I have seen this viridescent tinge mount to his cheeks, not, I must explain, because of the jealousy proverbially associated with that color, but from suppressed rage. The world to him was beautiful as he saw it, and in the sources from which his personal vision was derived, and he felt not much sympathy, I apprehend, with the different visions, sometimes more ambitious and inchoate, of certain other painters. He was never influenced in art by any fashions save those himself created or re-presented. Yet even his own willingness and ability to please — his enjoyment, for example, in providing for a patron the kind of room that would afford him gratification — showed a rare courage of his own, different from that of others: the courage to be alone in your art and epoch.

As was, however, to be expected, his success in each phase and enterprise brought in its train many imitators and, worse still, hundreds of unwanted commissions and invitations. Though he was young and enjoyed social life, these could have ruined his career, by preventing him from working, and

in order to avoid them he evolved, though not altogether consciously or deliberately, the special technique of vagueness
by which he was able to disengage himself from the cogs of
fashionable life in a manner at once charming and affectionate.
He hated to hurt people's feelings, and, in the warmth of a
genial moment, moreover, surrounded by friends, the invitation extended to him, and then pressed upon him, would seem
genuinely attractive, though with another part of his mind he
was aware, from previous experience, that he might feel very
differently about it the next day. And so, since it was impossible with grace to refuse, and not to spoil the spirit of the
moment, he, instead, accepted and forgot (because, as I have
said before, an artist is obliged to have a vista of free time before him in which to work, and Rex, realizing this, hated to be
pinned down to hours). Hence the opening sentences of so
many letters, received by different friends, but identical in
the sentiment expressed, probably under an exquisitely drawn
heading: "*Do forgive*" or "*I was so miserable*." And if this
vagueness must in part have been deliberate, a theory borne
out by the withering scorn with which he regarded the same
failing in others — for he was always present in person and in
mind when it was necessary, and he despised all kinds of
shoddy evasiveness — yet in his character, at once complex
but simple, there must too have been a contradictory and
underlying stratum of vagueness, the very complement of his
concise and definite judgments. Though had he been so hazy
as at moments he chose to give the impression of being, he
could never have achieved in his comparatively short lifetime
the enormous amount of work which he left behind him, yet
it would be true, I think, to say that, when he was painting,
time ceased to exist for him. Certainly I have known him,
when he had finished some commission upon which he had
been engaged, at four or five in the afternoon, to expect to
find luncheon ready for him at any of the neighboring restaurants, apparently quite oblivious of the hours that com-

monly prevail. Equally, his vagueness may have in the main
consisted in a fine indifference to things that did not interest
him, and an acceptance of those that did. We find examples
of both these factors in the anecdotes I am about to relate,
and since this vagueness — as we must still call it for want
of a more applicable and complicated term — was often to
be observed in him, it is fitting to record an instance or two
of it.

Rex Whistler lived first at 20 Fitzroy Street, and then at
29 Fitzroy Square, in both of which he had a studio attached
to his room. But in the spring of 1937, when he was executing
some very large wall paintings for a country house, their
size compelled him also, in order to work at them properly, to
rent for a time an enormous scene painter's studio off the
Horseferry Road, for in it was installed some special mecha-
nism that made it possible for the artist, by turning a handle,
to lower the canvases into slots in the floor, and thus be able
to attend to the upper parts without the whole time having to
climb ladders. . . . Here one afternoon I went to call on
him, after I had returned from spending a winter abroad.
The street of small, brown-painted houses was full, I recall,
of shouting children, who played under the gay lines and
festoons of flags and pennons hung across the street by the inhabitants to celebrate the Coronation. Mounting a staircase,
I found Rex, who had not long been installed, already with
one foot bandaged and wearing a slipper, because he had, in
a moment of inadvertence, caught his foot between the frame
that held one enormous canvas and the slot in the floor into
which it was lowered. I regarded the magnificent wall decorations on which he was engaged, and then, since we were
on intimate terms and I had not seen him for six months, and
also because he was in the habit of consulting me on matters
of business, I began by asking him two direct questions. I
had formerly, at his request, recommended to him the agents
who acted for him in anything connected with books and

journalism, for he found difficulty in discussing terms and fixing prices for himself. (And I may mention as an instance of the way in which artists are so often exploited, that he had been brought to the point of taking this step by a commission he had received from a firm of publishers. One of the principals had sent for him, and made a special plea to him to design a book jacket for a great admirer of Rex's work, who remained anonymous at his own request. This poet, typically unendowed, it appeared, with worldly goods, was yet paying for the cost of publication of his volume, and could in consequence only afford to offer the artist a very small fee. Under the circumstances, and with his usual good nature, Rex agreed to accept this trivial sum — three or four pounds — only later to discover that the pauper poet was in reality one of the richest heiresses in the world, with a name in this day proverbial for wealth as that of Croesus formerly.) So now, as I was explaining, I indicated the paintings and inquired:

"How much are you being paid for them, Rex?" Without turning round, but continuing to work, he replied nonchalantly:

"We haven't actually *mentioned* a sum yet."

"And how much do you have to pay for the studio?" I persisted.

"Well, that's another thing we stupidly forgot to arrange."

At this moment I turned round, and to my astonishment remarked the presence of an old Chinese gentleman with a thin beard, who was sitting in the darkest corner of the huge studio. He wore ceremonial robes and cap, and was smoking a short clay pipe. So still was he, and so much more consciously Oriental than anyone I had seen in China, that had it not been for the movement of the tobacco smoke from his pipe, I should have thought that I was beholding a ghost or had become the victim of a hallucination. Even as it was, I felt rather shaken by the experience. I turned to Rex, and, making a gesture in the direction of the Mandarin, contrived to form the syllables:

"Who-is-that-over-there?"

"Well, I don't really know. You see, he doesn't *speak* English. Apparently, he *likes* watching painters at work, and he's always been here. So he still arrives on the dot at midday, and stays here the whole afternoon. . . . No, he never utters. So I *can't* turn him out, can I, or make him alter his arrangements!"

Rex Whistler seemed, withal, to attract odd incidents of diverse kinds. For example, once at Renishaw, it was a cold autumn morning, and he had remained in bed longer than usual, his head almost covered by the clothes, so that nothing could be discerned of his presence by anyone entering the room. In consequence, an old woman from the neighborhood who was acting as rustic housemaid, and had been sent up to collect the hot-water bottles from the beds, failing to see him, put her hands between the sheets at the bottom of the bed to take out the bottle, and instead firmly grasped and then tugged his foot. It was a shock to her when the bottle moved violently and a voice shouted:

"Leave go of my toes, *will you!*"

His rooms in London were always beautiful, as well as clearly a place for work, and possessed an atmosphere of their own. . . . It was in Fitzroy Street, in an eighteenth-century apartment with its three high windows looking on the street, that very early one summer morning Rex Whistler saw his own ghost. . . . I relate the story as he told me it at the time; and he mentioned it first, I remember, because an incident somewhat resembling it had been the theme of a novel I had published in 1929, entitled *The Man Who Lost Himself.* . . . He had been working late, in order to finish a book jacket overdue. When he had completed the design he put it in an envelope which he addressed and stamped, and then

took to post in a letter box in Fitzroy Square. Purposely, he
had left the lights on in his room, and had refrained from
pulling the curtains, thinking that it would be interesting to
see the room from outside, and that it should look enchanting.
. . . The night was dark, it was a little after two in the
morning, and as he returned home along the other side of the
street, from which he could obtain a better view of the interior, he was amazed to see clearly a man seated at his own
desk in the furthest window, and apparently working. This
unexpected intrusion confounded and disturbed him, and he
stood still to watch: at that moment, the figure raised his
head, and looked straight at him — and he saw that it was
himself. While he struggled under this impact, the figure opposite dissolved. . . . I have known on one or two other
occasions persons who have claimed to have undergone a
similar experience as the result of overwork and exhaustion:
but the others I was not bound to believe. They may have
been trying to create an effect. But Rex Whistler was indubitably truthful.

When I think of Rex now, his image rises before me as I
last saw him. . . . He had been very critical and outspoken
in his views concerning Chamberlain's Peace-in-Our-Time
policy: for he cherished within him a high and generous ideal
of the national dignity. The Munich Crisis he had felt almost
as a personal anguish. Therefore, when war broke out, he
was eager, because of his principles, not to find the job which
his special combination of several talents would have so easily
secured for him — and which, indeed, on several occasions he
refused — but to play his own part in the fighting; though
all forms of destruction must have been to him, as a creator,
repulsive and terrible. Eventually he obtained a commission
in the Welsh Guards. It is needless to add that he quickly
won the esteem of all those in contact with him, or who
served under him. And a very smart and efficient officer he

made — though he admitted to me at dinner one night in Carlyle Square that he had created some consternation by appearing on Early Parade without a tie. No doubt, however, his willingness to help in his own inimitable fashion — the skill with which, to give only one example, he painted targets for rifle practice — quickly helped him to compensate for this omission, so truly appalling to the military mind. (I recall the earthquake which shook Chelsea Barracks in 1917, when I appeared at 4 A.M., having dressed during an air-raid alarm, wearing a hat belonging to my evening uniform, instead of that which should have graced the early daylight filtering through the windows into the Anteroom.) From parades he passed, when his regiment was mechanized, to tank drill: a still less congenial occupation, one would have imagined.

From time to time I saw him; though more rarely, for he was training in various parts of England, and I was living at Renishaw. Then, one morning in May 1944, after a long interval, we met again. . . . I was just turning from my house in Chelsea into the King's Road, at about eleven, when someone hailed me from a passing motor. The machine drew up, and out of it stepped Rex, in khaki, with all his old exuberance of greeting. I persuaded him to abandon for a short time the friends who were driving with him, and to join me in walking across the river to Battersea Old Church, and then to go round this spacious eighteenth-century edifice, which always seems to be deserted, as it so gracefully yet solidly floats above the dark swan-spangled waters of the Thames. He had never before visited it, and together we looked at the tombs, Elizabethan and Carolean, of deceased members of the St. John family — monuments that had been moved hither from the earlier church which had occupied the site — and examined the register in which is recorded the marriage of William Blake. . . . Then we walked slowly back, through the streets of dingy little yellow brick cubes, into the thoroughfares, across Battersea Bridge to the King's Road. . . . Is it merely imagination, and knowing the subsequent events, that edges that bright spring morning with a certain furtive fluttering of wings in the sad air? . . . I urged him, I remember, to design the sets for a film that was at the time being adapted from my story — *A Place of One's Own*. It was on the very point of being produced, and I hoped that, if he could be prevailed upon to undertake it, this might mean — since it was the policy of the Government to release artists for such work — that he would be obliged to stay in England (for all the world knew that we were shortly to launch an invasion of the Continent). I realized, of course, before I began, that the task I had set myself was hopeless: and though I persuaded him to do the drawings — indeed, they were the last commission he ever executed — nothing would induce him to apply for the full job, or to be seconded, even for a month, from his regiment.

So we proceeded to other subjects, to talk of many friends, now dead or separated from us by the war, and to speak of Renishaw. I recall, for instance, discussing with him during that walk, under the sound of the creaking trams, the exciting developments which he was planning (and which had occurred to him as the direct result of his experience of the theater in recent years) in the arts of landscaping and garden design. . . . Of this subject we had talked several times before. The recent improvements introduced into the making of papier-mâché and the other kindred substances now used by theatrical designers, and the increased durability of these materials, led him to propose to employ them in the open air, to make colonnades, aqueducts, great constructions of all kinds, even artificial hills. By their nature, these edifices would possess only a limited lifetime; they would be built to last at most for fifty years, instead of a thousand, but at the end of the period they could easily be dissolved or remodeled according to the ideas of the succeeding age. But within the boundaries fixed for them by their very essence, great effects could be obtained at little cost, panoramic visions of antique

[315   ]

cities, clusters of towers, gigantic statues, or glimpses of distant palaces. We spoke of the possibility that, when the war was over, we could build a vast colonnade at the end of the garden, and at the edge of a steep hill overlooking the lake at Renishaw, so that the expanse of view would be perceived through lofty, narrow arches, and would become all the more wide and dramatic for being thus framed. (My father had proposed something of the sort many years before, but had intended then to use for it brick and rubble.) . . . In any case, the plans Rex Whistler set forth that morning with so much imagination and enthusiasm are now incapable of achievement, for he was undoubtedly the only man living who could comprehend or undertake schemes of this kind: but I think even then, in May 1944, we both knew in our hearts that not only were the days for realizing such objective flights of the imagination ended, but that there would be no one to carry them out. . . .

On July 18th he was killed at Demouville, seven miles east of Caen.

CHAPTER XI

Arnold Bennett

⚘⚘⚘⚘RNOLD BENNETT! *Enoch Arnold Bennett,*
⚘ A ⚘ the novelist's full name, under which he started
⚘ ⚘ work, seems to me to retain, in the weight of its
⚘⚘⚘ syllables, as they fall through the air, more of the
clay and of the strength of the Five Towns, the life of
which he so ably depicted for future generations as well
as for his own, than does the more lissom *Arnold Bennett.*
Yet even this shorter version most aptly summons up his
image: the name is plain, solid, suggests material prosperity,
combines it with the gift of imagination, and has too about it
something that is portentous because so typical. How clearly
one sees the man, even now, as one murmurs the syllables.

It was again under Robert Ross's auspices, indeed almost
under his command, that I first made the acquaintance of
Arnold Bennett. . . . Our meeting took place in the marble-
lined hall of the Reform Club, an architectural monument so
impressive — obsolete as the Colosseum — as to seem to clamor
already for time to unroof it and allow the winds to race
through its wide-arcaded galleries and pompous marbled
corridors, and at the same time to sum up England, so that, as
my brother remarked to me, it seems the ideal background
for the opening of a novel by Jules Verne: the place, for
example, where two English club men would give breakfast
to an eager young French inventor about to set forth on a
perilous journey, the first ever to be made of its kind. It was
here, then, that the meeting took place, in the spring of 1918.
Robert Ross had, of course, invited me to meet the famous
man at luncheon because he was one of the pontiffs of litera-

ture; in this similar to, though in all else different from, Gosse, who walked delicately through the antique pastures of literature, culling the flowers; whereas Arnold Bennett was devoted to the present, and constituted to the readers of his age a living reminder that a great novelist — for such they considered him to be — could exist in others besides the Victorian reign, and could at the same time be (which no great Victorian had been) the best-paid journalist of any epoch. (I forget now what Arnold Bennett was said to be paid for a word — can it have been 2s. 6d. or 5s.? — but in any case, I know that when, many years ago, I was threatened with a libel action about a short story which had been published in a book of mine, and was advised to settle out of court, I computed that this had been the most expensive story ever written, because I had been obliged to pay out more per word than even Arnold Bennett earned.) At the time of which I talk, he was, as well, one of the directing heads of British war propaganda, under the press barons; in fact, every young author had to be presented to him, in the same way that every tourist in Rome must be taken to see St. Peter's. To sum up, he was a great figure of the epoch, the successor and heir, it seemed to many, of Charles Dickens; a famous publicist. His novels, his short stories, his literary criticism had won the respect of the middle classes in England and America, and were widely read throughout the English-speaking world; his reputation stood high in France and Germany. In America he had enjoyed the greatest personal success of any visiting writer for five decades. And his diaries, even today, reflect the people and spirit of the time with a singular and vivid faithfulness. Fifteen years after an author's death is the most difficult time at which to estimate correctly the contribution he has made: but whatever may be the ultimate importance or the reverse of Arnold Bennett, he cannot be omitted from any, even rather fragmentary, survey of the literary and social scene of the 1920's, and just before and after. Moreover,

I am not here concerned with him as a *writer* — though at the same time the fact that he was one accounts for his appearing in this essay — but as a person.

Even in spring days, the hall of the Reform, full of the funeral pomps of Liberalism, crowded with marble frock coats of the 1840's (a period in which Liberators were as common in England as they are abroad today), haunted by these heavy, white, side-whiskered ghosts of Prosperity, no less than by the more enticing shade of Soyer — who accomplished, in fact, so much more practical good for humanity than any of the originals of these Carrara images — is chilly, full of fog, though outside the boughs are breaking into green spray, and the soft winds blow. But we had only a moment to wait, for on the very stroke of one Robbie's other and chief guest materialized. Hedged off, as he was, with the laurels and bays of twenty seasons of fame, I felt a little frightened of him. And his physical presence, which combined that of a Midlands businessman with the rather solid panache of a great French novelist — the Parisian world-novelist of the mid-nineteenth century, with a touch, more than a touch, of Balzac, and a reminder, here and there, of Dumas the Elder, and of Emile Zola — did nothing to diminish this fear. His graying hair, his tired eyes — in which the expression of his often remarkable kindness could not at once be read — his corpulent habit of body, natural both to the vigor of his type and to a sedentary way of life (it was only in the last decade of his career that a desire to be more elegant, to be more ordinary in his manner of pleasing, or perhaps a sudden drop in his self-confidence, asserted itself and was responsible for a decrease in the volume of his figure), placed him a whole generation ahead of me, and made him seem — though I was, it is true, then only twenty-five — further removed in age than actually he was, in a manner in which one never felt my host, Robert Ross, to be distant. Nor can it be pretended that Arnold was an attractive or imposing, although he was a prosperous-looking, middle-aged man: his blunted, yet rather sharp and inquisitive nose, his bristly gray mustache and slightly protruding teeth, his creased, sallow face and recessive, dented chin, produced a far from handsome effect. I was puzzled, too, at first, by his fob of jingling gold seals and his coif of gray hair, which seemed to me — or would have seemed, if I had not gone in some awe of him — to be pretentious. Then, in an opposite, more naïve direction, I catalogued, for a final reckoning of character and attributes, a gold toothpick.

All these personal adjuncts, however, were in reality only another expression of the manner in which he liked to think things out, of the pleasure he derived from the everyday details of existence: clothes, food, walks and the decoration of his rooms. As one grew to know him better, one began to comprehend the breadth of his intelligent and informed joy in life. Moreover, just as I have, in an earlier chapter, mentioned that a pineapple, rising like a palm tree from a handsome dish in the center of his dinner table, constituted to him a visible emblem of his fortune, a token that the shadows of poverty, which had in early days surrounded him, had been securely dispelled, so, I think, every time he regarded himself in a glass, and saw the gray upstanding lock in the middle, above his forehead, his elaborate waistcoat and his seals, it brought home to him not only the same comforting assurance, but told him, too, that he now cut a figure in the world as one of the most famous of living novelists. Certainly, he liked looking in mirrors, and one could often, as he passed them, see him preen himself and observe his own reflection. Of this trait I can give the following illustration. A great friend of his told me that he had been to call on Arnold, who had just moved — in January 1923 — into a grander house, 75 Cadogan Square. The new owner had, however, at once been struck down with influenza, and his friend found him in bed, recovering. Noticing that the walls were hung with large mirrors, and that Arnold, lying propped up on pillows, and still looking excessively ill, was gazing contentedly at the repetitive perspective of images of himself thus afforded, his friend remarked:

"I couldn't lie there looking at myself reflected on and on into infinity like that!"

To which Arnold replied, in a tone of complacency:

"I . . . t suits me down to the ground!"

Though I was not present when these words were said, I can, as I write them, hear in them the exact tone and run of his voice; his voice which was so typical and easy to mimic. At first his always intractable and often outrageous stammer rendered me nervous for — and, in consequence, of — him. But, as one got to know him better, it became clear that his remarks actually gained in force and quality from the way in which his hesitation, so irksome to himself, obliged him to regulate his utterance, gearing it to various speeds, one or two slow words, then two or three fast, or a few slow, and then a run of fast, to get them in before the stammer caught him again. This physical drawback had forced on him a style of conversation that, like his voice, still rather rough, and retaining the broad, flat Midland *a*, as in *flax*, proved peculiarly suited to apophthegm and plain, nutty speech, such as when he said to me one day:

"The most important thing for a young writer is to write his stuff; the next is to know where to place it." Or when, after a well-known female novelist had been discussed, he announced:

"As a writer, there's . . . only-one-thing-wrong-about-that-girl [pause], she can't . . . write!" I recall, too, his verdict on a painter and writer, now growing elderly, whom I, like members of succeeding generations, had at first thought an entertaining character and talker; so entertaining that I had spoken of him much to Arnold, and had arranged to bring him to tea in George Street (this was in about 1920).

The day came. I took my brilliant friend there, but his customary essays in truculence Arnold treated with a genial indifference, and, as soon as he said good-by and left the room, remarked:

"That man's a . . . *bore!*"

Or to take a fourth instance: his warning words to my sister. She had been saying how low she rated the writings of an author whom I had lately named Muddleton Moral, when Arnold interrupted and said, "Spiritual Pride is a . . . terrible thing, Edith! Remember whatever I may think of your work, or you of mine, or both of us of Moral's, on the Judgment Day it will appear to the Almighty as pretty-much-the-same-thing."

Bennett's stammer, too, gave point to his enjoyment of a joke, whether his own or someone else's, for he would stammer in his laughter, his face would grow red-brown and he would laugh yet more.

On the first day I had met him, Arnold had been particularly tired, and his hesitation had been severe, indeed agonizing — it greatly varied — to witness. As was his wont, especially when it was extreme, he had kept on, throwing back his head, with his mouth a little open and with a look of troubled persistence in his eyes, and beating his knee with a regular rhythm, until at last he could get his words out: this being done, perhaps, not only to help himself, but also to lessen the suspense for those in his company who waited for him to speak. All the same, it gave the onlooker an uneasy suspicion that he might be disliked for being present when such a display of control was necessary: for many stammerers, on the days when their affliction is at its most acute, bear an involuntary grudge against their companions. But in Arnold Bennett's case it became plain in time that he harbored no ill will. . . . The conversation, though, had lagged. Arnold watched me with his shrewd, sharp gaze; to which was added the attentive, sidelong glance of the stammerer, in its origin due no doubt to his wish to see how others are supporting the strain of his prolonged struggle for words. Robbie took the burden of the talk on himself, just as, with his generosity of spirit, he assumed many other loads. However, I talked a good deal myself, for I am one of those whom an intense silence renders loquacious, anxious to do anything to prevent the coming of the inevitable silence that will never be broken; and so I had improvised a grievance which really I had hardly felt or had time to feel: the fact that the younger writers possessed no journal in which to vent their opinions or publish the writings of those whom they admired. Poetry, in those days, especially, was a Closed Shop, to which admission was only gained through friendship with the leaders or secretary, and, of course, by an absolute adherence to the birdloving tenets of the day. The mention of a blackbird or thrush in a poem meant you were a safe man, unlikely to give trouble to the Union. It was necessary also to take an interest in cricket. . . . Well, all this was true, odd as it may sound a generation later: but I was aware that on this topic I was saying more than I meant, talking too much, overvehemently and wildly. . . . I do not know how my host felt about it — he was probably too tired, after his efforts, to consider the matter — but for myself I was conscious, as I left the Reform, both of failure and of exhaustion. It seemed to me that Bennett had hardly troubled to say good-by.

It can be imagined, then, with what intense surprise I received a letter from him, the next morning, asking me to have luncheon with him alone, at a restaurant, early the following week, to discuss a matter of business. I could not think what it could be. . . . The day came, I arrived at the restaurant, and found my host waiting for me. No sooner had we sat down at a table than he asked:

"Did you mean what you said about wanting a paper for young writers?"

I said yes, I had meant it.

[323   ]

There followed a glazed pause, in which he looked at me dully. Then he continued:

"If you'll edit it, I'm willing to back it." And he proceeded at once, in the most businesslike way possible, to make arrangements for putting the plan into execution. "I'll give you a letter to take to Chatto & Windus. They've one great advantage over every other publisher: they've got a man with a first-class brain working there, Frank Swinnerton. He's a great friend of mine, and will fix it up for you."

In all truth, I was taken aback: as in some fairy tales, my careless wish had been granted too rapidly, almost before being formulated. I had not, until the luncheon I had mentioned, even contemplated editing a paper — after all, the war continued, and I was still in the Army — and so I was unprepared; my ideas were in chaos. However, I went the next day, and many times subsequently, to see Swinnerton; for Arnold insisted always that, if anything needed to be arranged, it should be done in proper, workmanlike fashion. The firm of Chatto & Windus, then in St. Martin's Lane, made a great impression on me, for it was the first publishers' establishment I had ever visited. A long dark passage stretched from the office into which the door opened, to a distant nucleus of inner shrines, unbelievably remote and sacred, and to which, I think, I was never, in the course of the next few years, allowed to penetrate: while, on the way between the office and these sanctuaries, in the straight, dark and narrow corridor you passed a number of doors, which led into airless dens, intensely small and confined, lit only by artificial light, and lined with books: closets which, as if to remove the feeling of claustrophobia that must assail anybody immured in one of them, were all open at the top, but above the level of the head, so that you could hear the conversations but could not see the talkers. These cramped boxes always seemed to me to be full of waiting figures, hopeless aspirants for literary fame; but sometimes, as I walked down the passage on entering or leaving, I would see the face of a friend, and the tall, lank figure of Aldous Huxley or of Lytton Strachey, two of "Chatto's authors" (for in such slavish terms do we talk), would elongate itself up through an open door, as if expelled therefrom by the pressure of space, in the manner — if such a contradictory yet accurate image be permissible — of a rather languid jack-in-the-box.

Though a good deal accrued eventually to my benefit through these visits, and through my several interviews with Frank Swinnerton, nothing came of them immediately. The project fell through, or, more accurately, fused itself with another: partly because I was still in the Grenadiers, and could not guarantee the time in which to edit a monthly magazine (and Arnold believed in a *monthly* journal, and would have nothing to do with a quarterly) and partly because, in the end, even the backing proved unnecessary, since, as I have explained in *Laughter in the Next Room*, Frank Rutter was at the time looking for two editors to help him to revive the quarterly *Art and Letters*, and offered one post to Herbert Read and one to me. But leaving these circumstances out of account, I fear that my lack of business habits and the fact that, out of consideration for him, I purposely refrained from continually plaguing him about the paper, although I had originally broached the matter, rather riled Arnold; who must have thought that I manifested, not only a certain dilatoriness, but a lack of interest.

Nothing, I said, came of the project directly — but still the amazing offer had been made: an affirmation of faith in young writers, and an effort — unparalleled to my knowledge in its generosity — to help them at the cost of a considerable personal sacrifice; for Arnold, having been poor, liked money and knew the value of it. It was, moreover, through these meetings with Swinnerton at Chatto's — and perhaps, even, through Arnold's more personal intervention, I do not know — that my first book of poems, *Argonaut and Juggernaut*, was published by Chatto's the following year. Several writers of my generation, painters and musicians (for he was interested in all the arts), must owe him a similar debt. I record all this because it is, in its essence, very typical of the character of a man who seldom in his lifetime or afterwards received credit for possessing, as he did in an extreme degree, the quality these facts display: indeed, to the contrary, I have often heard it stated about him in conversation, by those who must have been acquainted with him only very slightly, that he was penurious. I, on the other hand, know of many instances of what can justly be termed discriminating munificence on his part: notably one, in which he sent for a celebrated younger writer, in whose judgment he had faith, and said to him:

"Look here! I've made more money than I expected this year: here's a check for five hundred pounds for you to give away, as you think best, to younger writers and painters: there's only one condition — my name must not be mentioned in connection with it."

Moreover, he was as unsparing of his time as of his money: many of us used to consult him on numerous matters, and he would always find the necessary half hour in which to see us, though he liked to run his day's program to the fraction of a second. In the same way, if one wrote to ask him his advice on any point, he always answered promptly, and in a manner that proved he had given every consideration to the subject. Thus I remember consulting him by letter from Amalfi, some years subsequently, on which was the best literary agent to handle my writings, and on general lines of policy, and receiving an invaluable, and indeed masterly, letter of counsel in reply.

Above all Arnold Bennett rated such qualities as punctuality and personal competence. He preferred geniuses who could look after themselves to those who had to be looked after. He endured, and even appeared to enjoy, the company of businessmen, and he seemed to cherish a high respect for the makers of great fortunes and especially the holders of newspaper power. The name of Lord Beaverbrook, for instance, appeared to exercise a kind of spell over him. He liked people to lead tidy, punctual lives. His flats or houses he wished to be well run and, in the phrase of the house agent, well appointed. In addition they were always furnished with his own individual taste, handsome and to some extent original, influenced by a love of color, and of objects of solid worth. He believed in regular stretches of work, long walks and early hours. When I first knew him, and he and his wife, Marguerite Bennett, were living in their large flat in George Street, for formal dinner parties a notice, placed on the chimneypiece, would proclaim to the possible recalcitrant the ineluctable hint, "*Carriages, 10:45.*" In the years after 1923, when he moved from George Street to Cadogan Square, I used often, from the top of a bus, to espy him crowned with a bowler hat, a prosperous and somehow important figure, in a trance of thought, walking below through the crowded King's Road, or further afield. But, he told me, there were two kinds of walks he took: one to solve the problems with which the plots of his books presented him; the other, when he looked about him, to gather ideas, or to take in the atmosphere of a given neighborhood. It may be that his reasonableness, whether innate or acquired, sometimes betrayed him: for he believed that with the application of intelligence and the exercise of forethought, everything in human life could be arranged; whereas no doubt in the end he discovered that certain human faculties, attributes, emotions stand altogether beyond the scope of common-sense control.

After the first two encounters I have described, and although my failure as a man of practical affairs may have a little chagrined him, we nevertheless quickly became friends, and during the dozen years or so that followed, until his death in 1931, I saw much of him. Equally, my brother and sister delighted in his company. I do not remember how soon our friendship had ripened, but in 1919, he wrote to me, in answer to a letter in which, as I thought was fitting to an older and famous man, I had addressed him as "dear Mr. Arnold Bennett."

DEAR OSBERT, call me dear Bennett, dear Arnold Bennett, dear Arnold, dear Uncle Arnold, or anything you damned well like, but never again call me "dear Mr. Arnold Bennett." — Your affectionate Uncle, ARNOLD.

After receiving this, we always called him Uncle Arnold, and wrote to him in that style, and though, as I have said earlier, he had seemed, when first we met him, to be older than he was, in the years that followed we were continually surprised by his youthfulness, by — for example — his interest in the other arts. At the age of about sixty, he actually *liked* new ideas. About pictures, he knew a good deal: very much more than most authors; perhaps because, in addition to a natural feeling for painting, he had lived much in Paris, where writers pay attention to it. He numbered many musicians among his friends (he gave a magnificent party for Ravel, I remember, in his house in Cadogan Square), and he took an interest in the careers of young English musicians and conductors, such as Eugene Goossens. When, however, he played the piano himself, which occasionally he did, the effect was not happy. I have heard him play in George Street classical duets with Lady Ross; [1] and I recall my sister saying to me that the light clatter of their fingers on the keys exactly reminded her of the sentence said to be posed in schools where aspirates were taught as a test of pronunciation:

Hen's hooves hitting the hard highroad.

He was, however, an accomplished water-colorist, and I have in my collection a water color of his, representing a

---

[1] Lady Ross was the wife of Professor Sir Denison Ross, for many years head of the School of Oriental Languages.

convent in Portugal, which he gave me on his return from a visit to that country in 1920.

Youthful, again, was his sense of humor. It had no primness about it, as had that of the other pontiffs, and retained, in spite of the kindness of his nature, a certain inherent ferocity, which, for example, enabled him to enter into the spirit of the doings and sayings of my sister, brother and myself, apparently often incomprehensible to others of his age. This, I think, is manifest in what he wrote about us in August 1923, in the *Adelphi*: for it was a time when we were giving, and receiving, no quarter. In a moment, I will proceed to quote a sentence or two from this essay: but first I must explain, for the comfort of the rejected and as one more instance of how easily, and not seldom, publishers judge wrongly (I mean not only in matters of selection, but of selling books, which is their trade), that Messrs. Chatto & Windus refused my second book of poems. There had been a slump in books, and my first volume had come out the day the great railway strike had begun, so that it had not been given much attention. Now, let the reader understand that I am not so much complaining of their judgment of the poems as exploding the reason upon which they ostensibly based it: for the nice partner or director who saw me plunged delicately among the vibrating mass of a young author's feelings by saying, "I know that Arnold Bennett, who first sent you here and takes such an interest in your work, would be the first to be disappointed. He'd say, 'Why did he publish *now*: what are Chatto's doing to allow it? *Why* didn't he wait a few more years?'"

Of course, the refusal of this book did not help me with other publishers: but eventually Grant Richards accepted it. . . . Arnold knew nothing of all this, contrary to prophecy, but immediately wrote in his review of it:

Osbert's *Out of the Flame* is the longest stride forward by the Sitwells up to date. It made me reflect that the trio is still quite young, and may develop in astonishing ways. It really excited me:

for in my short-sightedness, I had looked upon Osbert as simply a satirist. . . . And lo! he is now creating ideal beauty. . . .

But the portion of what he wrote which shows, I think, a certain enjoyment in our exploits runs:

The Sitwells can all write. . . . Further, the Sitwells are all personages. Further, they all afflict the public — I mean the poetic public — which is a grand thing to do. . . . They exalt in a scrap. Battle is in the curve of their nostrils. They issue forth from their bright pavilions and demand trouble. And few spectacles are more touching than their gentle, quiet, surprised, ruthless demeanour when they get it, as they generally do.

To return to his youthful enjoyment of jokes and of fun, and to his high spirits, he records in a letter [2] dated 12.1.20:

I have begun to work again, and my health is much better. The mere thought of going to Portugal has had a marvellous effect. Strange! We went to the Olympia Victory Circus on Saturday night with the brothers Sitwell. It was a great thing. Especially the roundabouts. We came home with the brougham full of hydrogen balloons, which occasionally swept out on their strings through the windows into the infinite ether. . . .

How well I recall that occasion! The party consisted of Arnold and Marguerite Bennett, Aldous and Maria Huxley and Sacheverell and me. It was a night of bitter cold and deep snow, and the vast iron enclosure, within which the circus ring had imposed an attempt at form, was full of light yellow fog, splintered by arc lamps, and further darkened by peat dust; among which the Fratellini — it was the first time I had seen these famous Italian clowns — tumbled, cried and disciplined an imitation baby. The balloons, too, straining at the leash, were new to me, and a delight: as was Arnold's almost

[2] From *Arnold Bennett's Letters to his Nephew, Richard Bennett*. Messrs. Heinemann published this book, with a short preface by Frank Swinnerton, in 1936.

schoolboy pleasure in them. And I recollect his amusement, because they gave me an inspiration, and I outlined to him a new scheme: similarly to fill my father's invariable companion, the round air cushion, shaped like a lifebuoy, so that, just as that dignified, bearded gentleman was going to sit on it, in his accustomed place in the Reading Room of the British Museum, it would either soar with him aloft, as the eagle once carried Ganymede to Olympus, or, eluding him, would go bumping up to the ceiling by itself. (He always took an interest in my father and his books, and used often to ask me to read aloud to him a particular page, mostly of acknowledgments, from one of them; while he would sit chuckling and slapping his leg.) So, on parting, we piled the balloons into Arnold's brougham, and watched them drive away, through the snow, into the fog, a balloon every moment bobbing out of the window, until, quite soon, the vehicle was lost to sight.

It was after his return from the visit to Portugal to which he alludes at the beginning of the letter I have quoted that he gave me the water color I have mentioned, in return for presents that my brother and I had brought him from Spain the previous year: two genuine sombreros, one brown, one black. He had seized on them, as we had thought he would, with delight, though it required a degree of courage to wear them, for they would have appeared unusual in any country except that of their origin. They carried immensely large, stiff brims, in a perfect circle, and stiff crowns, too, tapering gradually to the top, and had leather straps which fastened tightly under the chin. I have no doubt that he wore them, for to do so would have been part of his fun. He took the greatest trouble over his appearance, went to the best tailor, and imported shirts — his day shirts were always a delight to his friends no less than those he wore in the evening — from the most famous of Parisian shirtmakers. To behold him, however, at his finest, most typical, one had to see him in full evening dress — preferably at a first night. Yet I do not think his reflection in the glass afforded so intense a realist any illusions concerning his exterior; he saw too straight for that.

Just as children sometimes stand without terror in the very path of tigers, and are alleged to be thereby preserved from danger, because the beasts admire a display of so much courage, so, too, Arnold remained resolutely unafraid when confronted with new ideas or their promoters. And it was for this reason that, when Sacheverell and I organized in August the first exhibition of modern painting of the Paris School to be held in London since the outbreak of war in 1914, we asked Arnold to write the preface for the catalogue.[3] As I have written, in addition, we had hoped, of course vainly, that the position he held with the public, and his admirable common sense, might suffice to quiet the outburst of popular rage that would undoubtedly otherwise ensue at the sight of a few modern masterpieces. The two Post-Impressionist Exhibitions at the Grafton Galleries should have stood as a warning to the crowd: but no! Though Arnold wrote in the foreword, ". . . It is the first exhibition of its kind since the war, and the best of its kind since the celebrated exhibition at the Grafton many years ago . . ." the public would not accept his hint, and though he openly tipped them the work of Modigliani as a winner (this was the first time his paintings had been exhibited in London), yet did the heathen roar, rave and, after prowling around the gallery, howl hideously together in the newspapers.[4] The result, one which they would have understood, was that they lost the chance of a valuable investment. On my advice, I am glad to say, Arnold bought — he says in his diary for fifty pounds, but I believe it to have been for sixty — a very beautiful reclining nude by Modigliani: that which I considered the finest picture in the exhibition. He notes in his journal for August 1929:

[3] See *Laughter in the Next Room*, p. 168.
[4] See *ibid.*, pp. 168*ff*.

Eight years ago I bought a portrait of a woman by Modigliani — certainly one of the greatest painters of this century — for £50. So that when I received an invitation to a private view of Modiglianis in a West End Gallery, I accepted it at once. There were no £50 items in this show. I halted before the picture which pleased me most, and asked the price of it. The Manager replied "A Paris dealer offered me £6,000, but I refused it. . . ." [5]

Arnold himself, in the great slump, parted shortly afterwards with his own Modigliani at a huge profit.

That, indeed, is as it should be. I need hardly say that this man, accused so often of avarice and stinginess, this author, the most highly paid of his epoch and the continual victim of overwork, had agreed to write the preface — and no one except a fellow author can estimate the nuisance value of having to break off what you are working at, in order to write something else, however small it may be — without payment of any kind, solely in order to help two young writers in whom he believed, and whom he knew to be undergoing a difficult time financially. But, in truth, there was always something big and generous about him, just as there was about his physical personality, even though it may not have been prepossessing at first sight, a delightful quality of exuberance; which in itself plainly proclaimed him to be no skinflint. In London or Venice or Paris, in great world or little, he remained always, as the result of the conditions of his early life, that happiest of beings, a provincial on holiday — a comfortable provincial of genius on holiday. This accounted for his interest in large hotels (all businessmen from the provinces enjoy a similar Babylonish thrill when they arrive at a famous place of fashion or luxury), for his attention to clothes and innumerable other details of life. He still dared to take nothing for granted, but was in no sense uneasy: yet this verdict must be modified, since he was naturally at home with the arts. As he grew older, there was no shrinking of his spirit, as some-

[5] Arnold Bennett, *Journal*, 1929. (Cassell, London, 1930.)

times there is. . . . One night, in the last months of Arnold's life, I dined in Chiltern Court with H. G. Wells, who occupied a flat in the same block, a few floors down, and only half the size of that into which his contemporary, friend and rival for fame had lately moved. The talk turning on his neighbor, a reflective look came into H. G.'s eyes, and he remarked in a confiding tone, and his very personal voice, so characteristic in the way it went high and low:

"The trouble is, whenever I do a thing, Arnold does it too, but twice as posh."

CHAPTER XII

Colophon

🌸🌸🌸🌸EHIND US, under the Arch of Time — in sub-
🌸 **B** 🌸 stance, by its very nature, transient, yet abiding
🌸 🌸 because its span is that of each generation — it
🌸🌸🌸🌸 has been possible to catch final glimpses of a few
figures upon whom the last hours of sunlight have fallen with
a peculiar flourish and prosperity. But now the gate has shut,
and within the gallery we have just left brood once more the
darkness and peace of night.

At last I have clothed fully with flesh the skeleton, the first
idea of which, and the labor it would impose upon me, came
as I walked by a dry and stony river course in Italy twenty
years ago: then, ten years after, staying in the mountains by
the Grande Chartreuse among the aromatic airs of that high
and herb-strewn region, I drew the frame upon a sheet of
paper, indicating the articulations, and a decade has been
required of me to finish my task. Now, if I am not to spoil the
design, I must leave adventures and friendships of other years
for a later incorporation or embodiment, though alas, this
compels me to abandon many people and places I would have
liked to describe for you. . . . Let me elaborate a little before
I end. I have referred to, but I have not told you of, as I meant
to have done, the appearance of Manuel de Falla, of how his
somber head might have been cut from Spanish stone, and
of the precision with which his appearance matched that of
the Gothic Spanish saints, standing on the ledges of their cathedrals; nor have I written of how Maurice Ravel was brought
to dinner with me in my London house, and of how the glittering shapes it contained in blue and pink glass and in shellwork

caught his fancy, and he played with them as a child might with a toy. Nor have I, in the course of the preceding volumes, been able to try to present for you Tchelitchev, great artist, greatest of living draftsmen, nor to summon up for you the transcending magic of his amazing and illuminating discourses, conducted in several languages not native to him, and with gestures, frequent and illustrative, of his fine painter's hands. King Francis the First was supposed once to have said that it was worth while to have lived if only to have heard Leonardo da Vinci talk for an hour; and so, too, with Tchelitchev, an artist whose mind, except that it is Slav, approaches in type that of the Italian Master; an hour's conversation opens wide for an instant whole vistas hitherto closed, lights the distances, and makes you too behold them while he speaks, proving by ineffable similes the miraculous ways of Nature and of the Spirit, showing for example, it may be, how all creatures, all crystalline and vegetable forms, are subject to the same immutable laws of structure.

Again, there are so many countries I should have liked to describe for you, in the same way that I wrote of my home in Italy. I could talk to you, Reader, for many minutes, if the plan permitted it, of the Street of the Paper Hangers in Peking, best to be seen from the Jesuit Observatory, just at that instant when the ten days' season of the Chinese spring flames suddenly, in the course of some forty or sixty hours, into an emeraldine summer, and a city turns to a forest as the trees assume their thick estival fleece. I could tell you of the Great Wall of China, as it sweeps for miles over gray and brown mountains down to the sea, and I would like to attempt to paint for you too the Highlands of Guatemala, where the little golden Indians trot briskly along their paths and the trees carry on their branches the stove plants, ringed with brilliant red and blue, of English hothouses, epiphytes that flourish dreamily in the warm mists of the Andes; or I would endeavor — and how difficult it is! — to conjure up for you a sight and sound

of the famous pig market of St. Francis, highest in the world
and alive with its own sound, situated at some twelve thousand feet above sea level, and of the hundreds of Indian
farmers, in their thick, striped blankets, who there talk together and smoke cigars, while on a long piece of string each
of them leads, like so many pet dogs, twelve or fourteen
squealing porklings, straining to escape, screaming loud with
the eager lusts of greed or the wish to explore these barren
uplands, fields of rock sprinkled with agaves as though darts
had pierced the clefts, under the burning tent shape of the
sky; or I would speak to you for a moment of the *douanier*
at the jungle border of Salvador, and of his customshouse that
was a cage of tame monkeys, and also of parrots, their wings
aflame with scarlet and green, chattering and squawking
through the heat of the day and the gloom engendered by
impenetrable orchid-strewn tropical wastes. I would like to
stop to tell you — it would take five minutes — of my visit
to Mycenae, of the wasp-waisted people who still live in it,
and of how I dreamed, ten years later, of the two journalists
just as they were kidnaped there by the insurgents; or to try
to make permanent in words the large white roses of Olympia flowering coolly and fragrantly upon houses built of
bricks of brown mud; or of torrid noons in Morocco, spent
in an open motor in a burnous of dust, under the flashing
sun, while a wheel was hammered incessantly for hours;
or of the afternoon when my dear friend Ethel Sands took
my brother and me to look for peonies in the High Atlas,
and of how we reached a village filled with almost naked men
and women, with one exception — a respectable French couple who ran a café and issued out in thick French bourgeois
dress, speaking banal phrases in the most civilized of languages. . . . But all this must wait until, if I am allowed the
time, I write another book I plan — *The Four Continents*.
. . . There are all kinds of small episodes I should have liked
to relate, to stress in their own place, as — to give you one

example — an account of that golden Syracusan April morning I spent in a boat with my friends Marion Dorn, Ted McKnight Kauffer and Adrian Stokes, in search of the Nymph Cyane within her fountain, and of how, on the way up the glassy stream, between banks lined with the large green-fringed heads of papyrus, the homeric boatman caught small, darting crabs, and crunched the shell and legs of the living thing between his teeth, saying "Vair goot," "*Molto buono*," and of the bull's skull we found, gleaming in its dry, white and forever isolated beauty, near the fountain which seemed to hold within its depths, not only the Nymph herself, but the cool and united reflections of every color of the neighborhood, in the same way that the unique substance, Sicilian amber — baked by the fires and under the lava of Etna — holds within it all the colors of the world. Or I would like to converse with you once more and at some length of my father, recalling certain things, and passing them on to you: little details, as, for example, how he gave a quick sideways glance at the evicted tenants who had come back to Montegufoni to put in a day of glum staring at the changes that were being wrought before their eyes, and with a typical misinterpretation of their sullen look pronounced to me:

"You see, *I* can always make myself popular when I want to!"

Or I would picture for you, at greater length than I can do now, the first day I spent at the Castello after the war, and how, though the tides of destruction and men of several armies had passed through its hall, and albeit, in the next room, in what had been my father's study, the brown-tiled floor was littered with charters and ancient parchment deeds, torn and trampled, relating to the family estates in Derbyshire and Yorkshire, yet in his bedroom his round air cushion hung still in the cupboard, and the eighteenth-century rapier, nacre-handled, which he kept as a protection against burglars, still lay on the table, beside the huge gilded bed, with its rococo masks, under the coved ceiling, where flying cupids pelt down flowers from a sky swimming with light. These many incidents, great or small, humorous or the reverse, are enclosed between the shattered and tragic walls of the present time.

As we turn away from the past, to regard the path in front of us, we must all of us realize that it leads inexorably and with certainty to personal oblivion, and probably to darkness in a more general sense. Therefore have I stirred the embers of my memory, that they might give a flame before the arch itself begins to sag. It frames a desolate scene; for the huge horizons which once we saw with the vision of childhood or with the eyes of youth have dwindled to dust, and in this dust, in the infinite universe comprised or reflected in it, lies the threat which I outlined for the reader at the end of the preceding book. Only the sounds remain the same from childhood, the piercing scream of the bitter-beaked seagulls flying in and over the white, wintry shore, and the ominous words, which have followed me all my life, since they were first chanted or slyly insinuated so early in the morning under the dawn sky, "Rags and Bones."

"Rags and Bones," or "Look under the flesh for the skeleton, and in the construction of the skeleton for the fiery core, and the swift, fierce chance of immortality. . . ." Let us, before we part, then, take one more glance at the phoenixes and phantoms who in this ultimate book of my autobiography have shaken on their contours and colors for us once more. The gallery is now dark and peaceful, and they sleep again, untroubled by dreams, or if a memory stirs in them, it is as a tendril of a vine stretches towards the sun. As they rest there alone, and before we go to join them — as sooner or later we must — we will turn to salute them; for at least let it be said of me, as my apologia, that, undecided as my character was in much else, I have nevertheless followed the lines I traced for myself in the right hand, rather than those inalterably incised in my left, and that I have traveled from far countries, down the long roads I have described, from Normandy and Anjou and Italy, from Derbyshire and Ireland, and with the innumerable and unknown currents of blood that all human beings share, to find my home in the end, and for the first time truly, in the arts; that I recognized an artist whenever I saw one, whether the scale of his creation was great or small, and respected him, that I perceived in art the spirit made concrete and the flesh made eternal, and that accordingly I have admired talent and adored genius on each occasion that I met it. And so I take my farewell of these noble essences and, Reader, of you, before my world closes down, and the rending cry "Rags and Bones" becomes no longer prophetic, but universal and of the present time.

RENISHAW
  June 30, 1949

APPENDIX A

From *Things that Have Interested Me*

by

Arnold Bennett

STILL MORE about the censorship. In June last a firm of picture-dealers in London, very honorably known, ordered from Amsterdam fifteen etchings by Félicien Rops at a total price of £127. Last month the consignment had not reached these chaste shores, but the picture-dealers, after long inquiry, had learnt that it had been held up by the British Post Office, on the ground that some of the etchings were "indecent." On the 24th ultimo the picture-dealers reasoned gently with the Post Office. They pointed out that Rops was regarded by competent authorities as one of the greatest modern etchers, that his works (including many of those held up) had been publicly exhibited in London, amid the plaudits of the most respectable journalistic critics, that all the impugned etchings are to be found in the Public Library of Washington, and that Rops is well represented in all the great collections. Also that fully illustrated books about Rops, written by first-rate authorities, can be bought from any good second-hand bookseller in London. Hence the picture-dealers hopefully asked for the release of the consignment. Fond picture-dealers. Four days later they received the following epistle from the G.P.O.: "I am directed by the Postmaster-General to inform you that as certain of the prints contained in the packet in question were undoubtedly of an obscene character the packet was properly stopped in the post under the regulation shown at page 17 of the Post Office Guide. *Its contents have been destroyed in ordinary course"* (my italics) . . .

8 *February*, 1919.

A question was asked in the House about the destruction of Rops' etchings. The Postmaster-General admitted all the facts, and stated that he would do nothing to alter the system which permitted the highly cultivated human products of our public schools to destroy at their own caprice the works of genius. However, the present exposure has probably accomplished some good, for even anonymous officials hate to be made ridiculous in the public eye.

22 *February*, 1919.

The scandal of the destruction of a whole series of etchings by Félicien Rops has not yet abated. Last week the Postmaster-General offered to the House of Commons a new defence of his vandalistic subordinate, in which he remarked *ex cathedra* that it needed no special training to judge whether or not a work of art was obscene. . . .

8 *March*, 1919.

APPENDIX B

THE POET AND THE MIRROR [1]

by

Sacheverell Sitwell

⧉⧉⧉⧉OMETHING of a soldier is each poet;
  ⧉ S ⧉ At least both share like triumph in their dreams,
  ⧉   ⧉ Though poetry comes quicker than a plan of
⧉⧉⧉⧉   battle,
And it blows through shriller trumpets for attack.
After the sharp rivers that run down like swords,
The hills, and the baffling clouds men hide behind,
Victory, when it comes at last,
Through the veins of these two races runs the same,
They are lifted and stand still like eagles in the wind;
For both there should be halls made ready for their feasting
Filled with the false sunlight that burns pale by morning
And loud with music, though the throbbing music dies,
And nothing now is left of it,
For the poet, like music and the lights, dies back again.
How can the poet live and feast through time?
For only the soldier gets the spoil to take away.
Poor are all poets born beneath the starrèd shade,
They must live and while their days last
The showering gold may comfort them,
Sun by day and moon by night
Their purse and bread,
While grass grows to sleep on and the leaves will give them
    shade:
They may stand long in the cold snow with stars for crumbs,

[1] From *Selected Poems* by Sacheverell Sitwell. (Gerald Duckworth & Co., 1948.)

[343]

Rain will give them water, and the light from houses warm
  them
As they stand outside.
Cold does the wind blow, neck deep do they wade in it,
While the pavers stretch their icy plain beneath the feet.
This is his campaigning and its flags wave on the chilled air,
That air through which his words go, from which his words
  are made,
While out of that thin substance, though he dies, yet do his
  thoughts live.
All brave soldiers, though they die, are not remembered
And so it is with poets however high they climb to die:
How, then, can his memory live who had not strength to win
  his battle,
Who shivered in the snow, and in the sun was parched and
  thirsty?
No one will remember him, himself his only friend
And all the tears that fall but his own brackish sorrow.
If no one will remember me, somehow I will make a mote
That smarts however strong the eyes
And lodges there like dust to tingle,
Living in their vision like the fire heart in all smoke,
And so each time they look
My mote smarts and they rub their eyes:
Deep as the deepest sea, unruffled, never cut by wind,
This mirror is the water where I write my name,
Eating earth up inch by inch
As the tides do, tilting at us out of the salt sea.
I stand before this mirror and I walk away,
While my image, like the dying tide, ebbs before its change:
It walks out of the mirror as though I climbed out of the
  water,
But yet it never ruffles and I hear no lapping waves:
These waters like the Dead Sea
Keep us floating though we cannot swim.

Acknowledgments

ON BRINGING this Autobiography to its close with a book very different from its predecessors, but still part of my whole design, I should like once more to thank all those whose help I have previously acknowledged, and to name those who have aided me in the production of this final volume. Taking the order in which these *Characters* are present, I have in the first place to thank Sir Leslie Farrer, for allowing me to print the letter of the late Reginald Farrer, given in *Portfolio*.

I am indebted to Lady Dorothy Charteris, Messrs. William Heinemann Ltd. and Harper & Brothers for authorizing the use of various quotations from Sir Evan Charteris's *Life and Letters of Sir Edmund Gosse*. I am also obliged to the editor of *Horizon*, where this chapter first appeared.

Messrs. Gerald Duckworth, London, and New Directions Ltd. have been good enough to allow me to quote from the works of Ronald Firbank and publish my essay on him, which, in its first form, appeared under their auspices.

Wilfred Owen's brother, Mr. Harold Owen, has helped me greatly, and I am much in his debt and that of his sister, Miss Mary Owen, for authorizing the use of extracts from the poet's letters and works. Mr. Frank Nicholson has kindly allowed me to quote his letter about the poet. And Messrs. Chatto & Windus and New Directions have also given their consent for me to reprint various passages from letters and poems. The chapter is included here by arrangement with Mr. John Lehmann, editor of *The Penguin New Writing*, in which it was originally published. The first form of the essay on D'Annunzio, which has since been rewritten, appeared in *Discursions* and Messrs. Gerald Duckworth & Co.

Ltd. have allowed me to publish it here. I am grateful to Mrs. Guy Wyndham for material from *Letters to the Sphinx from Oscar Wilde and Reminiscences of the Author*, by Ada Leverson, and to Mr. Vyvyan Holland for the quotations from letters and telegrams from Oscar Wilde reprinted from that work.

I should like once more to place on record my great gratitude to the late Miss Thérèse Lessore, for the help she gave me over many points in my *Character* of her husband, W. R. Sickert. The chapter first appeared in *Orion*, to whose editors I make this acknowledgment, and subsequently as Preface to *A Free House* published by Macmillan.

In the chapter on W. H. Davies I am permitted to make the quotations from his *Collected Poems* and his *Autobiography of a Super-Tramp* by the generosity of Mrs. W. H. Davies, of Mr. Harrison Smith and of the publishers, Messrs. Jonathan Cape Ltd., who have also allowed me to include the poem that later appears in the chapter on Violet Gordon Woodhouse. And I acknowledge the kindness of Mr. Robert Herring, editor of *Life and Letters Today* in which the *Character* first appeared.

Mrs. Dorothy Cheston Bennett and the Viking Press, Inc. have very graciously given me permission to quote from the *Journals of Arnold Bennett;* Mrs. Bennett has also allowed me to quote from that author's *Letter to a Nephew, Richard Bennett* and from an article in the *Adelphi* and the Public Trustee and Doubleday & Company, Inc. have allowed me to quote from Arnold Bennett's *Things that Have Interested Me* (In *Appendix A*): and I again have to thank Mr. John Lehmann, as editor of *Orpheus*, in which magazine the *Character* first appeared.

The Poet and The Mirror is printed as *Appendix B* by kind permission of my brother, Sacheverell Sitwell and the publishers, Messrs. Gerald Duckworth & Co. Ltd.

And finally I wish to thank Mr. Bernard Shaw for writing half a page of my autobiography.

INDEX

Index

"A Terre" (Owen), 122

Aberconway, Lady, 291

Adelphi, 329

Adey, More, 111, 116–117

Agnew, Messrs. Thomas, 222

Alfonso XIII, King of Spain, 280

Alma-Tadema, Sir Lawrence, 186

Annunzio, Gabriele D', Regent of Carnaro, 125, 137; his literary work, 125, 128, 142; his love affairs, 125–126; author's contacts with, 126, 138 ff.; and Fiume, 127, 128; and the Press, 128–129; and war, 129, 130; his influence, 132–133; his fleet, 134; and the English, 135–136; his army, 136; his apartments, 137; his appearance, 138–139; leaves Fiume, 141; libels on, 141

Arbos, E. Fernandez, 287

Argonaut and Juggernaut (Osbert Sitwell), 25, 325, 326

Aria, Eliza, 177–179

Arlen, Michael, 230

"Arms and the Boy" (Owen), 121

Art and Letters, 86, 122, 325

"Asra, Der" (Heine), 28, 32

Atkin, Gabriel, 84, 95

Autobiography of a Super-Tramp (Davies), 233, 238, 240, 241, 244, 252–253, 256, 266

Barrie, Sir James, 176

Barrington, Lord, 267, 271, 282, 285

Bartolozzi, Francesco, 279

Baudelaire, Charles, 3

Beardsley, Aubrey, 154, 158, 213, 304

Beardsley, Mabel, 158, 164

Beaufort, 8th Duke of, 80

Beaverbrook, Lord, 327

Beddington, Mrs., 146

Beerbohm, Constance, 176

Beerbohm, Lady, 61, 175

Beerbohm, Sir Max, 61, 146, 171, 174–176, 193

Before the Bombardment (Osbert Sitwell), 178

Bell, Clive, 218, 220

Bennett, Arnold, 8; and Wilfred Owen, 118; and evening dress, 239, 331–332; and W. H. Davies, 257–258; at the Reform Club, 317; compared with Gosse, 318; his literary work, 318; his appearance, 319–320; his stammer, 321–322; his essay on the Sitwells, 329–330; at the circus, 330–331; and Exhibition of Modern French Art, 332–333; his *Journal*, 333; H. G. Wells on, 334; passage from his *Things That Have Interested Me*, 341–342

Bennett, Mrs. Arnold, 327, 330–331

Benson, E. F., 72–73

Berners, Lord, 98

Bernhardt, Sarah, 145, 274

Berrenger, Oscar, 273

Berry, Mary, 52

"Bird of Paradise, The" (Davies), 246–247

Black and White, 153

Blake, William, 198, 250, 255, 257, 284, 314

Blunden, Edmund, 104, 108, 119

Borenius, Dr. Tancred, 114, 221

Boulestin, Marcel, 145, 163–164

Brooke, Rupert, 45

Brown, Ford Madox, 49, 56

Browning, Robert, 49

Buchanan (cat), 57

Burlington Magazine, 111, 116, 185

Burne-Jones, Sir Edward, 116, 160

Burton, Miss, 114, 117

Byron, Lord, 125

C——, Marchesa, 94

Campbell, Mrs. Patrick, 87

Caprice (Firbank), 77, 94, 97

Carisbrooke, Lord, 280

Carlyle, Thomas, 53

Index

Carpenter, Nettie, 287
Carrington, 14
Casals, Pablo, 287
Chaliapin, Feodor, 305
Cham (Vicomte de Noé), 216
"Chances, The" (Owen), 122
Chatto & Windus, Messrs., 324–325, 326, 329
Childe, Wilfred, 85
Christ (Epstein), 28
Church, Richard, 254–255, 291
Churchill, Arabella, 52
Clemenceau, Georges, 120
Clotilde, 151–152
Cobden, Richard, 195
Cockerell, Sir Sydney, 68
Colefax, Lady, 45
Colette, 163–164
Collins, Churton, 43–44, 57
Colonel Newcome, 164
Colvin, Lady, 71
Colvin, Sir Sidney, 50, 71–72
Conder, Charles, 200
Connolly, Cyril, 10
Courtneidge, Cicely, 277
Coxe, Judge, 284
Cranbourne, Viscountess. *See* Salisbury, Elizabeth, Marchioness of
Curzon, Lord, 65, 133–134

Danby, Frank, 177
Dante (vessel), 134
Davies, W. H., 8; at Sickert's breakfast parties, 211, 217; and Nina Hamnett, 230, 231, 237; his birth and upbringing, 232–234, 241–242; and Violet Gordon Woodhouse, 234, 267, 291–292; his likeness to Irving, 234–235; and evening dress, 239; goes to America, 242–243; returns to London, 243; his first poems, 243–244; as a tramp in England, 245–246; and Francis Thompson, 246; his "The Bird of Paradise," 246–247; marries and leaves London, 247, 266; his home in Great Russell St., 248; his likes and dislikes, 248–253; and Belgian refugee, 254–255; and Walter De la Mare, 255–256; and Sir Henry Newbolt, 256; Epstein's sculpture

of, 257, 270; and Robert Nichols, 257; and Arnold Bennett, 258; and Sickert's etchings, 258, 270; and Haraldur Hamar, 259–261; and the police, 266; his illness and death, 268–271
Davies, Mrs. W. H., 266, 268, 269
Davis (nurse), 35, 37, 38
"Dead-Beat, The" (Owen), 122
Deffand, Mme. du, 147
Degas, Hilaire, 186, 195, 197, 200, 213
De la Mare, Walter, 236, 255
Dell, Ethel M., 97
"Deranged, The" (Owen), 111
Descriptive Catalogue, A (Blake), 198
Diaghilev, Serge, 263, 290, 305
Dieren, Bernard van, 28–32, 218, 291
"Disabled" (Owen), 121, 122
Discursions on Travel, Art and Life (Osbert Sitwell), 166
Dolmetsch, Arnold, 273
Dorn, Marion, 338
Doughty, C. M., 67–68
Douglas, Lord Alfred, 113, 172
Downman, John, 83
Drinkwater, John, 46
Duncan, Isadora, 87
Duse, Eleonora, 125

Earp, Thomas, 85
Eden, Sir William, 215
Elgar, Sir Edward, 277
Eliot, T. S., O.M., 45, 291
Elizondo, Brother, 288
English Review, 111, 171
Epstein, Jacob, 28, 257
Exhibition of Modern French Art, 332

Falla, Manuel de, 235, 290, 335
Farrer, J. A., 19
Farrer, Mrs., 18, 19
Farrer, Reginald, 17–28
Father and Son (Gosse), 40
Fauré, Gabriel, 78
Field, Mrs. (nurse), 159
Firbank, Lady, 80, 90
Firbank, Ronald, 8; his works, 77, 79, 80, 93, 96–97; his appearance,

78; his ancestry, 80; in Egypt, 80, 98; at Oxford, 81–86; his *objets d'art*, 82–83; and dinner in his honor, 84–86; in Italy, 86, 170; his visit to Augustus John, 89–90; in France, 91–92; and Marchesa C——, 94; his palm tree, 96; in London, 96; his illness and death, 97–98; and Ada Leverson, 143; author's observation of, 165

Firbank, Sir Thomas, 80

Flower Beneath the Foot, The (Firbank), 77, 88

Forster, E. M., 46

Fratellini, the, 330

Free House, A (Sickert; ed. Osbert Sitwell), 184

Fry, Roger, 63, 185, 193, 210, 218, 230

Futurist Exhibition, 77

GAINSBOROUGH, THOMAS, 52, 248

Galsworthy, John, 176

Garibaldi, Giuseppe, 136

Gaudier-Brzeska, Henri, 63, 230

"Gebir" (Landor), 51

Georgian Poetry, 45, 75

Gertler, Mark, 63

Gide, André, 15, 69–71

Gilbert, Sir John, 187

Giolitti, Giovanni, 136, 140

Glenconner, Lady, 301

Godfrey, Mrs. *See* Churchill, Arabella

Goff, Thomas, 273, 282

Good-Humoured Ladies, The (Scarlatti-Tommasini), 263

Goossens, Eugene, 328

Gosse, Sir Edmund, 7, 8; his literary works, 40–41; and the Sitwells, 42, 47, 61–63, 72–76; visits Tennyson, 43–44; and younger poets, 45–47; and Pound, 46; his Sunday gatherings, 47, 56 ff.; his hands, 47–48; and Swinburne, 47, 49, 53; and D. G. Rossetti, 49, 53–54; and Stevenson, 50–51; and William Morris, 53–54; and W. M. Rossetti, 55; his drawing room, 56–7; Librarian of the House of Lords, 58, 64–65; his dinner parties, 61–62;

his snobbery, 64; and C. M. Doughty, 67–68; knighted, 68; and André Gide, 69–71; and Sir Sidney Colvin, 71–72; and E. F. Benson, 72–73; at Hawthornden Prize giving, 73–76; at Hardy's funeral, 176; compared with Arnold Bennett, 318

Gosse, Mrs. Edmund, 48, 57–59, 61

Gosse, Dr. Philip, 40, 44, 48, 66

Gosse, Sylvia, 59, 61

Gosse, Tessa, 59, 61

Gould, Gerald, 79

Grainger, Percy, 287

Grant, Duncan, 186

Graves, Robert, 45, 291

Great Morning! (Osbert Sitwell), 77

Green Carnation, The (Hichens), 155

Greene, Robert, 245

Grey of Fallodon, Viscountess, 301–302

Guevara, Alvaro, 211, 218, 259

Gwynne family, 273, 290

HALDANE, LORD, 58, 60, 65

Haldane, Miss, 58

Hamar, Haraldur, 259–261

Hamnett, Nina, 63, 211, 218, 230–231, 237, 248, 257, 259, 260

Hard Times (Dickens), 169

Hardy, Thomas, 49, 176

Hare, Augustus, 163

Harris, Frank, 173, 213

Hawthornden Prize giving, 73–76

Headlam, Rev. Stuart, 159

Hendecourt, Vicomte Bernard d', 221

Henley, W. E., 51

Hodgson, Ralph, 255

Horizon, 175

Horner, David, 181, 308

Howard's End (Forster), 46–47

Hulbert, Jack, 277

Humphreys, Arthur, 157

Hunters and the Hunted, The (Sacheverell Sitwell), 28, 31, 219

Huxley, Aldous, 45, 211, 218, 258 291, 325, 330–331

Huxley, Maria, 330–331

Hydra, The, 110

"Ill Winds" (Osbert Sitwell), 120
Importance of Being Earnest, The (Wilde), 158
In Russet and Silver (Gosse), 50
Irving, Sir Henry, 177–179, 188, 235

Jack the Ripper, 211–212
James, Henry, 49, 147
Jim (toad), 268, 270
John, Augustus, O.M., 83, 89–90, 94, 136, 259, 261
John Bull, 119
Journals of André Gide, The, 69

Kauffer, E. McKnight, 338
Keats, John, 46, 71, 99, 106
Keene, Charles, 194, 213
Kent, William, 304–305
Kindler, Frida (Mrs. Bernard van Dieren), 30
Kindler, Hans, 30
Koanga (Delius), 290
Konody, P. G., 219

Labouchère, Max, 285
Lafayette, Marquis de, 257
Lamotte de Valois, Mme. de, 29
Lancet, 114
Lara, Isidore de, 155
Laroon, Marcellus, 222, 225–226
"Last Laugh, The" (Owen), 121
"Last Word, The" (Owen), 121
Laughter in the Next Room (Osbert Sitwell), 9, 45, 112, 175, 301, 325, 332
Lawrence, Katie, 201
Left Hand, Right Hand! (Osbert Sitwell), 163, 287
Letters of Robert Louis Stevenson (Colvin), 50–51
Letters to the Sphinx from Oscar Wilde and Reminiscences of the Author (Leverson), 143, 158, 159
Leverson, Ada, 8; her literary work, 143; letters from Oscar Wilde to, 143, 155, 159, 160, 171, 172; author and, 144, 145, 147, 152, 160–161; and Oscar Wilde, 144, 145, 146, 153, 154–157, 158–160, 163, 172, 174; her appearance, 145, 149, 163, 165; and Henry James, 147–148; her letters to author, 148; and Sir George Sitwell, 149–150; and Arthur Waley, 151; and Aubrey Beardsley, 154; and the Caribou, 157–158; in the nineties, 160–161; and Boulestin, 163–164; her travels, 166; at Renishaw, 179–180; her death, 180
Leverson, Ernest, 158
Leverson, Violet, 146, 157, 163, 181
Lewis, Percy Wyndham, 63, 218–220
Life and Letters of Sir Edmund Gosse (Charteris), 49, 53, 62
Lindsay, Norah, 284
Londesborough, 1st Earl of (grandfather), 216

"Machine Breaks Down, The" (Osbert Sitwell), 171
McLeod, Irene Rutherford, 45
Magnasco Society, 221
Malatesta, 132
Man Who Lost Himself, The (Osbert Sitwell), 312
Marchesi, Blanche, 290
Marinetti, 137
Marsh, Sir Edward, 46
Marziale, Théophile, 49
Masques and Phases (Ross), 164
Massingham, H. W., 112, 131, 218
Maugham, W. Somerset, 235
Melmoth, Sebastian (Oscar Wilde), 172
"Mental Cases" (Owen), 111, 121
Meredith, George, 176
Millar, Gertie, 214
Miller, Max, 305
Mitchison, Naomi, 60
Modigliani, Amedeo, 63, 230, 333
Monro, Harold, 257
Montegufoni, Castello di, 10, 170, 338
Moon, The (Sacheverell Sitwell), 34
Moore, George, 61, 173, 187, 214
Morrell, Lady Ottoline, 219
Morris, William, 49, 53
Myself, My Two Countries (Boulestin), 145, 163

Nash, John, 63
Nash, Paul, 63

Index

Nation, 112–113, 131, 218

Nevinson, C. R. W., 63, 81, 218

Newbolt, Sir Henry, 256

Nichols, Robert, 45, 46, 61, 112, 257, 291

Nicholson, Frank, 108–109

Normanby, Marchioness of, 67

Oiseau de Feu, L' (Stravinsky), 77

Old Huntsman, The (Sassoon), 110

Olivier, Edith, 302

"On Hearing Mrs. Woodhouse Play the Harpsichord" (Davies), 292

Orioli, G., 131, 134

Our Mutual Friend (Dickens), 50

Owen, Wilfred, 8; his poems quoted, 101, 102, 104, 105, 106, 107, 121, 122; and author, 101, 117–118, 122–123; letters quoted, 103–104, 108, 109, 110, 111, 112, 119, 120–121, 123; Tailhade's letter to, 107, joins Army, 107; in hospital, 108; and Frank Nicholson, 108–109; and Siegfried Sassoon, 110–112; at Robert Ross's, 117–118; his appearance and personality, 117–118; his letter to author, 120–121; and Violet Gordon Woodhouse, 122–123, 291

Owen, Wilfred, The Poems of (Blunden), 104, 108

Oxford and Asquith, Lady, 218, 232

Oxford and Asquith, Lord, 232, 247, 251

Paderewski, 146, 288

Paolo, Giovanni di, 115

"Parable of the Old Man and the Young" (Owen), 121

Parker (parlormaid), 56, 59–61

Patti, Adelina, 290

Paul (waiter), 223–224

Pavlova, Anna, 87

Payne, Helen. *See* Davies, Mrs. W. H.

People's Palace, The (Sacheverell Sitwell), 34

Pepys, Samuel, 302

Picasso, Pablo, 63, 289–290

Picture of Dorian Gray, A (Wilde), 154

Pinto, Vivian de Sola, 85

Pirate's Who's Who (Philip Gosse), 66

Pissarro, Camille, 200

Place of One's Own, A (Osbert Sitwell), 315

Poems and Ballads (Swinburne), 53

Poet and the Mirror, The (Sacheverell Sitwell), 343–344

Poetry and Drama, 257

Poor Minnie, 167–169

Post-Impressionist Show, 77, 332

Pound, Ezra, 46, 59, 291

Powell, Mrs. (housekeeper), 206

Prancing Nigger (Firbank), 77

Price, Dr. Harry, 6–7

Prinsep, Val, 221

Prometheus (Scriabin), 78

Public Address (Blake), 198–199

Puccini Among Friends (Seligman), 146

Punch, 153, 180

Quarterly, 43

Rachmaninoff, Sergei, 290

Rainbow Bridge, The (Farrer), 24

Raleigh, Prof. Sir Walter, 220

Rape of the Lock, The (Pope), 304

Ravel, Maurice, 328, 335–336

Read, Herbert, 325

Renishaw, 179, 180, 182, 271, 272, 293–294, 312, 314, 315–316

Renoir, René Auguste, 186, 200, 203

Reynolds, Sir Joshua, 257

Richards, Grant, 81, 329

Richardson, Frank, 164

Rita, 37–39

Robins (butler), 306

Robins, Betty, 306

Robinson, Charles, 227

Robinson, W. Heath, 227

Rodin, Auguste, 290

Rootham, Helen, 263, 264

Rops, Félicien, 83, 216–217, 341–342

Rosenkavalier (Richard Strauss), 78

Ross, Alec, 114

Ross, Lady, 328

Ross, Robert, 42, 45, 61, 101, 109, 112, 113–117, 143–144, 160, 164, 171–172, 174, 232, 317, 319, 323

[353]

Rossetti, Dante Gabriel, 49, 52, 53, 56, 59, 160, 221

Rossetti, W. M., 55, 59

Rothenstein, Lady, 213

Rothenstein, Sir William, 213

Rubio, 273, 287–288

Ruskin, John, 221

Rutherston, Albert, 83, 213

Rutter, Frank, 325

SALISBURY, ELIZABETH, MARCHIONESS OF, 215

Salisbury, Georgiana, Marchioness of, 215

Salisbury, Robert Cecil, 3rd Marquis of, 215

Sands, Ethel, 337

Sandys, Frederick, 221

Santal (Firbank), 77

Sarasate, Pablo de, 287

Sassoon, Siegfried, 45, 46, 60, 84, 101, 102, 110, 112, 117, 122–123, 257, 291

Scarborough, 36, 66, 119, 178

Scarlatti and His Times (Sacheverell Sitwell), 287

Scarlet Tree, The (Osbert Sitwell), 17

Schiff, Mrs. Sydney, 144, 146

Schönberger, 273

Schuster, Frank, 16

Segovia, 287

Seligman, Mrs., 146

"Sentry, The" (Owen), 122

Shaw, George Bernard, 40, 42, 174, 176, 243, 244, 274–278

Shelley, Percy Bysshe, 46, 99, 128, 139, 241

Shenstone, William, 302

"Show, The" (Owen), 122

Sickert, Mrs. Christine, 187, 204–205, 207

Sickert, Walter Richard, 8, 63; his drawing of Ada Leverson, 161; and Oscar Wilde, 174; and Denton Welch, 175; and Edith Sitwell, 183; his works, 183, 184, 196 ff.; his writings, 185, 188, 197, 209; and Roger Fry, 185; as an actor, 188; at Swan Walk, 191 ff.; his appearance and personality, 191–195; his studio, 195, 199, 204; and Conder,

200; and Whistler's pictures, 201; and auction of forged pictures, 203; and author, 205–211, 218–219, 220–226; and Jack the Ripper, 211–213; and George Moore, 214; and W. H. Davies, 217, 258; and Percy Wyndham Lewis, 218–220; retires to Broadstairs, 226–227; and Sacheverell Sitwell, 227; his "Echos," 228–229; Nina Hamnett's drawing of, 230; and W. H. Davies and Aldous Huxley, 258

Sigurd the Volsung (Morris), 53

Simmonds, William, 282

Sitwell, Dr. Edith (sister), and Reginald Farrer, 17; episode of her early childhood, 34–39; at poetry reading, 45; and Sir Edmund Gosse, 47, 62; and review of "Vainglory," 79; and Robert Ross, 112; her editorship of *Wheels,* 121, 122; and Wilfred Owen's poems, 122; and Ada Leverson, 148; visits London at Christmas, 161; and Walter Richard Sickert, 182–183, 204, 205, 218; Nina Hamnett's drawing of, 230; and W. H. Davies, 237, 244–245, 263–265, 267; and Violet Gordon Woodhouse, 290; and Arnold Bennett, 322, 327

Sitwell, Florence (aunt), 182

Sitwell, Sir George (father), and Reginald Farrer, 19; at Scarborough, 37, 38; his cautionary phrase, 131; and Ada Leverson, 149–150, 179; visits London at Christmas, 161, 162; at Montegufoni, 170; and W. H. Davies, 264–265; and G. B. Shaw, 276; and Rex Whistler, 294; and arches at Renishaw, 316; his air cushion, 331; and Arnold Bennett, 331

Sitwell, Lady Ida (mother), and episode of Edith's childhood, 35, 37, 38; and Ada Leverson, 149–150; visits London at Christmas, 161, 162; at Montegufoni, 170

Sitwell, Lady Louisa (grandmother), 17

Sitwell, Sir Osbert, in Spain, 10–16; and Lytton Strachey, 14–16; and

Reginald Farrer, 17–28; and Bernard van Dieren, 28–32; and Sir Edmund Gosse, 40–76; and Ronald Firbank, 77–100; in the Army, 77, 78, 190, 204, 222, 314, 324; edits *Art and Letters*, 86; and Wilfred Owen, 101–124; and Robert Ross, 112–113, 117; his poems published in the *Nation*, 112–113; as parliamentary candidate, 119; and Gabriele D'Annunzio, 124–142; and Ada Leverson, 143–181; and Isidore de Lara, 156; in Italy, 165 ff.; and Sir Max Beerbohm, 174–176; and Eliza Aria, 177–179; and Walter Richard Sickert, 182–229; and W. H. Davies, 230–271; and Violet Gordon Woodhouse, 272–292; and Bernard Shaw, 274–278; and Rex Whistler, 293–316; and Arnold Bennett, 317–334; and libel action, 318; and editing of literary paper, 323–325; Arnold Bennett's essay on, 329–330; at the circus, 330–331; his farewell to his portrait gallery, 335–340

Sitwell, Sacheverell (brother), in Spain, 10–16; and Bernard van Dieren, 28, 32–33; his early manhood, 33–34; at poetry reading, 45; and Sir Edmund Gosse, 47, 62, 63; at Oxford, 81; and Ronald Firbank, 84, 87, 97–98; and Robert Ross, 112; and D'Annunzio, 130 ff.; winters in Italy, 148, 165, 166; visits London at Christmas, 161; and Poor Minnie, 167–169; and Sir Max Beerbohm, 175; and Walter Richard Sickert, 190, 205, 227, 228; at dinner party at Carlyle Sq., 218; at Magnasco Society banquet, 221; and W. H. Davies, 231, 249, 250, 255, 259; and Haraldur Hamar, 259–260; his "The Poet and the Mirror," 260, 343; and Violet Gordon Woodhouse, 275, 288, 290; his *Scarlatti and His Times*, 287; and Arnold Bennett, 327–328, 331; at the circus, 330–331; and Exhibition of Modern French Art, 332

Smith, Logan Pearsall, 61

Smyth, Ethel, 79, 273, 287
"Soldiers' Dreams" (Owen), 121
Soyer, Alexis Benoît, 319
Sphinx (Ada Leverson), 145 ff.
Sprigge, Sir Squire, 114
Squire, Sir John, 45
Steer, Wilson, 187
Stevenson, Robert Louis, 49, 50, 51, 56, 71
Stokes, Adrian, 338
"Stone Ginger, A" (Sickert), 189
Storr, Paul, 303
Strachey, Lytton, 9–10, 14–16, 325
"Strange Meeting" (Owen), 105, 122
Stravinsky, Igor, 139, 290
Street, George, 164
Study in Temperament, A (Firbank), 81
Stulik, 94
Swan Walk, 62, 123, 191, 218, 259, 291
Swinburne, Algernon Charles, 47, 49, 52, 56, 63, 128, 174
Swinnerton, Frank, 218, 322, 323
Swinton, Mrs. George, 183
Symonds, J. A., 51

Tailhade, Laurent, 106, 107
Talk and Talkers (Stevenson), 51
Taylor, Walter, 208–209
Tchelitchew, Pavel, 336
Tennant, Hon. Stephen, 301–302
Tennyson, Lord Alfred, 43, 49, 109
Terence, 151–152
Terry, Ellen, 290
Things That Have Interested Me (Bennett), 341–342
Thompson, Francis, 245–246
Thornycroft, Sir Hamo, 46, 48
Tiscote, Mrs., 167–169
Tollemache, Denis, Lt. Col. the Hon., 280, 285
Tonks, Prof. Henry, 297
Toulouse-Lautrec, H. M. R. de, 213
Tree, Sir Herbert, 176
Triple Fugue (Osbert Sitwell), 74–75
Tull, Henry, 285
Turner, Reginald, 171–174
Tusitala (Stevenson), 50

Index

VAINGLORY (Firbank), 77, 79, 90
Valmouth (Firbank), 77, 85–86
Vandervelde, Mme., 17, 22, 23, 45, 218
Vecchia, La (Sickert), 183
Vechten, Carl van, 97
Victoria, Queen, 294
Vines, Sherard, 45

WALEY, ARTHUR, 5–7, 9, 151, 291
Walker, Emery, 275
Walpole, Horace, 52, 147
Walter, Bruno, 290
Walton, William, 9, 148–149, 167, 218
Watts-Dunton, Walter Theodore, 49
Weg (Gosse), 50, 51
Welch, Denton, 175
Wells, H. G., 118, 334
Welsh Prince (schooner), 233
Wheatley, Prof. John, A.R.A., 203
Wheels (ed. Edith Sitwell), 121, 122
Whiskers-and-Soda (Richardson), 164
Whistler, Daniel, 302
Whistler, James McNeill, 186, 192, 194, 196, 200, 201, 204, 213, 221, 302
Whistler, Mrs. James McNeill, 201
Whistler, Laurence, 298, 300, 301, 302, 304
Whistler, Rex, his appearance and personality, 293–296; as an artist, 297, 298–301, 304–306; his birth and background, 298–299, 302–303; threatened with eye defect, 301; and William Kent, 304–305; and Robins, 306; and Rossini's opera, 308; his letters, 309; his houses and studios, 310–312; and payment for his work, 311; his rooms, 312–313; and his own ghost, 313; in the Army, 313–316; and designs for *A Place of One's Own*, 315; and landscape design at Renishaw, 315–316; his death, 316
Whistler, Rex, His Life and Drawings (Laurence Whistler), 304
Whiteley, William, 240
Wilde, Oscar, 113, 143, 144, 145, 153, 154–161, 163, 171–173, 174, 177, 213
Williams, Vaughan, 287
Willy, 163, 164
Wilson, Richard, 115
Wood, Sir Henry, 290
Woodhouse, Gordon, 267, 271, 282, 283, 285, 286
Woodhouse, Violet Gordon, 79; and Wilfred Owen, 122, 123; and W. H. Davies, 234, 267, 268, 269, 291–292; her genius as an executant, 272–274, 285 ff.; her family, 273; plays for G. B. Shaw, 274–278; her appearance and personality, 278–279, 280–281; her houses, 281–284, 289; her musical life, 285–289; and Pablo Picasso, 289–290; plays for author's birthday, 291

YEATS, W. B., 68
Yellow Book, The, 160–161